W9-ALM-327

"The one way of tolerating existence is to lose oneself in literature as in a perpetual orgy."

—Gustave Flaubert,
in a letter, 1858

B·O·O·K·S
& Co.

939 Madison Avenue
New York City 10021

'phone (212) 737·1450

DAVID ROBILLIARD

September 13–October 6, 1990

CARLO MARIA MARIANI

October 11–November 3, 1990

PIERO MANZONI

November 8–December 1, 1990

PIERRE ET GILLES

December 6, 1990–January 8, 1991

HIRSCHL & ADLER MODERN

851 Madison Avenue
New York, New York 10021
212 744-6700
FAX 212 737-2614

Catalogues Available $15pp.

CONJUNCTIONS

Bi-Annual Volumes of New Writing

Edited by
Bradford Morrow

Contributing Editors
Walter Abish
John Ashbery
Mei-mei Berssenbrugge
Guy Davenport
Elizabeth Frank
William H. Gass
Susan Howe
Kenneth Irby
Robert Kelly
Ann Lauterbach
Patrick McGrath
Nathaniel Tarn
John Edgar Wideman

Bard College *distributed by Random House, Inc.*

EDITOR: Bradford Morrow
SENIOR EDITORS: Susan Bell, Elisabeth Cunnick
ASSOCIATE EDITORS: Martine Bellen, Karen Kelly,
Yannick Murphy
MANAGING EDITOR: Marlene Hennessy
EDITORIAL ASSISTANTS: John Cumpston, Inge Schaefer

CONJUNCTIONS is published in the Spring and Fall of each year by Bard College, Annandale-on-Hudson, NY 12504. This issue is made possible in part with funds from the New York State Council on the Arts and the National Endowment for the Arts.

Editorial communications should be sent to 33 West 9th Street, New York NY, 10011. Unsolicited manuscripts cannot be returned unless accompanied by a stamped, self-addressed envelope.

Distributed by Random House, Inc.

Copyright © 1990 CONJUNCTIONS

Cover art copyright © 1990 Tim Rollins + K.O.S.

SUBSCRIPTIONS. Send subscription order to CONJUNCTIONS, P.O. Box 115, Bard College, Annandale-on-Hudson, NY 12504. Single year (two issues): $18.00 paperback, for individuals; $25.00 for institutions and overseas; $45.00, cloth. Two years (four volumes): $32.00, paperback, for individuals; $45.00, for institutions and overseas; $85.00 cloth. Patron subscription (lifetime): $500.00, paperback. Overseas subscribers please make payment by International Money Order. Back issues available.

Stills from Dusan Makavejev's "Montenegro" and "Sweet Movie" reproduced courtesy of The Museum of Modern Art/Film Stills.

All rights reserved. No part of this book may be reproduced or transmitted in any form or by any means, electronic or mechanical, including photocopying, recording or by an information storage and retrieval system, without permission in writing from the Publisher.

Printers: Edwards Brothers. Typesetter: Delmas Typesetting. Cover artwork and typography by Tim Rollins + K.O.S.

ISSN 0278-2324
ISBN 0-679-7-3515-1

TABLE OF CONTENTS

The editor would like to express his gratitude to everyone who helped keep CONJUNCTIONS alive this last year, while we were in search of a new publisher. To Walter Abish, Susan Bell, Martine Bellen, Mei-mei Berssenbrugge, Leon Botstein, Mary Caponegro, Bruce Duffy, Forrest Gander, John Glusman, Leo and Linda Hamalian, William Kalvin, Deborah Karl, Karen Kelly, Robert Kelly, Ann Lauterbach, Jamie Linville, George Plimpton, Perdita Schaffner, Jim Sitter, Jean Stein, Nathaniel Tarn, Marjorie Welish, Paul West, Diane Williams, Andrew Wylie, heartfelt thanks for the advice and generous assistance given through a rough time.

Congratulations to contributing editor Guy Davenport, who was awarded a MacArthur Fellowship this year.

In Memoriam Seth Morgan
1949–1990

The First Voyage of Somebody the Sailor
John Barth

ONCE UPON A TIME I was twins; my other half didn't quite make it into this world.

I remember her.

Like many another solitary though not unhappy child, young Simon William Behler invented playmates. "Bijou" especially, with her tidewater eyes. We two had long conversations, high adventures; no doubt they've colored my memory from this distance. But we were together back there, more or less conscious through the last trimester, and my kid sister (I've never thought of her otherwise) was game for anything. In our liquid world we slid and turned like a brace of young otters. We even told stories—*I* did, anyhow—about what we imagined was going on: what was out there, who we were, who *they* were. In these tales of adventure, love, and mystery there was no *Once upon a time.* Our language had no tenses. My stories were perhaps no more than a rendition of what took place.

In the last of them, Bijou and I make ready for what four decades later will be called Extra-Vehicular Activity. Pressure's on. We know it's risky, this shift from one world to another; we're edgy but eager. A comradely last hug; then I thrust myself headfirst into the Passage. My faithful friend and audience is right behind me. See you there, Bijou! Two. One.

He awoke in the strange though familiar bedroom of his older brother, Joseph "Joe Junior" Behler, in the family house in East Dorset, Maryland. Sunday morning, July 1, 1937: Simon W. Behler's seventh birthday.

Bijou's, too.

"Familiar" because our parents had lived in that house since before we were born; "strange" because the night just past was the first I had slept in my brother's room. Today they would bring Mother home: my birthday present, Aunt Rachel said. (Bijou's too.) But she was still too sick to sleep in her and Dad's room, and so yesterday Dad and Uncle Josh had moved my twin bed back into Joe Junior's room. Today we would move the rest of my things, and Mother would take the spare twin.

Neither my brother nor I was happy with this arrangement. Joe Junior was thirteen and wanted privacy; I was used to rocking myself to sleep and talking to Bijou. But it was for Mother's sake, and just for a while.

Those twin habits of mine, however, were of long standing and not easily put by. I rocked on my left side; all my pajama tops wore through at the right shoulder from friction against the bedsheets. When I was mostly awake, talking quietly to my sister or telling our stories in my head, I had a way of rocking that made nearly no noise. But as sleep took over, sometimes I would rev up enough to set springs and bedframe going. On the door between her and Uncle Josh's room and mine (and Bijou's), Aunt Rachel would tap "Shave and a haircut"—tap tata tap-tap—and say, "Sy?"

"O*kay*," I'd answer. Wearily. For a while then I would lie still, and sometimes fall asleep without further movement. But well into my teens I woke up rocking. What would I do, I used to wonder, when I had college roommates? When I had a wife right in bed with me?

Now my brother said "Quit rocking." Joe Junior's room had an odd rank smell, not sweat not dirt not garbage. Matter-of-factly he declared, "You got to quit that now, big baby," and added in a singsong, "Happy birthday to you happy birthday to you happy birthday dear Simon happy birthday to you. Amen."

The room was hung with his flying-model airplanes, rubber-band powered, their hand-razored balsa frames painstakingly tissued, doped, decal'd. Testors glue and banana oil were part of the smell, but not all of it. Spad, Fokker triplane, Flying Jenny, Ryan trainer, and my favorite: Stinson Reliant, with its ring of nacelle blisters around the navy-blue engine cowling. An airplane pilot was what I was going to be.

After Sunday breakfast with his family, young Behler and his older brother went off as usual to Sunday School.

Our family were indifferent to religion, except that Dad, perhaps out of civic-spiritedness, went regularly to Men's Bible Class at East Dorset Zion Meth-Prot while we boys attended Sunday School. But we "went to church" only on special occasions, did not say mealtime grace or bedtime prayers, and never spoke of

God, Jesus, the soul, the hereafter. Probably we thought that Uncle Al, mustard-gassed in Belgium in 1918, waited to rejoin us up there somewhere, meanwhile looking after Bijou. But our disposition was entirely secular. Joe Junior and his buddies spent their Sunday School hour teasing girls, twisting the words of the hymns, and making plans for the interval between the ten-fifty benediction and our one o'clock Sunday dinner. I myself took more interest in the exotic but vaguely depressing world of the illustrated lessons—camels and palm trees, figs and dates and anointing-oil, sandals, robes, unbarbered hair and beards—than in the strange agonies and paradoxical imperatives of the lessons themselves, presided over by cheerful matrons of the neighborhood: *Whoso loseth his life shall find it*, and the rest. *Let the lower lights be burning,* we sang together at the end:

Send a gleam across the wave.
Some poor sinking, suff'ring seaman
You may rescue, you may save.

Joe Junior and his friends changed *sinking seamen* to *stinking*, adding the *t* just lightly enough to escape detection. Since boats and beacons, unlike palms and camels, were the daily furniture of our tidewater lives, I wondered as always why the hymnist called for lower rather than higher lights. A forward range light, perhaps. But in that case, why more than one lower light? It was only a hymn, Mrs. Travers explained.

In the ten-minute break between Sunday School and Church, as others mingled and chatted in the steamy shade of maples out on the bright sidewalk, my brother's gang and I made our way back along Maryland Avenue to Maple Street, past rows of crabfat-yellow clapboard houses, mean but tidy. I hurried ahead to say hi to Mother. Our big black LaSalle was out front as always on Sunday mornings. Surrounded by used white handkerchiefs on the screen-porch glider, Dad was reading a section of the *Times.* Aunt Rachel was at work in the kitchen; Uncle Josh was off somewhere in their maroon Nash but would be back soon. I ran upstairs through the odors of roast chicken and cigarette smoke.

Mother was propped on pillows in the spare twin, wearing a light bedjacket over her nightgown despite the heat. She looked sick, all right, and the room smelled different. She had her glasses on—I used to think she looked prettier with them on, like a pretty schoolteacher—but the magazine section of the *Times* was lying beside her on the bedsheet, open to the untouched crossword puzzle. On my maple nightstand were a small white enameled basin, a box of Kleenex, and a pencil for the puzzle. My wastebasket had been set in front of the nightstand; quite a few used Kleenex were in it already, and a couple more on the floor beside it.

"Mother's *so* tired," she said after we had carefully hugged and kissed and she had wished me a happy birthday. "She wasn't able to go shopping for you this year."

That was okay, I told her. The powder on her cheeks was thicker than she used to wear it; you could see it caked on, as if new powder had been put right on top of old. I sat on the edge of the spare twin, holding her wrist as she held mine. On hers was still the name-bracelet from the hospital.

"Is Joe Junior home?"

"He's coming."

He and I would have fun in the back bedroom together, she assured me. Would I promise her, now that I was seven, to try not to rock in bed?

I promised.

She really was tired. We didn't say anything else for a while. Presently, however, it occurred to me to ask her whether she could tell me something about my sister.

"Your sister!" She laughed a little, in her chest, and that made her cough, and she had to spit into a Kleenex and close her eyes and lie back against the small headboard. "There's nothing to tell, honeybun. She didn't quite make it into this world, is all." She considered. "We called her BeeGee, for Baby Girl Behler, 'cause she didn't live long enough to get a real name. Then you took to calling her Bijou after Schine's Bijou Theatre uptown."

Those things I knew. "Was she born alive and then died, or born dead?"

Mother had squeezed my wrist while she coughed; now she patted my forearm. "Some of both, I guess. Once in a while it happens that a baby gets hung up being born, and that's what happened to little B. G. Behler."

I had more questions, but Mother was so tired, and I heard my brother taking the steps two at a time, calling "Mom?" Anyhow, I had learned a considerable piece of news. I went down to help Aunt Rachel set the dining room table and asked her what made a baby die being born. "Now *there's* a nice Sunday dinner question!" she scoffed in her way, but then explained while stirring gravy that sometimes the bellybutton cord gets twisted around a baby's neck and strangles it while it's being born. Doctor Fowler and everybody had been upset, but there wasn't a blessed thing anybody could have done. They had been relieved then that I came out okay, because with two of us swimming around in there, she guessed things could get right tangled.

I was astonished. Hadn't I been born first, as I'd always been told?

"No no no no no," Aunt Rachel scoffed, and tapped her stirring-spoon smartly on the edge of the roasting-pan: tap tata tap-tap. "Who ever told you such a thing as that?"

"Everybody!"

Good-humoredly but positively she declared, "They never did! You got that idea from being older than your sister ever since. But she came first and she went first: 'Girls first!'"

This second revelation, more momentous than its predecessor, made me almost dizzy. I could not, in fact, recall ever having been told in so many words that I had been born before "BeeGee"—though surely I had never been told otherwise, either, and that omission struck me as extraordinary, even somehow culpable. I urgently wanted verification, but Mother was resting now, and with Dad you had to say things too loud, and Uncle Josh wouldn't know any different from Aunt Rachel. I summoned the family to dinner and, on the way back from the screen porch, asked my brother whether *he'd* known that BeeGee was born first.

Nonchalantly he asked back: "What's the difference between a duck?"

The talk at table was of the strike at the local tomato cannery: of how much better off were the Albany Brothers workers than the people in war-torn Spain and China, who would count it a blessing to eat spilled tomatoes right off the *street* and would give their eye teeth for a dinner of stuffed roast chicken and succotash and mashed redskin potatoes with giblet gravy. That was a Christ fact, Uncle Josh had to admit, but even so.

"I heard another truck got turned over," Joe Junior announced loudly to our father. "And a picket beaten up and arrested."

"I doubt he was beaten up and arrested both," Dad said. Uncle Josh chuckled and said "It happens." Aunt Rachel thought they should arrest them all and ship them off to the U.S. Army.

"Nothing can stop the Ar-my Air Corps!" Joe Junior sang out, with the grin that meant he was in on something I wasn't. Aunt Rachel crooned admonishment—"Joe *Jun*-ior . . ."—pitching the

second note higher, like our door chime. My brother said "Tee hee" and made a neat volcano of his mashed potatoes, with gravy lava. "Isn't it something to have Mother back for your birthday!" Aunt Rachel asked me, and I agreed it was, and Aunt Rachel said to Uncle Josh in a knowing tone "The poor thing's tired, though."

Over tapioca pudding the fire whistle blew. When the sound had risen and fallen once and then re-risen, Joe Junior told Dad "Fire whistle," and Dad said "Hah" and excused himself to join his fellow volunteer firemen, blowing his nose as he left the house. Almost an hour later he telephoned to say that the fire had been an Albany Brothers warehouse and now there was an emergency town council meeting and he didn't know when he'd get back. We had cleaned up dinner and were all on the screen porch waiting to take our Sunday ride, which Mother had insisted we ought to go right ahead with, never mind her. It was the first time I could remember Dad's ever telephoning home.

"Well!" Aunt Rachel said when she came back out on the screen porch. In her cheery-scoffing tone the word whooshed out with lots of breath: "*Hwell!* We'll just take our little ride in the Nash, the four of us."

Joe Junior said, conversationally, "Yippee."

We didn't *have* to take a ride, I offered. "'Deed we do," Aunt Rachel replied, "and it's a pity Mother and Dad can't come along, 'cause it's your birthday surprise. Howja like *them* apples?"

"Eee-urr-*room*!" Joe Junior went, imitating first the sound of a diving Spad and then its chattering machine guns: "Khuh-huh-huh-huh-huh-huh-huh-huh!"

Uncle Josh said mildly "That'll do, Joe," and folded his section of Sunday paper.

"You have a good time, honey," Mother bade me when I went upstairs to say good-bye. "Mother's sorry she can't go with you, and you'll love your surprise, I know." She was lying down now, her glasses folded beside the basin and pencil on the maple night-stand. I bent over and was weakly hugged and kissed. While her hands were pressed to both sides of my face, an awful question occurred to me, so important that I went ahead and asked it despite her being sick and Joe Junior's standing right behind me:

"Was it her own bellybutton cord that Bijou tangled up in, or mine?"

"Geez, Sy!" my brother objected. A blush scalded over me.

But Mother didn't seem to mind. She laughed, airlessly, and

shook her head. "The things you think of!" Her hands were on my shoulders now; she squeezed and wearily let go.

Joe Junior crowed to our aunt and uncle: "This *drip*!" We were turning off Maple onto Maryland in the maroon Nash, Uncle Josh driving with his deerskin gloves even in July, his black cigarette holder between his teeth. "He *asked* her that, while she's sick in bed!"

"Mother didn't mind!" I said hotly. But I was impressed both by the accusation of tactlessness—which, once I heard it, seemed shamefully justified—and by my brother's superior discernment, which clearly impressed him too.

"I'm sure Mother didn't mind," Aunt Rachel soothed. "That all happened years ago, and there wasn't a blessed thing any soul could do."

Seven years ago *today*, I thought, stinging. And *I* could have gone first.

"Nhow!" Aunt Rachel declared: "What we need to know is what Simon William Behler intends to be when he grows up."

Joe Junior at once replied, "A bigger baby," but not in his really needling tone: more as if he were still rolling his eyes at my dumb question to Mother.

"A famous pilot," I declared, glumly. They all knew that very well, in general.

But Uncle Josh grinned in the rearview mirror. "A *famous* pilot?"

"That's the ticket," Aunt Rachel approved.

What had happened was that the first time Joe Junior had declared at table his ambition to be an engineer and I mine to be a pilot, the grownups had pointed out to us that there were many sorts of each: highway engineers, electrical engineers; harbor pilots, coastal pilots. When my brother then specified locomotive engineer and I airplane pilot, they had good-humoredly chided us both: Such people (Dad and Aunt Rachel maintained) were no more than glorified truck drivers. We should set our sights higher; make a name for ourselves. Joe Junior had subsequently decided he would be the other kind of engineer, the kind that designed and built locomotives; that way he'd get to drive them as often as he wanted to, to make sure they were okay. For a while I had reckoned I would do the same with airplanes. But "aeronautical engineer" sounded too close to what my brother would be doing, and I had in mind to be a lot more important than he would be. So, without mentioning it till now, I had revised my ambition.

"Get a load of Charles Lindbergh," Joe Junior mildly jeered. I blushed, but was pleased to sense he was envious of my having thought of celebrity. I was ready to point out to him, when necessary, that there *were* no famous locomotive engineers, in the desirable sense: Who wanted to be Casey Jones? But it was not necessary yet.

There was something going on.

"My father's father was a famous pilot," Uncle Josh remarked around his cigarette holder.

Joe Junior laughed. "Was not!"

"Sure he was," our uncle maintained. Aunt Rachel smiled at him.

All we knew of the Vernon family was what we had been told. "He was a farmer!" I insisted, considering however that in those early days a person might somehow have been both. "Was he a crop duster?"

"Some people might call it that," Uncle Josh allowed, twinkling. "But actually he was a manure pilot: *Pile it here; pile it there. . . .*"

As we duly groaned, I saw we were about to turn left off Maryland onto Bridge Avenue, toward the Chaptico River bridge itself and Avon County, instead of right as usual toward the canneries and marshy lower Dorset. "Hey, what's up?"

"Price of eggs," cracked Joe Junior.

"Price of tomatoes," Aunt Rachel predicted, "soon enough."

"*Airplanes* are up," declared Uncle Josh, cocking his cigarette holder at a jaunty angle like President Roosevelt as we headed north over the blue Chaptico.

"What goes up must come down," my brother said, and made his dive-and-crash noise: *Eee-urr-room-pulghhh*!"

Young Behler's family had arranged a marvelous birthday surprise.

"Where're we going?" I demanded, beginning dizzily to suspect. Aunt Rachel said "You'll see, birthday boy."

We were across the bridge and headed for Avondale, where the region's only airport was. As often as I could persuade them to, my parents took me there to watch the planes take off and land, but that was not often: Our father always said that the Eastern Shore begins at the south bank of the Chaptico; he had no interest in prosperous Avon County, with its gentleman farmers and waterfront estates. It was these that the Avon Airport largely served: There were no scheduled commercial passenger flights, but many of the "C'meres"—people from Washington, Wilmington, Philadelphia, even New York, who "came here" to their vacation or retirement properties—owned private airplanes or hired air taxis to and from the city. Sometimes we would sit for half an hour among the Pipers, Cessnas, and Grummans and see no planes move at all. Once, however, we saw a trimotored Ford "Tin Goose"; another time, just a few weeks past, a brand new Douglas DC-3.

But being merely taken to see the airplanes again, so soon, was not likely my birthday surprise. I became uneasy. *"Are we going up?"*

Uncle Josh steered smiling through Avondale. "You couldn't get *me* up in one of those things!"

Always-game Aunt Rachel said she would give her eye teeth to go up again; years ago she'd had a beau who was a barnstormer. (He was that, Uncle Josh agreed.) But we would just see.

"*You're* going, aren't you?" I asked Joe Junior anxiously.

"What's the matter, big baby? Cold feet?"

As we approached the familiar corrugated-metal buildings on the far side of town—and the windsock, the beacon, the grassy runways—those brightly painted airplanes parked in rows no longer looked like large gay toys. They were formidably real, not particularly friendly machines. Where we lived there were neither mountains nor tall buildings; I had traveled no farther from home than Baltimore, once, but there had not been time then to go up in a skyscraper. The highest off the ground that I could remember having been was the top of the Ocean City ferris wheel.

"It'd better be a Stinson Reliant!" I said. "I guess if it's not that blue Stinson Reliant, I'd just as leave skip it."

Joe Junior chortled: "Listen to the big baby!"

"I don't *have* to go!" I made clear. "It's *my* birthday!"

"Boo hoo hoo!"

"Peace on earth good will to men!" Aunt Rachel chided us. "I'd go up in a raspberry Model T if somebody offered!"

Uncle Josh said he bet she would, too.

The blue Stinson Reliant I had admired on other visits "belonged to somebody," they guessed. Anyhow, it did not take passengers up for hire. What kind was it, then, the one they'd rented?

Incredibly to me, they didn't know what kind: a regular little one, they supposed. On our last ride over here, the family had seen a sign for airplane rides, and Aunt Rachel had phoned ahead this morning while we were in Sunday School, to confirm. The pilot was expecting us.

"Manure pilot!" said Joe Junior. "I'll go with you, big baby."

I was much relieved. "But I can decide, okay? When I see what kind of plane it is."

We did not go from the maroon Nash right out onto the airfield, but into a small office entered from the grass parking-lot side of a nearby hangar, where a red-on-yellow hand-lettered sign advertised AIRPLAИE RIDES $5. The office was floored with worn-through green linoleum; a chipped oak desk was strewn with grease-soiled manuals and papers, box and crescent wrenches, ashtrays filled to overflowing; the walls were hung with finger-smudged maps of Avon and Dorset counties and calendars from sparkplug companies, with all-but-naked women on them. A thin-faced man in yellow sport shirt and slacks and red porkpie hat swiveled his beat-up desk chair to face us, mouthing an unlighted cigar. An ancient black oscillating fan stirred the humid air.

It was me he looked at. "You're the feller wants to be a pilot?"

I cleared my throat. "Yes sir."

"It ain't no way to get rich!" he laughed to Aunt Rachel and Uncle Josh.

My aunt informed him with mock asperity, that I was going to be a *famous* pilot.

"Oh, well, then!" The man's laugh loosened phlegm. He spat into a rusty metal wastebasket beside his desk and said "'Scuse *me.*"

"Wiley Post!" my brother offered: "Eee-urr-*pulghh*!"

"Well I'm Howard Garton," the man said, shaking hands with me and then with Joe Junior, "and I say don't let *no*body make fun of wantin' to be a pilot."

My uncle said that that was the ticket.

"What kind of plane do you have?" I asked Howard Garton, and he said why didn't we all just go take a look. We were going simply to inspect the airplane, I imagined, after which we would return to the battered office to discuss the flight plan, and I would make my decision. But Howard Garton led us through the small empty dirt-floored hangar behind his office and out to a Bellanca four-seater, red and yellow like his clothes or Aunt Rachel's Bon Ami can, with painted flames streaming back from the exposed cylinder heads and the wheel pods. He opened the thin door on the passenger side, tipped down the right front seat-back, and said to Joe Junior "In you go, bud. We'll let the birthday boy ride up front. You coming along, Ma?" he asked Aunt Rachel, and explained to Uncle Josh, "Can't sit but four of us."

"You bet your bottom dollar I'm coming along!" Aunt Rachel scoffed, and then added "How 'bout three for the price of two?"

Things were happening too fast. Where were the helmets and goggles? The parachutes? I thought of offering to wait on the ground with Uncle Josh. But Howard Garton chuckled and said "Make it twelve-fifty," and Aunt Rachel said to Uncle Josh, "Kiss me good-bye, love; I'm off to the wild blue yonder," and let Howard Garton help her up into the rear seat beside Joe Junior. I didn't have nerve enough not to climb in too.

It was better when Howard Garton threw away his wet cigar, stepped up into the pilot's seat, and stashed his red porkpie into a stretchy pocket in the door. His head was bald, bumpy, freckled. "All right, sir," he said: "What's your first name?" I told him. "Let's you and I fasten our safety belts, Mister Simon, and Mom and Brother do the same, and we'll see if old Bessie feels like running today."

"Aunt Rachel's our aunt," Joe Junior reported. As if in a spirit of mere inquiry, I asked "Where do you keep the parachutes?" Howard Garton laughed. Joe Junior said "What good are a *pair o' chutes* for four people? Get it?" Aunt Rachel told me to go ahead and ask all the questions I wanted to, and Howard Garton explained then that parachutes were used only on warplanes and maybe by stunt pilots and test pilots; if old Bessie's motor conked, we would just look around for a nice place to park. He started the engine—not nearly so loud a noise as I'd expected; like a big fan, really—and now I understood that of course we didn't need helmets and goggles in a closed cabin, any more than in Uncle Josh's maroon Nash or our black LaSalle. The Bellanca had dual controls; I knew what every one was for, from my reading. Howard Garton let me move the ailerons, the elevators, and the rudder while we were still parked.

"Not when we're up in the air, though," Joe Junior warned from behind. Howard Garton said we would just see. Now all my fear was gone; though we had not yet moved, I loved Howard Garton and old Bessie and flying. Uncle Josh stepped back and waved his gloves; we three waved back. Howard Garton advanced the throttle—I admired the way his bony, freckled hand rested so lightly upon the knob—and we rolled forward.

"Off we go!" sang Aunt Rachel. "Do you like Stinson Reliants?" I asked Howard Garton, who squinted judiciously out the side window and replied, "Stinson Reliant. They're a right nice airplane, I reckon. Out of *my* class." I declared Bellancas to be good airplanes, too—though in fact I was impressed by the apparent flimsiness of old Bessie's construction. As we bumped along toward the runway, the plane seemed not all that different, except in scale, from one of Joe Junior's balsa-and-tissue flying models. Even the quietly fluttering propeller sounded rubber-band powered....

Until, in takeoff position at the head of the runway, Howard Garton advanced the throttle while braking the wheels, and the Bellanca roared and trembled and strained to go. "That's more like it!" cried Aunt Rachel. I watched an instrument needle climb; my skin buzzed. I had expected radio talk with a control tower, but there was none. Howard Garton merely looked around, released the wheel brakes, and opened the throttle all the rest of the way. As we gathered speed, the Bellanca's tail lifted; now I could see the grass runway rolling swiftly under us, the windsock almost limp above the distant hangar before which Uncle Josh waved. In no hurry at all, at a certain point Howard Garton drew toward him ever so slightly the little steering wheel on his side, as I knew he must. Mine came back in tandem with it. We were airborne.

I had not anticipated the untidy decrepitude of Howard Garton's office, the unglamorousness of the little man himself, the homely insubstantiality of old Bessie's interior appearance; but about the experience of flight itself my imaginings proved prescient, and I was as perfectly at home in thin air as in the waters of the Chaptico. My boyish ambition to be a pilot, however, fell lightly away from me with the tree- and rooftops of Avondale. Oh, I might fly a Stinson Reliant for recreation when I was grown, but commercial aviation (I realized already from this first altitude, as clearly as I had realized while taxiing that we didn't need helmets and goggles), even piloting a brand-new DC-3, was ... *an insufficient destiny.*

Things were exactly as I had known they would be: the little airport, already well below and behind us; tree-shaded Avondale; the highway leading south through farmland to the Chaptico bridge. I was glad that Joe Junior and Aunt Rachel were behind me; glad also that they were too absorbed to speak much. In a calm, non-boyish voice I asked Howard Garton whether we had time to fly over the river to Dorset; above the engine's drone and the rush of air past the Bellanca's thin fuselage, it was like speaking to our father.

"I reckon," Howard Garton said. The steering wheel in front of me turned just a little, and we banked left on the light west wind we had taken off into. "It don't take long to get there in this baby."

Already I saw the blue-gray Chaptico ahead, so much wider below our town than above it. Just under us was the smaller Avon, its tributary, flecked here and there with sails and scored with the wakes of motorboats.

"Hey, neat!" Joe Junior said. "There's the bridge! I bet we see our house!"

I knew we would, and more, for there was the world exactly configured, a living map. There was the rivershore, the general hospital with its seawall; there were Maple Street, Maryland Avenue, the other mapled streets and avenues of East Dorset. Our house was mostly shrouded by those maples and by our Chinese-Cigar trees, but I saw part of our shingled roof, under which Mother lay ill and tired, and a white clapboard gable, and now the black LaSalle out front; so Dad was there, too, probably on the screen porch with the *Times,* deaf to the plane humming high overhead. There was the squat gray granite belfry of Zion Meth-Prot; there was East Dorset Elementary, and behind it the shiny new standpipe of our ward. There was Dorset Creek, lined with packing houses, dividing our town into East and West; the creek bridge leading to the business district, with Behler Maintenance & Improvement somewhere in it, on the street behind the fire house. Howard Garton banked left again before I got a good view of West Dorset, where the waterfront park and the better residential section were. But to westward when we leveled off I had a long view out toward the hazy great mouth of the Chaptico, miles wide where it joined Chesapeake Bay at what remained of Piney Island; and to southward now stretched the endless marshes of the lower county: a maze of reedy necks, meandering tidal creeks, and spattered low islets. Now we banked left yet again, to head back to the airport, and I could see the poor colored ward and the spread of Albany Brothers canneries, from one of which rose smoke. There now was Island Creek with its several channel markers, exactly right. I could see where the twin creeks eventually came together at the municipal cemetery, making a larger island of East Dorset itself. I could even see the shoal that the Island Creek day beacon perfectly marked, extending to meet it underwater, and the little indentation in the shore nearby, where Bijou and I, once upon a time—

To hide my sudden distress, I pressed my face to the glass. *Though this should have been her birthday gift as much as his, Simon Behler had not even thought of his sister, much less narrated to her, since the family reached Avon Airport in the maroon Nash.*

My narrator's voice was hollow now, wrong. Dismayed, I regarded upshore beyond the Island the grounds and buildings of the Eastern Shore State Hospital, and beyond them, where the slightly higher ground of the upper county commenced its quiltwork of woodlots and tomato fields, the new county cemetery. That was not yet where our dead lay, but it would be: The Behler plot in Dorset Municipal, where BeeGee Behler was, was full; so was that whole old graveyard, which had served our town since its incorporation two hundred fifty years ago. Dad and Aunt Rachel had bought space for the future in the bare, newly laid-out county spread, formerly one of Captain Philip Albany's tomato fields.

"*Hwell!*" my aunt exclaimed just then, behind me: "There's home!"

"Right pretty to look at, i'n't it," Howard Garton said.

Announced Joe Junior: "I see the seawall!"

En route home in the maroon Nash, I was teased for my odd behavior, mainly by my brother. But Aunt Rachel, too, declared to Uncle Josh she didn't know just *hwhat* had come over our Simon. When Howard Garton had invited me to take the wheel for a minute and hold old Bessie steady as she goes, I had politely declined, saying I was content to let him do the flying so I could just look. "It is right pretty," Howard Garton had admitted. Back at the hangar, standing beside the Bellanca's yellow wing-strut, I had felt subdued, taller and more serious forever. I shook Howard Garton's freckled hand and thanked him for a good flight.

"You don't seem too het up," Uncle Josh observed kindly in the car. "Stomach woozy?"

"No, I feel great. It was great." Even to me my voice sounded peculiar. To hear it again I said "I sure thank you-all." I was relieved that they pretty much left me alone then: My small dismay at forgetting Bijou had quickly passed; the exhilaration of flight remained, but I felt too serious about it and other things to join in Aunt Rachel and Joe Junior's Did-you-sees as we recrossed the Chaptico bridge. I worried, too, that they would ask whether I still wanted to be a famous pilot, and then think it was out of fear I had changed my mind, when in truth . . .

On the screen porch, Dad took off his glasses, smiled, and asked "How'd it go?" "Great!" I called back. Aunt Rachel declared that the whole Eastern Shore of Maryland looked from up there just like the fire company Christmas garden. Except no snow, Joe Junior corrected her, and went off on his Silver King bicycle—hollering "Contact! Switch off! Eee-urr-*room*!"—to tell his friends where he'd been.

Still feeling tall and grave, I *ascended* the stairs to thank Mother for the airplane ride. It was the neatest birthday present I'd ever had, I said truthfully. In that room my grave voice and manner seemed less affected. She held my hand as I sat on the edge of the spare twin and told her what I'd seen from up there. That was nice, she said. She believed Mother might be feeling just a little bit better.

Then I asked her whether Dad and I could ride over to the town cemetery before supper: I wanted to put some flowers on my sister's grave.

Surprised, Mother said "What a thoughtful idea. But I know Dad's tired, honey. And we don't have any flowers."

I stood my ground. "Just to visit, then."

"Well. Ask your father, or maybe your Aunt Rachel. No: She'll have her hands full with supper. And your Uncle Josh has been driving already."

I could see the problem tiring her out. All the same, gratified that Joe Junior wasn't there to tease or maybe even ask to ride along, I put the question loudly to our father.

"Cemetery?" he repeated.

Uncle Josh was on the screen porch too, looking through the travel section of the *Times*. He raised his voice for Dad to hear: "Boy wants to say happy birthday to his sister! I'll ride him over, directly."

Aunt Rachel called from the living room: "The boy's father can drive him, Joshua." She stepped out onto the porch, wiping her long hands on her apron. "I think that's a *good thought!*" she said to me, loudly enough for Dad too. "I wish we had flowers for the whole kaboodle!"

Dad blew his nose and put on his seersucker suitcoat, though temperature and humidity were both in the mid-eighties, and we went off in the black LaSalle. Even with windows down, it was an oven inside that car until we had driven across East Dorset to the creek bridge, for Dad never parked in the shade of the silver maples where starlings would drop all over the paint. In the black LaSalle it was even harder to talk to him; as he couldn't hear the big engine idling, he often raced it and engaged the clutch too suddenly. But when we had crossed the trestled swing-bridge over Dorset Creek (rank even on Sundays from mountains of crabshells rotting in the sun beside the packing houses) and lurched onto Cemetery Avenue, I saw blue cornflowers and white Queen Anne's lace wild along the rusting fence and asked whether we could pick some for Bijou's grave.

Dad guessed not.

"They're just weeds!"

He smiled and shook his head. "Don't belong to us, son."

That was that.

We turned off the creekside street of peeling clapboard houses and into the old cemetery, wound through its crushed-oystershell lanes of tombs, and stopped beside an ancient cedar. Dad took a cigarette from the pack with its desert scene like our illustrated Sunday School lessons, tamped its end against the horn button, and pressed his thumb against the cigarette lighter on the dash. A clear glass bead in its knob would glow red when it was ready. "We're over by those holly bushes," he told me, pointing with the unlit Camel. "You take your time."

The air was still and steamy; already cicadas rasped in the trees. Our plot was marked by a polished gray stone the size of a single-bed headboard, lettered BEHLER. Before it the individual grave-mounds bore low footstones. WILHELM BENJAMIN, 1850–1933, and ROSA HERRON, 1855–1934: my grandparents, who had come over from Germany and whom I scarcely remembered. JOANNA PARSON SIMONS, Mother's mother, not really a Behler, 1863–1935, after whom I'd been sort of named; her too I could but half recall, though she had lived with us in her last years, ill and indifferent. FLORA, Dad and Aunt Rachel's elder sister, 1885–1929, who had never married or left home and had died of a cancer the year the market crashed. CPL. ALBERT WILHELM—older than

Dad, younger than Aunt Rachel, 1891–1918, mustard-gassed in Belgium. And BABY GIRL BEHLER, the only one of us with our last name on her stone, as she had never had a first: DAUGHTER OF JOSEPH BENJAMIN AND PAULINE SIMONS. BORN AND DIED JULY 1, 1930.

The mound above her footstone—had I ever really seen it before?—was tiny. Here is where she had been, winter and summer, while I was growing up and doing every kind of thing. I considered saying some sort of prayer for her soul, but it occurred to me not to believe in any such thing. The people in the coffins under those mounds were just skeletons now—Grandma Simons maybe not quite, as she had died only two years ago—and their souls weren't anything. Chemicals came together to make a holly tree or a sea nettle or a person; then after a while they dissolved like Piney Island in the mouth of the Chaptico. Fifty years ago, Dad had told us at the dinner table, Piney Island had had farms and woods and a village of three hundred people, with a general store and a Methodist church; now everything was washed away but a small stand of loblollies and the skeleton of a pier. By the time I grew up and had a wife and children, there would be nothing left of Piney Island but a shoal under the water, marked with a light.

Same with Bijou: When the time came that I forgot even how I used to narrate my life to her, that would be that. Same with Mother and Dad and Aunt Rachel and Uncle Josh, eventually, and me and Joe Junior and whatever children *we* would have. The tide would still come in and go out; that had nothing to do with us.

Not far from our footstones was a single clump of dandelions in bright blossom. I checked to see whether Dad was looking; couldn't tell through the reflections on the windshield; went ahead anyhow and plucked the whole clump. The five or six blossoming ones I laid atop my sister's mound. Anybody watching from behind would think I was kneeling to pray. One dandelion had gone to fuzz; to make up for having picked the clump, I puffed its seeds over the whole plot.

As we crossed back into East Dorset in the black LaSalle, Dad surprised me by remarking, without turning his head, "I want you to *be* somebody, son." I supposed it was a birthday wish; or perhaps my wanting to visit the cemetery had impressed him. On the other hand, maybe he meant I wasn't measuring up. To ask, at a shout, was too awkward. Without turning my head either, I nodded shortly.

My father went on, still looking forward down Maryland Avenue: "Make a name for yourself."

It was odd, in bed that night, to look up through the dim reflected street light at Joe Junior's hanging models, even the blue Stinson Reliant, and feel myself measurably older. Now I didn't know *what* I would be. Odd also to realize—as I could easily do now by imagining myself up there just then, looking down on us all from Howard Garton's red-and-yellow Bellanca—that the whole town of Dorset, asleep and awake, was *going on*. The entire world was going on while I lay there, and Joe Junior lay over in his bed, asleep already or pretending to be, and BeeGee Behler, who had gone first and was gone now, lay out under her little mound. Tigers in the jungle, Chinese people in China, whales in the oceans of the globe—all *going on*.

Under my head my Ingersoll Mickey Mouse wristwatch ticked. Bijou's dandelions were already dead and curled. Down by the Island Point day beacon the tide would be sliding silently, in or out.

So that my brother, if he was awake, would think me asleep, I breathed slowly and evenly. Presently from his side of the room came a muffled slap slap, his more urgent respiration, and the smell. Some time after that I heard the breathing of his unfeigned sleep. East Dorset was by then so silent that I could hear the dinging of the Dorset Creek bridge bell, many blocks up Maryland Avenue from Maple Street. Even at this late hour on a Sunday, they were opening the draw to let some vessel out upon its business. Then that sound, too, ceased.

Ever so slightly, ever so lightly I rocked, and it was not long before I reached that state between two worlds where distances go strange and the familiar is no more. I was in black space, suspended, or as it were with one eye open above some surface, one below. Little suspected by his family (my narrator resumed in a new voice, to a different audience), our unnamed hero verged upon an alternative and very different life, in a very different realm, to the threshold whereof his lost twin had led him, but into which not even she could follow.

India
Yannick Murphy

I DO NOT KNOW if I have been to India, but I can see men with sticks walking behind white cows and I am beginning to think that, yes, when I was young my mother and father took me to India and I saw great things. There I rode an elephant, I'd like to say, and I slid down its long grey trunk and held its ears for balance when stepping to the ground. Or are these just things my mother and father told me about India and I remember them so well I think I was there. I do not know for sure and I can only say that I am beginning not to trust myself with information. Tell me you have been to Greece and walked the black sand beaches and I might go home and dream I have been on those beaches and in the morning I will tell my children of some Grecian ways.

In Spain I knew a boy from Jaén. There his family picked the olives from the olive trees. In the high hot sun the boy would not leave the house and instead he would stay inside and look out at the hills and he would see his mother and father reaching up and coming down to pick the olives from the trees and the boy thought that the way one would reach up while the other went down, that his mother and father moved like a wave and that the hill they were on was the ocean. And now, when the boy cannot sleep, he imagines his mother and father in the olive field. When I cannot sleep I also think of this man and this woman picking olives as if the man and the woman were waves on the hill in the high hot sun.

In India the men with the sticks turn around to look at me as they walk behind the white cows. I see the men's teeth. Their teeth are whiter than the cows who have stains at the bottom of their legs from walking through the mud.

There is an old aunt who tells me I have never been to India, that my father and mother and I took a ship to India but I was sick and could not go to shore. Instead my parents left me on the ship with a doctor who said I had a fever from a rash on my hands. Every day the doctor came by boat to me to rub fat from animals onto my hands and then he would wrap my hands in sheets so I would not scratch at them. This aunt who told me this lives far away and when I go to visit her she does not get up from bed. She opens up a box of chocolate and then wipes the chocolate off her fingers by reaching up behind her head and wiping them on the pillow. Her pillowcase has chocolate fingerprints around its borders.

Here comes the chief of the Montagnards, his testicles swollen so big from the stream water that his wife pulls a wheelbarrow beneath him that holds his testicles so that he can walk without his testicles ripping from his skin and falling to the ground.

My mother takes my hand and brings me closer to her while we stand and watch the chief and the wife and the wheelbarrow go by.

I have seen my father wake in the morning when it's dark to go and meet with the Montagnards. My father sits on his bed and his body is white in the light from the moon and he pulls on his shirt and the whiteness of his arms disappears and then he pulls on his pants and the whiteness of his legs disappears. My father has a long nose and he looks at my mother sleeping before he leaves and I can see his long nose and then he turns away and leaves the place and I can't see his long nose any more so then I listen for his footsteps as he walks toward the mountain.

The day my father goes to see the Montagnards, my mother and I go to the great room and lay in our silk skirts on the woolen carpet catching moths.

It is summer and my mother and I dress in the pink light of dusk into our silk skirts. They are tight skirts that show where we are strong in our legs and the colors of our skirts are as bright as the cloths the Montagnards use to wrap up their dead.

My father goes in the morning leaving his sandals behind, saying they would find him talking with the Montagnards if they found sandal marks on the side of the mountain. Later my mother puts the sandals under his pillow so no one will know. This day we watch them walking to where we live, opening the doors, counting heads, they come to our door and we open it before they can. They touch my mother's leg and put their hands up her skirt and my mother tells them it is my birthday and my mother asks them don't I look nice and they say I do but they look at my mother and my mother smiles at me and her black hair looks almost red in the pink light of dusk.

It is summer and the moths are eating the woolen carpet in the great room and no one knows what to do because it is not ever done to roll up the woolen carpet in the great room where the great ones once walked. This day my mother says we will be great ones and she takes me to the great room when the men aren't watching. We walk the borders of the carpet and then we walk to the middle of the carpet where the moths are flying slowly by our legs and we lie down. The moths find our skirts are made of silk and they fly up between our legs and my mother lays her hand on her leg, waiting to catch them before they fly up. When my mother catches a moth she gives it to me and shows me how to rub the dust from the moth's wings over my eyes so that when I look in the great mirror my eyes are bigger and shine as if half moons were above them and I look like she does, like my mother does so then I turn around to look at her lying on the carpet, but she is not there any longer and has moved to stand by the window. "You can see the Montagnards from here," she says. I go to see if I can see the Montagnards as well but I cannot. I see the black mountains. Then my mother licks her fingertips and wipes the dust from the moth's wings off my eyes and we go.

My father had long fingers and my children have his fingers as well. These days, with me not trusting myself with information, I am beginning to think that because my children have my father's hands that they also have his memories. They never knew my father, he died before the first was even born, but they move like my father did and when they talk their hands talk like his talked, and if they point I cannot look at what they're pointing at and instead I see their fingers, those of my father's hands.

In a way, I think of this as unfair, that my father's memories are locked inside my children's hands and not in mine. It is as if he had played some part in overseeing the growth of my children in the womb, a part I could not see or even did not know about. As if my father made my children not my own but his.

I am seeing the men with the sticks behind the white cows so many times that the faces of the men are changing. They are changing into the faces of my mother and my father as they turn around to look at me and it makes me miss seeing the faces of my mother and father and I wish I could really see them again, I do not need to talk to them or to hold them but if I could see them I think I would remember how things used to be.

The boy from Jaén had an aunt who worked in the olive fields as well and one day the aunt put a gun in her mouth while the mother of the aunt was sweeping in the upstairs room and when the gun went off and the bullet went up through the ceiling, to the floor where the mother passed the broom, the mother kept on sweeping into a pile the bits of wood from the hole in the floor and the bits of the brain and the skull of her daughter.

This boy from Jaén says he would like to live in the caves in the mountains made by the gypsies, and with him he would bring some books and one loyal dog. He says he would spend his nights looking at the luna. Luna llena.

Driving down into Cadaques you can pass through mountains with rich green ridges like steps cut into the sides of the mountains and maybe you think to yourself even though you have never been to Peru before, that these mountains must be like the mountains of Peru.

This aunt has been to the black sand beaches in Greece. She has told me of the men who dance in a circle at night on the black sand beaches, and in the mornings the women come and clear the ouzo bottles away.

I have told my children that the Greek men raise their bottles while they dance, not to the moon, but to the waves in the ocean because they believe that after their deaths they will come back as waves, each wave being the soul of a different man.

My children ask me if I have been to Greece and I tell them of course I have been to Greece, how else would I know these things, these Grecian ways.

Outside I can see the doctor coming aboard. In his hands, as if he holds a child, he holds the sheet he uses to wrap my hands. This day the sun is red. I am not sure if it is morning or evening. The doctor does not knock and he comes into my cabin without a word of hello. I am the first to talk, "Have you seen the white cows?" I ask him. I think maybe he has not heard me because he does not answer and instead he puts his hand over my head. I think maybe I have died and next he will shut my eyes for me, then, finally, the doctor says, "I have told you before, I see the white cows everyday." "And the men walking behind them with the sticks," I say. "They are always with the white cows," the doctor says. "Tell me again how the legs of the cows are black with mud," I say. The doctor unwraps the sheets and I can feel the air beginning to touch my hands. "You've been scratching your hands," he says. "No, I haven't." "You must be doing it in your sleep," he says. "I dream," I say. "You must dream your hands are rid of this rash," he says, he takes out a tin and with two fingers he pulls up the yellow fat and spreads it onto my hands. "I've slid down the elephant's trunk," I say, "I've held its ears for balance when stepping to the ground." "Next time we will use lemon juice," the doctor says, "to draw the pus and dry the rash." "Tell me," I say to the doctor, "how the men bend down and with leaves they wet in the river, they wash down the muddied legs of the white cows."

The doctor takes the old sheets from my hands and throws them out the window to the ocean but I cannot hear them hit the water. He puts his tin of fat back into his robes and he says, "I will come back late at night and I will bring you out under my robes, then into the boat and I will take you to the shore of India and you will see the white cows and I will sit you on an elephant so that you can slide down its long grey trunk, but for now you must dream that your hands, like the hooves of the white cows, are strong and can take you anywhere."

After the doctor left I slept and I dreamt I was a white cow and I saw the streets of India as I turned my head from side to side. At my back a stick would push me so I did not stop to watch for long the things I saw on the streets of India.

My mother asked me what I preferred, the Chinese in me, or the French. At the time we were at my wedding, and she was falling down drunk, that's at least what she always was when she was drunk, falling down. I have a picture of her sitting up, I think it's her passport picture blown large, and whenever I look at that picture I think I should turn it on its side, give it the falling down look. Chinese, I said because Uncle Pouz was at my side with a red chinese envelope, the kind that always held money. My mother could pull her thumbs back down so they touched her wrist and that's just what she did back then at my wedding when she asked what I preferred, the Chinese in me, or the French. Or that's what she did when I answered, when I said, Chinese and not French, which is what my mother was. She used to do that thumb thing for us when we were little so when she did it at my wedding I felt like I wasn't getting married, that I wasn't anywhere near being grown up because I still liked to watch her do that thumb thing the way I used to like to watch when I was young because, I guess, I could never do it myself. It was after that that my mother fell down. Uncle Pouz gave me the red envelope with the money first and then we took her up under the arms and brought her to a chair.

It is neither the french nor the chinese that I prefer.

After my mother would fall down she'd get up again and try to go somewhere. At the wedding she went to stand where I stood to take the vows and afterwards she turned to me and said, "You didn't mean it when you said it all." I said, "Said what?" she said—"That you prefer the chinese in you." I told her it was true, that I didn't mean it all. "You love your mother don't you?" she said. I wanted to ask her to do that thumb thing again. I wanted to watch her do that all night. I didn't want to dance at my wedding. I didn't want to be in my wedding. "Go dance," my mother said to me, and then she fell down again, so I picked her up under the arms once more and made my way back to the chair with her and told her *this* was dancing.

Some nights before I go to the bed I say goodnight to that picture of her. Even though it's just a passport picture she looks proud in it. You wouldn't think a proud woman would always be falling down, but she was a very proud woman. She would always ask me for a cloth or a pillow to put down on the chair before she sat in it, she would be hanging in my arms, her skirt maybe split from the awkward fall a drunk always takes and she would say, wait—can't you put a cloth down on that seat first.

Oh, there were times when I took her hand in mine, years later and I kissed the back of her hand. You know she never really kissed me, only in the french way, on the cheeks. "What did you kiss the back of my hand for," she said, then she said, "Your husband was no good, I stood where he stood when you both took the vows and it was him who didn't mean it all." I brought her gardenias and she would look at the plant and say tomorrow this bud will bloom and then she would sit back in the chair as if to wait to see it all happen before her eyes in that slow motion speed that seems to run in the world of a drunk.

It rained so hard we could not work to hold back the river banks because the wooden shovels kept slipping from our hands. The chief of the Montagnards was uncomfortable because his swollen testicles kept rising and floating in the rainwater that collected in the wheelbarrow that his wife rolled around for him so his wife used a bowl to scoop out the water so the chief's testicles could go back down again and to rest at the wet wood bottom of the wheelbarrow. My father and some others asked the men if we could stay in our places for the day and not work on the river because the shovels kept slipping from our hands. The men let us and I remember sitting on the floor of our place with my mother and my father while we played a hand game. I would put my hand on the wooden floor and then my mother or my father would try to slap it before I moved it away. I still remember the way it sounded when we played the game. It sounded as if they weren't hands hitting the wooden floor but feet walking around and the pace of the walk was fast and angry. We played the game for hours in the dark of the rainy day and we did not say anything to each other while we played. At night I put my hands face down on the pillow because it felt cool on my hands that I had been hitting the wooden floorboards with all day. I saw that my mother went right to sleep but that my father put his sandals under his pillow and left the place again to meet the Montagnards. I remember thinking how good his hands must feel to be out in the rain and I wondered if my father held his hands face up so the rain could fall on his fingers.

You ask the boy from Jaén what will happen when living in that gypsy cave so long his one loyal dog dies and the boy from Jaen says it won't matter, he too will be so old by then he will not remember the dog or that he ever had the dog.

The boy from Jaén has fallen in love with me. He is dark like a Moor. His name is Jesus. And the taken name from his mother is Jesus of the Snow.

In his town the women make their own chorizo and Jesus has brought me the chorizo his mother has made. It comes in strange shapes because casings of pigs are not always the same size, Jesus says. Oh, there was the pig, Jesus says, who stayed in the bar and took walks down the street and back into the bar, Jesus says. He was a fat pig, Jesus says, and the men gave him beer and olives and put a hat on his head. The way the Andalusians do it is they drop their "s"s so to say more or less they say *ma o meno* and now, after so many years, I still cannot say more or less without wanting to say instead ma or meno. So *ma o meno,* Jesus said, the pig was our mayor, people went to him—a man went to the pig in the bar and told the pig his wife wanted to leave him and go to Madrid and what asked the man of the pig, should I do. The pig said nothing and the pig stayed where he was under the table in the bar by the man's dusty feet, dusty from the work in the olive fields where it seldom rained, and the man then left after talking to the pig and he went home to his wife where she was making chorizo and the man said nothing to his wife and he did nothing the same as the pig had done nothing and the wife never left the town of Jaén for Madrid and the men in the bar dropped olives to the floor for the pig and straightened the hat on his head.

Ma o meno, Jesus says, this is how the story went.

My father beat me. Every week I would go in to see him and he would ask me what I had done wrong and he would beat me after I told him and if I told him I did not do anything wrong he would beat me anyway. I loved my father's clothes. He wore gabardine shirts that when he moved looked like they held a wind inside of them and they billowed as I watched his hand raise and then fly to hit my face. When he hit me I always hoped the wind he held inside his gabardine shirt would come up so I could smell my father's chest. If he hit me more than once his smell became stronger.

When I think about it I saw things when he hit me and I smelled the wind he held in his shirt. I cannot remember now what it is that I saw. I might have seen people I had seen walking on the street that day. I might have seen a sun setting in the cold weather so the sun looked as sharp as glass. I might have seen India. The ocean. A ship. I would close my eyes to see these things better and my father told me to open up my eyes again.

My father was beautiful and I could not look at him for very long. I would always want to turn my eyes away and then to turn them back on him when he wasn't looking at me. I thought that someone so beautiful must be dangerous. The smell held in his gabardine shirt might kill me, it might be a wind so strong I am knocked over, my eyes closed and left to seeing things I can only imagine and things that maybe never took place.

Under his robes I touch the Indian doctor's belly. I want to see if dark skin feels the same as my skin. "Are the sheets slipping from your hands?" he asks me. "No," I say and I have forgotten about my hands being in sheets because we are now in the small boat and the doctor is rowing and my head is on the middle of his chest and every time his arms go back and then forward to row the boat it feels as if he is just about to put his arms all the way around me and to hold me but he doesn't and his arms go back again to pull the oars through air so he can once again pull them through the ocean and we are on our way to India.

"There are the white cows," the doctor says to me and I cannot look because I think he is not telling me the truth and like his arms almost coming around me in the rowboat but never coming full around, I will never see the white cows with the men walking behind them, pushing the white cows with sticks. "Look," the doctor says and takes me out from under his robes and I stand barefoot and I think how good the dust and the small rocks of the ground feel to my feet and then I look ahead and I see the white cows. But in the moonlight the cows do not look white and instead they look silver and I say to the doctor, "These cows are not from India," and the doctor asks me what do I mean and I tell him that the cows I have heard of are white and are not silver looking like they have been sent down from the moon." The doctor tells me I have been looking out from my bed on the ship at the moon too many nights now to know white from silver. Some days the sun is so bright it looks white off the water and I think my ship is resting on snow, not the ocean. What glistens at night may be small fish but I think it's crystals of snow. How can this be India, I think. My hands itch and wrapped in sheets I rub them together, it may be that the animal fat has been rubbed on so many times my hands are becoming paws, or better yet hooves. "What are you doing to me," I ask the doctor. He takes me up under his robes again and then he unties his pants and we go down to lie on the ground. I can see out through the neck of his robes, as if like the wind that billows my father's shirt, I am the wind inside my doctor's robes ready to come out. From under his robes I can hear the men talking softly to the cows—silver cows, they push with sticks on down the road.

Polar bears now they say can only be spotted on the white ice and snow by their black noses so they take up by their claws pieces of snow and hold them to their black noses so nobody finds them. This is what the Eskimos say and this is what others say is not possibly true. Eskimos say they've seen the polar bears do this, and the stories of the sightings have been passed down to Eskimo children and grandchildren.

I was with Jesus de Nieve when I went down the road to Cadaques. It was he who told me the mountains looked like the mountains of Peru. He had never been to Peru either, but because he told me that the mountains looked to him like the mountains that would be in Peru, I thought they did also. Jesus said seeing the steps in the sides of the mountains made him want to stop. He asked, "When you see steps like that made by God don't you feel as though you have to walk up them?" I told him that you can see where the steps go, they just go up to the top of the mountains. "*Ma o meno*," Jesus said, and then he lead the way down into Cadaques.

In the great room my mother says this room is breathing. The great carpet heaves up and down. The day after the rain has stopped it is so windy that the glass windows ripple and the space between the floorboards and the woolen carpet in the great room catches the wind as well so that the woolen carpet looks as though the great ones live under it and move as if they are the backs of sea monsters, undulating up and down. The white moths are gone to hiding in the corners of the room. "I dreamt of your father," my mother says, "He went to live in the mountains," she says. "He became a Montagnard and he left us here, with the men, and he never came back to get us and instead we would sometimes see him walking the face of the mountain." I thought of my father's nose, how it must have been for my mother in her dream to see my father on the face of the mountain and how she could tell it was him because of his nose when my father turned to the side.

We call my sister Poulet, they call me Tian—it's short for Christiane. My mother's name was Marcelle and my father's, Yeu. My father made Marcelle sound like a call a bird would make, he would say it so many times. Marcelle, Marcelle, Marcelle. I learned English and I could not believe the whippoorwill was the very sound it made. Around the house he called her and she did not come to him but he would find her. He would walk through the rooms of the house. Marcelle—Marcelle. He had an idea he had to tell her. I never heard what the ideas were or if I did I do not remember them. I remember watching him stand in front of her. Yeu in front of Marcelle, my beautiful father in front, standing before my mother and my mother listening to him, maybe holding my sister in her arms at the same time, the baby sleeping. My father would not sit down until he finished telling Marcelle his idea, what he had to say, and then he would sit by Marcelle, take hold of the baby's foot or Marcelle's arm and he would look out as if what was in front of him was a window with a view of the woods, birds going back and forth in the trees.

Eating Disorders
Jay Cantor

WHEN I GO TO THE MOVIES my heart fills with intense expectation, and for the first half hour or so of almost any movie I am unreasonably pleased, so in awe of the wonderful technology of the spectacle, of a world so accurately reproduced yet enlarged, that I think I'm watching a great movie, when really I am just—at least for a while—delighted by the glamour of movies. I gawk at the sheer size and light of the thing, as if what was shown escaped mere representation, *as if* I were not seeing images but something like the delicious body of the world itself. (But better: no need to fear the anxiety caused by another body.)

I gawk at the stars' glamour, too, an aura the more mysterious to me because it comes not from their beauty (stars are often far from pretty), but from their magnificent self-absorption, an attitude so long perfected that it seems almost generous of them to show themselves to me. The star has learned to want herself first, learned to love the shape of her own nose, its cunning little bump; and I love her for seeming to love herself—a masochistic passion, for that very quality means she will never need or love me. So large, so smooth (the screen shows abrasions and crannies yet remains forever unbroken, like the most perfect skin), so whole (all on one plane, she and her world are a perfect fit), the star is inedible by me or by time. By comparison, I'm needy, cracked, vulnerable, hungry; and my shame at my body only adds to the star's glamour. (And how fans abused Elizabeth Taylor for betraying stardom by being hungry, getting fat!)

But a desire to see glamour is only a small part of my excited expectation at the movies; and perhaps, too, it's the empty food I accept when I know my more profound appetites won't be fed. For mostly my heart leaps to greet a film because I expect to be *transformed* by the meeting. At the movies, I expect (though it rarely happens) to find new fragments (of style, of attitude, of gesture, of magical fantasy) to add to the inner assemblage that *is* my psyche, fragments that properly assembled might be curative of those first images of union and of severance that have shaped me. For I like the psychoanalytic view of the self (maybe because it reminds me of movies), that the personality is a raggle-taggle montage of the unlikely fantasy-images and pieces of the world that out of love and fear of loss, you swallowed up in childhood—a delicious breast, a moustache, a comforting fragment of a cloth coat you once felt against your cheek, a melodramatic threatening hand, a melancholy carriage to the body. Supposedly one often gets such fragments at films, so that after a movie, members of the audience leave the theater walking like James Dean, mumbling like Brando, but in my experience the images are too perfect, too hard to be truly broken up, mixed with the saliva of the imagination, and swallowed.

I know it's a fairy tale expectation to think that I'll find magical fragments to re-make the mosaic of myself at my local mall's wickedly uncomfortable octoplex. And, of course, I'm almost always disappointed. After an hour, I twist about in my seat. We've been cheated! There's nothing transformative here, nothing nourishing! I turn back to the screen, and in the absence of food, I accept more glamour; but it tastes a little bitter to me.

Once upon a time, though, I think many people felt that popular culture gave them something more to feed upon, something to help them in their remaking. In the Sixties, it was as if Bob Dylan or the Beatles or Aretha Franklin were growing up before us, and sent back, as if from the frontline of a new adulthood, reports of their discoveries and their quandaries. A *new adulthood,* or so we thought (and *not* just a Peter Pan-like endless childhood), with an insistence that morality and ecstasy could be reconciled, that the questions of pleasure (what are its sources? how is the deepest pleasure to be formed? how are we to be worthy of it? what are its dangers?), if sounded deeply enough, pursued rigorously enough, would instruct us in how to shape a new human solidarity. We even thought that the joys of art might lead us to a new rationality, a reason of the heart, where pleasure would guide the connections between realms, and satisfying organic form would be as rigorous in setting limits as any imposed order. In this enterprise, rock & roll drew heavily on—or stole from—black popular music, for nowhere else have the questions of pleasure been as profoundly asked as in black secular and gospel music, where to move together might make a congregation, and pleasure and morality join in the ecstasy of bodily possession by the holy spirit. Maybe that spirit can take one both in Church and on the dance floor; in the Sixties black secular and religious combined to make "Soul" music, the most enthralling and wrenching popular art of that time.

There was oodles of *Teen Scene Magazine* illusion in our sense of connection with popular artists, but not just that—though the artists did grow rich (and distant) from our adoration. Still, the artists' wealth seemed less important to us than the questions we thought we shared, as if money merely gave them greater scope and leisure to carry out experiments on our behalf. And what they discovered, we were sure, would be—like sex, the three basic rock & roll chords, or a hit of windowpane acid—cheap thrills, democratically available. After all, why should beauty only be rare and difficult?

I also had a sense of questions shared, of bits of answers for us to use within our selves in the filmed essay-stories, the research reports, of Jean-Luc Godard, and in the more generous, more sweet-tempered films of the Yugoslav filmmaker Dujan Makavejev. And Makavejev remains especially valuable to me in his continuing attempt, through the greedy eighties, to rally the scattered dispirited remnants of the party of pleasure. Even in his less successful films the questions remain: What is the instruction pleasure might offer? Why do we fear it? What is the shape of the community pleasure might make? And will it look grotesque to our eyes? (So much the worse for our eyes!)

Makavejev's greatest films are *WR: Mysteries of the Organism*, a free form fantasia-documentary inspired by Wilhelm Reich (patriarch—or sacred monster—of the party of pleasure), and *Sweet Movie*, an original mixture of allegory, fantasy, and documentary. These films of the early Seventies describe, in terms witty, shrewd, vulgar, and blatant, the ways we've tried to free our bodies, and the ways history has mutilated them. *Sweet Movie* follows a special "Miss World" pageant, whose winner's prize will be marriage to the richest man in the United States. (His pleasure is the degradation of his wife. To consummate the marriage he'll reward her with a urinous "golden shower.") Alongside this story we follow the ship of Captain Anna Planeta (CP), called *Survival*, as it moves forward through a city's canals with a huge papier-mâché bust of Karl Marx on its prow. To lure people on board she promises them open-hearted comradeship, sensual pleasure, redemption on this earth for their bodies. That is to say, the Communist

Party coopts comrades from the party of pleasure. This time she attracts a fellow named "Bakunin," from the ship *Potemkin*, representing the early,and betrayed, promise of the Russian revolution; and with sweets and a striptease she also seduces three teenage boys to join her. The party of pleasure, it seems, is ripe for betrayal; desperate to deny the death instinct,the attraction of the gun pointed at others or at oneself, it makes ecstasy too easy a matter, purging it of all violence. So the repressed returns: "Bakunin" willingly submits to what he knows will be the deadly caresses of Captain Planeta. She bites his neck, and he says, "That's good, go on . . . Everything cannot be explained . . . I felt so jealous when Vakovlinchuk was killed." Then she stabs him to death in a bath of sugar. "I brought a lot of sugar," CP complains later, "but I can't get rid of the bitter taste." She murders the teenagers and has the crew put a tear under Marx's eye.

We also join a commune in Amsterdam for a saturnalian meal of the greatest grotesqueness, a theatrical counterculture dinner whose intent feels therapeutic. At this feast a communard takes a huge sausage out of his pants, lays it across the table and whacks slices off for everyone with a big knife; communards drink urine, and vomit freely; a man shits on a platter, and his bowel movement is carried about as the "Ode to Joy" plays in the background. This carnival of a world and a body turned upside down is followed by a painfully literal and self-conscious ceremony of re-birth in which a fat, hairy man, covered with blood and feces, has his comrades beat on his stomach to mimic the painful contractions of giving birth—in this case, to himself. The whole community swaddles, powders, and nurses him as he mewls and pukes. (Rebirth is celebrated. But the other stages of life, the *deathward* ones, as we ripen and rot, seem once again omitted.) The communards then dance with a hippety-hop motion that filled me alternately with a desire to move with them, and a wish, like Miss World—who becomes anorexic at the commune—to get as far away as possible (perhaps to sell real estate and watch T.V.). At the conclusion of the film Captain Planeta is arrested,and the corpses arise again, like the countries of Eastern Europe. Is their re-birth only a trick of the camera? Are they alive, or not yet alive? That decision, (and the how and why of re-birth) is left to the viewer.

Makavejev's next film, *Montenegro,* was released in 1981, as the once frolicsome party of pleasure—including delegates from the left misled by Anna Planeta, weary former communard feasters from the counterculture, gay erotic adventurers afraid of sexually transmitted diseases (and the growing rumor of worse to come)—became tuber audiences to a T.V.-provided history. (With T.V. you needn't fear the anxiety caused by another body.)

In *Montenegro,* Susan Anspach frighteningly incarnates an American housewife in Sweden, Marilyn Jordan, wife of Martin and mother of two, thoroughly uncomfortable in very comfortable circumstances. She runs away with a theatricalized theater troop of Yugoslav immigrants, has an affair with one of them—Montenegro—murders him, and returns home to poison her family.

"There is enough food in this country," a customs inspector says, confiscating a young immigrant girl's pig. Probably there is; but Makavejev wonders if it's good to eat. Near the beginning of the film, Anspach offers a bowl of milk laced with poison to the family dog. "It's your decision," she says to the dog. "But if you ask my advice don't do it." And her husband's grandfather, who has been made wacky by time and American pop culture until he thinks he's Buffalo Bill, looks suspiciously at the glass of milk that Marilyn brings him, and says, "What is in this milk?" (In fact, it's the grapes that they should all be looking out for, that's where she'll place the poison.) Would *we* know the right food? This film's flavor is not the unsatisfying bitterness of glamour, but an irony that tastes to me like spoiled milk, a sourness that comes, I think, from a distrust of the ecstasies that Makavejev and I had, we fear, once foolishly found nourishing, yet fear we might be more foolish to surrender. So we grow to doubt our ability to tell good food from bad, as if the rottenness were in us as well, in our judgment.

That a woman should offer poisoned food to her family is almost unbearable to me. There must be an explanation! Something must have curdled her milk. I first saw the film as a story—more or less—of a woman's failed liberation: an oppressive husband, a try at independence of a wife driven so mad that she was unable to bear the food (the delicious lamb, the strong, illegal brandy) of freedom. In this version of the film the emblematic dialogue is the obtuse businessman's telephone conversation with his runaway wife, whom he believes has been kidnaped: "Will they [the imagined kidnapers] accept a check? How much do they want? It must be a fortune!" To which Marilyn angrily replies, "It's more than you can begin to afford, my darling." (Martin doesn't mean to be disparaging by counting Marilyn's cost; that his wife would be worth a fortune to the imagined kidnapers also measures her worth to him.)

Marilyn's madness made me anxious, and I wanted to calm my nerves by *explaining* her. But my interpretation was too bland, already chewed. And a contrary outcome to Marilyn's failure, the many victories for independence won by the women's movement, hadn't, so far at least, led to the triumph of pleasure. So I went back to the film wondering what made Marilyn destroy her ecstasy and poison others.

I thought, too, this might tell me something about why the party of pleasure has faded so. The explanation for Marilyn's unhappiness would be one answer to Freud's question—by now, I think, his most quoted phrase—which is also one of the movie's questions: *what does woman want?* Perhaps the questions of pleasure can be phrased in this way because women's pleasure has been found threatening for so long (by men—and perhaps sometimes by women, too), and because our earliest memories of pleasure are bound up with a woman's body.

This time I think that it's film (that often disappointing but still crucial ecstasy), the means by which her story is told, that has curdled Marilyn Jordan, made her murderous towards her pleasure. (And it is, as I say, a drug I frequently consume, too!) So the movie *intends* to leave a bad taste in my mouth, for the film's not just about Marilyn Jordan poisoning others, but about film poisoning me. Makavejev wants to warm me against his own medium; perhaps he dreams, too, that film might be the kind of poison that, used properly, might cure.

Each art, during the course of its development (and even—as *Don Quixote* shows in the case of the novel—near its beginning, before a sense of its dangers was drowned by the din of its triumphs, its effective distractions), has offered warnings, and homeopathic cures for the diseases that the art itself might cause. *Madame Bovary* (whose irony is at least as unsettling in flavor as Makavejev's) is the nearly poisonous narrative that would be the cure for romantic narratives. Brecht wished to make theater an instrument against the distractions—the harmful identifications and soporific inattention to one's actual bitter conditions—that theater produced. Godard's films borrow Brecht's techniques, and his characters, self-consciously the children of Marx and Coca-Cola—which is to say, of film—reproduce for us the "automatisms" caused by a love affair with the mechanical medium, movies. Each of these sometimes artists, directly, in exposition, in plot, or in allegories that describe the medium of the story even as the story is told, warn us of the dangers of artistic representation, and produce from this doubled message about their own medium an anxious quality and a sense of depth. It's a difficult job *to film* the dangers of film, and not simply to theatricalize one's self-suspicion—making the critique of the show another part of show business. (I think something like that happens, for example, in Antonioni's *Blow Up.*) But most recent movies—like the Eighties retro-style Hollywood films—don't try to critique their medium. They seem simply nostalgic for earlier representations, and just want to repeat them to manufacture a flat distraction in the present. (But in this endless Peter Pan-like second childhood you'll have money to buy better toys, niftier special effects.)

In *Montenegro* film becomes the subject near the beginning of the story, in Marilyn Jordan's kitchen, as she cooks dinner for her family. Marilyn furiously pounds veal as if all the hatred of her life could be put into the mallet's swing, and then, in one of the more chilling scenes in a very frosty film, she teaches her daughter a

recipe, as if she was teaching the little girl a witch's curse. But, as in a fairy tale, the witch's curse imprisons the witch: "This life," Marilyn concludes angrily, "this movie—all so damn predictable." The child asks, "What movie?" Marilyn replies, "The movie we're in." The child demurs, "I'm not in a movie. I'm in the kitchen." And Marilyn concludes, frighteningly, "In the kitchen like the schnitzel in the hot fat." Then we see Marilyn eating a pile of schnitzel, eating, as we find out later, *all* of her family's dinner, and as she tears at the meat she looks both dazed and imprisoned, an empty spirit in vacant space.

Makavejev is always fascinated by how we animals eat. In the communal meal in *Sweet Movie* the communards grossly, savagely, conflate eating and defecation and sex. Which is which, and where? Where does it come from, and where does it go, and what farcical torments must we go through if we are ever to get it right? In *Montenegro* there's a small reprise of the commune's feast when we watch the Jordans stuff themselves with spaghetti till it tumbles out of their mouths, while the young son gleefully describes a Frenchman who died gorging himself on snails. The Jordans seem to be having a good time, but they would be shocked if they saw how grotesque they looked. (The communards of *Sweet Movie* would be shocked, I think, if they *hadn't* looked grotesque to me.)

I'm not sure that the director has some settled position on how or what we should eat, except that he doesn't want to let us forget that we are animals when we eat (as, of course, we always are). Starting from our animality might be a way to discover a deeper, though for the moment uncomfortable, sense of solidarity, and even, perhaps, possibilities for more satisfying activity. So food provides Makavejev with many ways to phrase the questions of pleasure: What are good table manners (that is: a decent—sometimes *too* decent—social order) and what is our proper food? (Why do we feel hungry all the time, our bodies unsatisfied?) Eating is a metaphor, too, for how we symbolically feed upon the body of the world to form ourselves, swallowing bits we like to form the montage of the self. (Why can't we find better pieces to add to our montage?) So eating is the infant's first version of the question of how pleasure might make the self, and Makavejev continues, often in an infantile way, the child's investigations: *Do I feed upon her destructively?* becomes, must we waste each other, in work and in sex? Or, to give a utopian extension to his metaphor, is there some way that the dream of the communion meal might become real on this earth, so that the communards might joyously eat and joyously offer themselves, through all that their bodies can do, as symbolic food?

Marilyn—we learn as we watch her devour the family's schnitzel—is voracious. And she thinks herself imprisoned; not by her husband, precisely, but because she's in a movie, trapped there—as if she were food—like schnitzel in hot fat. Of course, she *is* in a movie, one directed by Dujan Makavejev; made up of images, she is an image, and what she eats is an image. No wonder her appetite is so unappeasable—is there an *image* of food that can satisfy? A woman who is "in a movie," a woman made up of images, is a version of the person (common outside movies, too) who acts "as if" she feels; so her emotions are only what she successfully portrays for others, what they take her as portraying. Severed from the inner sources of her own appetites, she can never be satisfied or truly satisfy.

This schnitzel scene reminded me of the gluttons' punishment in Dante's hell; they fall all over themselves in their rage to stuff mud in their mouths. Of course the "food" doesn't satisfy them, so they have to eat more and more of it. After Freud, though, I think Dante's sinners might, like the rest of us, be analyzed more remissively. The punishments that Dante doles out are not the result of their crimes, but their cause. They were voracious here on earth because the food they were given was like mud to them, and couldn't satisfy. Neither the glutton, or an anorexic like "Miss World," can find the food they truly want to eat. (And perhaps they sometimes poison others, so they, too, won't be satisfied.)

When I was watching Anspach's angry, bewildered face, I wondered why Makavejev had made his damned glutton an American. (Of course, I mean *Marilyn's* face, but when a movie performance so seems to fit the actor's body I forget which is role and which the player. Bogart becomes Hammett becomes Sam Spade. John Wayne becomes the American West embodied, a hero off screen because he walked like a hero on screen.) Is Makavejev unfairly having at us, as if we Americans poisoned others because we were too puritanical, or too prudent, and couldn't stand our own pleasure? Miss World, for example, Makavejev's representative American lass in *Sweet Movie* can't fuck for business reasons; her "cherry" is, she feels, her most salable asset. But what country revels more—however restlessly—in its hedonism? Have we really created bodies so made for work, or so intolerant of the flesh, that we're incapable of pleasure? I think we have to grant Makavejev that we *are* restless, yearning, dissatisfied, and perhaps (more than some puritan stain) it's because we've given ourselves over to the endless teasing of the spectacle, to images *as* commodities, and commodities as mostly images—so a thing is as much the brand name, and the fantasy of its advertising, as it is the work it might do. The ability to anneal trademark and product is part of the genius of images—like film's ability to unify the character and the actor. "When people eat chocolate, the brand we advertise . . . I want them to feel they're eating you," one mock movie director in *Sweet Movie* says to Miss World, as she's filmed circling her breasts with chocolate. But when you buy the product, you don't really get the delicious body of the world itself, you're *not* really eating it. This sort of symbol—product + image—can be bought, but not eaten, for this symbol wasn't meant to be used *by* you in your self-construction. (It was meant to shame you.)

This describes, in part, the inevitable dissatisfaction of human sexuality, which, like advertising, begins in fantasy. We dream of

the breast when it isn't there; when it returns the real isn't *quite* the same as our star-fantasy, not as perfectly satisfying as what we had imagined. So image-culture's airbrushed fantasies play upon the disappointment of sexuality, magnify it, intensify it to the point of a restless insatiable madness. The images, compared to *our* bodies, rebuke us for our gross appetites (we're so imperfect, so needy compared to the stars). And the images, compared to the food we might find, seem so perfect, so flawless, yet, when we try to use them they are, because of that very perfection, so inedible, so unsatisfying!

Perhaps if you bought *enough* image-commodities they might, almost, turn your own body into something watched—so although you can't *use* the images within yourself, you might almost *become* one. Swaddled in designer clothes you can have, for a few moments, the feeling that you're in an ad, have become a hard enduring image, an immortal self-satisfied movie star, rid of the muck and appetites of the body, neither eating nor being eaten. (Or, like Marilyn, you might feel you're trapped in a movie.) As Alex, the Yugoslav paterfamilias, says to Marilyn—when she has, by a nice concatenation of plotting, gone to live with the immigrants at their theater-compound, "Many people have Gucci shoes. You have a Gucci foot." He means this as a compliment, but it's also another curse, for not just the shoe you wear, he is saying, but the foot itself, has become a brand name, an image in a spectacle—a star's foot, masochistically loved by Alex because it doesn't need him; it requires no tickling, no fondling.

Marilyn's husband, worried by his wife's endless dissatisfaction, seeks out a psychiatrist for her, Dr. Aram Pazardjian. This doctor, with his bowl-cut white hair and enigmatic smile, is a creepy charismatic fraud who looks remarkably like Andy Warhol. Dr. Pazardjian's power (and perhaps some of Warhol's as well) comes from an open admission of fraudulence. "He would like you to know," his receptionist says, demanding payment in advance, "that he is only interested in money." In this free display of his vulgarity he is like the Yugoslavs Marilyn will meet later; after long denial, such open vulgar appetite, such bad taste, can be a new and fascinating flavor. (O my Madonna, my newfound land!)

Dr. Pazardjian feeds Marilyn a few gnomic fortune cookies—"what's the difference between one chicken?" and "How long is a piece of string?" Marilyn's need to be joined to a saving power turns Dr. Pazardjian into a healer who cares about her, so she tries to answer his K mart koans. To the first she replies, "You mean a chicken looking in a mirror?" Then "You can't escape someone if that someone happens to be yourself." And in reply to the second, she mimes hanging herself.

She is saved from more therapy when, accidentally stranded at an airport, she's serendipitously taken up by the Yugoslav immigrants who I think of as gypsies—for in tales of a housewife who needs to be saved from her husband it is often the gypsies who fulfill the role. The Yugoslavs are, as it turns out, a charming troop of performers. Part of their sweetness is a gift of the movie maker: The bourgeois household has been shot in very harsh light, and fill-light has been used throughout to give a cold, evenly lit, inedible, almost clinical effect to the scenes. The immigrants, by contrast, are shot in smokey, soft, romantic, light. And like the commune in *Sweet Movie,* the immigrant's encampment-showplace (ZanziBar) is a libidinous soup. The *Sweet Movie* communards' attempt to recapture, to re-awaken their bodies (are we alive or dead?) were frightening, grotesque, willful, and repulsive in their purgative, shitting, puking effort to get all the bad stuff out of themselves. This group of Slav performers seems to have been given a pass on history; easy in their appetites, they have nothing to mend. By contrast to *Sweet Movie*'s cock-sausage, the lamb that we've seen Montenegro carry across his back, butcher, roast, and serve at ZanziBar simply looks delicious. (In the Makavejev film that follows this, *The Coca-Cola Kid,* the drama of an American placed among the libidinal denizens of a forest of Arden is played out, even more improbably, by contrasting a tightly wound American businessman—brilliantly acted by Eric Roberts—with . . . Australians. Makavejev, I think, has grown desperate for "a world elsewhere"—anywhere! In this Makavejev reminds me of the way radicals turned about looking for allies and noble saviors free of society's distortions—schizophrenics? women? blacks? students? the third world? . . . Australians?

In ZanziBar gypsies brawl with elemental anger, take knives in the head and blows from a shovel across the skull—but no one dies. And sexual play, in its free unfolding, causes no anxiety: Alex and a woman fuck athletically at the bottom of the bed where Marilyn sleeps; the bed collapses, enraging the young woman, who then snuggles under the covers with Marilyn. ("What do we need him for?" the woman says of Alex, as she pets Marilyn. "That feels good," Marilyn replies with a quizzical but accepting look.) ZanziBar is rich in moments of charming communal improvisation. At the airport Marilyn has broken a heel from her shoe, so Alex's former wife slips hers off to provide for the guest. If Marilyn needs a towel for the shower, the ex-wife whisks a table cloth into service.

The slippers that Alex's ex-wife gives Marilyn fit; this Cinderella story ends darkly, but it's filled with fairy tale elements. At the airport, for example, Martin doesn't recognize his wife's broken shoe, even when it is held in front of his face by Alex: this certifies Martin's unsuitability. At ZanziBar, after a battle over her, Marilyn revives a seemingly dead Montenegro, thus showing they're fated for each other.

Makavejev has always liked the style of fairy tales. *Sweet Movie,* for example, retells "Hansel and Gretel": the bad witches of both capitalism and communism use and distort our desire for sweets to lure us to our destruction. Communism promises the "real" sweetness of a satisfying community, then pushes its citizens into the gulag. Capitalism coats its images with a patina of sex to make its products seem sweet, but the world then becomes images that can't satisfy. I think Makavejev is drawn to fairy tales because in them the character's (and the reader's) unconscious wishes suddenly, surprisingly become symbols, fragments of fantasy rich with one's unknown necessities for connection and for death, magical food and drink that can change one's personality.... Or does Marilyn simply delude herself about her suitability for Montenegro—as one might say sarcastically, "She's trying to turn life into a fairy tale"? Are such stories of ecstatic transformation (like my memories of Sixties popular culture) just self-deception? Makavejev's irony, which tastes to me like my own self-distrust, makes it hard to decide.

Maybe Makavejev simply loves his theatrical gypsies because they're a better subject for the camera than the world outside ZanziBar. He has always had a goat's appetite for popular stagecraft, bawdy songs, vulgar burlesque. And unlike their intuitive sexuality, the Slavs weren't simply born more colorful, for Makavejev shows us how they have *made* themselves interesting—whatever the risks—as part of their seductive vaudeville. A photo they take of themselves, for example, before rushing a wounded man to the hospital makes a more engaging snapshot than the Kodak of the family Marilyn has left, because in the gypsies' Polaroid one of the characters has a knife sticking out of his head. They're willing to die for their picture, for only the knife in the head allows the gypsies to compete with the many other entertainments available to us. (But in ZanziBar, if it weren't for the beautiful American, no one need really *die*).

Is it only me (and not the director) who's suspicious of Makavejev's recent worlds elsewhere, his ZanziBar, his "Australia" (still green because the Americans, the Coca-Cola Corporation, haven't eliminated the charming native soft-drinks)? These gypsies remind me sometimes of a fond memory of communal living, which, in reality, did give many ecstatic moments but also had more of the actual slog and abrasion of people living together than ZanziBar does. (Why are there never any towels not spotted with Chianti, or any dry table cloths!) And sometimes, in their efforts to theatricalize themselves, the Slavs remind me, too, of the way so many in the Sixties seemed greedy for publicity, made themselves grotesque in order to become good subjects for the camera. The party of pleasure's desire to purge ecstasy of its destructiveness, its wish to deny the death instinct, contributed greatly to this lust to become an image—for images, like stars, need never die.

These desperate performers stay alive by entertaining people—as Martin does with the mass produced "sculptures" he sells ("ball bearings in a strait-jacket," the psychiatrist calls them), as Dr. Pazardjian does with his gnomic patter, as the pathetic applicants to be Buffalo Bill's wife do when they mug for the video camera that Martin's children hold on them. All the world's a stage. In *The Coca-Cola Kid,* the Coca-Cola executive wants an "authentic Australian sound," for his T.V. ads, and on the street in Sydney he finds a fairy tale character, a raggedy gray-bearded aboriginal gnome who plays a horn made at the beginning of time. Of course, the musician offers the executive his business card, and asks him to get in touch with his agent.

Probably, like me and the aborigine, the gypsies have agents, too, for they're greedy for things as well as for attention. Several of the women want Marilyn's fur coat, the young girl wants her hair done to look like Marilyn's, and Alex wants to sleep with her because "she's a lady." But these simple greeds are easy enough to accept. It isn't so much that our greeds ensnare us (though they do, they did!), or that, as Lenin wrote, the small bourgeois ceaselessly gives rise to the large, but that the small theater troop goes to Broadway, the Polaroid picture dreams of becoming the De Mille epic, and the ZanziBar vaudeville show probably wants to use our adoration to grow rich and distant from us, and themselves become part of what makes us at once yearning, passive, and dissatisfied, become ... television. As, alas (whether Makavejev wants it or not), did *Montenegro.* The last time I saw the movie, it was on cable T.V.'s Movie Channel—introduced by an "as if" good-old-boy, Joe Bob Briggs, on his "Drive in Theater Show." "Joe Bob" had once been a Texas newspaperman who reviewed grade c movies in a comic red-neck persona. But the man and the mask annealed, and the reporter was fired when Joe Bob's reviews grew offensively racist and misogynist. (Some men wear fancy boots, but Joe Bob had grown shit-kicker feet.) He's made a comeback on cable. Last week, Joe Bob announced,the programmers had goofed and sent him a foreign film. Still, it wasn't as bad as he thought it would be. It had, he said, eight shots of naked breasts.

The second act of the gypsy show includes several of the naked breasts as a young girl does a striptease, clearly enjoying her own performance. There isn't any innocence to be found in

Makavejev's movies. He thinks that's another fantasy, like table manners, or movie stars, that people use to repress themselves, for they fear their pleasure. (Such magical eating might change us, and we want to remain forever as we are, never dying.) The young girl is chased by a plastic penis on wheels until she submits to being mock-fucked by it, and is fork-lifted into the heavens above the stage. Marilyn is then carried off by her prince charming, her legs wrapped around him in the most shamelessly clichéd pose of romantic pornography, like the trashy novel we'd seen her reading in bed with her husband. The smokey light and tinkley music of this shot may mark that the director knows this is hokum, Marilyn's cliché-fantasy of satisfaction. But is it Makavejev's too? And if *I* still find it hokey is it because I fear pleasure now? Or because I snobbishly disdain honky-tonk thrills, the grade c movies that I, too, once had a goat's appetite for—just because they want to be on television? (And where do I want to be?)

Marilyn, angry at her own need, produces a scene for her internal theater where she has protested her desire, where she has no appetites, where she was—in the scenarios she's staging for her super-ego—taken against her will. She hits Montenegro in the most theatrical of ways. Then they fuck, rolling about in the grain. Fireworks—literally!—go off outside their bedroom, the climax to the gypsy show. Again, like the tinkley music, this is an irony, undercutting the glorious "did the earth move?" aspect of their fucking—yet, like so much irony, allowing us also to *have* the sweet romantic feeling without thinking ourselves simpletons. After more fireworks—feu d'artifice—the show ends. The next morning, Marilyn walks out of ZanziBar, and we see Montenegro's body, his blood pouring out on the ground. Was Marilyn angered because she was satisfied with him—so she *has* needs (she isn't a star)? Or because he didn't please her—for how could an image satisfy? Is she terrified by her ecstasies (she isn't an image, she will die) or maddened by their absence (she remains trapped in a movie, surrounded by unsatisfying images)? Enraged, she's taken a knife to the screen, but now that we are ourselves a scene seen, she's also ripped into flesh.

In a talk of Makavejev's on Ingmar Bergman he said: "From Tausk's 1919 paper 'On the Origin of the Influencing Machine' we learn that each schizophrenic has his own all-powerful dictating machine. This machine is our genitals, projected and seen as foreign, determining our lives, the source of life. Bergman's depiction of the parts of a projector is his declaration of his machine, so conceived." The projector is the source of life—if life is an image. But if life is just an image—or *the wrong sort of image*—we can't incorporate it, but only watch it, and sink into a stupor of acceptance (of shame, and a yearning for glamour) and we grow ravenous. Or murderous.

Marilyn rejoins her family, and all she has done becomes a story around the dinner table. "There was a lamb that was slaughtered . . . Two men fought a duel . . . she saved one of the men who was her lover."

Her son asks, does the story have a happy ending?

"Yes, they all lived happily ever after," Marilyn says, as is appropriate to a fairy tale become Hollywood movie.

But, a title tells us, the fruit she gives her family was poisoned—the grapes she gave her family, the apple Eve took, the movie we have watched.

Well, it's only a movie—in this case one in part about the dangers of movies. But then another title tells us that it's not just a movie. It was based on real events.

A troublesome ending; once again it left a bad taste, and not, this time, because of Marilyn's smiling savagery as she places poisoned grapes in her children's mouths. Once upon a time, I don't think Makavejev would have appealed to any authority outside of his fiction, wouldn't have thought that fiction was made *more* powerful, believable, by appealing to reality. Isn't it images used in some new way, images made more edible, made into symbols rich with our nutritive necessities, that may save us? I would think a film maker must believe so. Fantastic images (of castration, say) produced by our own Imaginary Film Company made us, and not *acceptance* of reality, but new fantastic images will remake us. We do have unconscious needs, of course, and only those fragments of fantasy will change us that embody those necessities; but I think Freud has shown us—and against his own wish for mastery—that there is no way, outside of fantasy, of metaphor and symbol, outside of finding the fairy tale elements in life, that those needs *can* be embodied (then eaten, incorporated) and our bodies re-formed. Do we feel we can no longer tell—let alone create!—a transformative fantasy from a glamorous momentarily pacifying, but eventually maddening, image?

There is in Makavejev's earlier films, like *Sweet Movie,* and *WR: Mysteries of the Organism,* a conjunction, an intercutting of images of communism and of capitalism. Each revealed the failed attempt at re-formation within the other. But there *was* a failure each system suffered, and it was in its attempts at making the truth of utopia real on this earth, that is to say of making a world where our fantasies might be used by us to make ourselves, and not simply be sold to us in seemingly sweet but inedible images. Now I feel in my life, in Makavejev's recent movies, the lack of that revealing conjunction, the lack even of failure.

I count on Makavejev to find a way to ask the questions of pleasure again, and not give way, as he almost did in his next film, *The Coca-Cola Kid,* to despair. At the end of that movie, Eric Roberts is shocked from his faith in Coca-Cola (a product that has annealed for him with "the miracle of America . . . the American way of life"), when a small Australian entrepreneur who made fine fizzy fruit drinks blows up his bottling plant and himself rather than have his factory taken over by Coke. Roberts quits the business world to set up house with the libidinally free daughter of the dead bottler, and her open-hearted child. They make a charming family unit. We see a mouse nose about a doll house, looking for a home. But the pleasures of home are, Makavejev thinks, less than we require. There is a world still to be changed by pleasure, till it satisfies our bodies. Or apparently Makavejev thinks we will destroy it: A title says, "A week later . . . while cherries blossomed in Japan/The next world war began." It *hasn't,* and most of the time I'm happy enough in my mouse house with my VCR and big screen T.V. Occasionally, though, like a name I can't quite remember, I'm troubled by the fading specter of the party of pleasure's questions. (What was it they wanted to know about? Food? . . . drink? . . . break? . . . wine?) But I find it hard to imagine how one might now even ask such questions without sounding preposterous!

The Horse Killers
John Hawkes

It was a dark night. A stormy night. There was rain. There was wind. The beaded trees were helpless but to accept their drenching. The pitch-black air was unnaturally heavy with summer heat. Not a light shone.

There was a road, a morbidly narrow road, empty and slippery, that went its way—somewhere—through the stormy night. There was a horse trailer, there was a pickup truck that pulled the trailer along the empty road. Inside the trailer were two horses separated by a shoulder-high partition covered in worn and tattered padding. Side by side in the cab of the pickup truck were a man, a boy and a girl. A father and son. A girl. The father and son were large and fat. Massy. They were dressed identically in sweatshirts and tight jeans and western style boots that proclaimed in every way that the boots were intended to be worn by large men or boys who spent most of their time on horseback. The son was indistinguishable from the father except for his hair, which was shoulder length and black and stringy, oily. And for the frightened look in his eye. The girl drove. She was a mere sliver of a girl, short and skinny, who always spoke in a high-pitched twangy whine. She was known as Sissy. The boy, who sat between the girl and man, was Bo. The father, Stanley, sat to the outside with the window down and the crook of his arm protruding into the storm. He spoke. He laughed. The father.

Two horses. London Bobby and Sweet William. Poor Bob, as I called him. Willy, as I was to Bob.

The trailer was small and decrepit, it lurched from side to side or swayed and slid precariously on the slippery road, though we were moving at a slow pace. An uneasy pace. Feeling our way. It was darker inside the trailer than without, and the noise of the wind and rain was louder. The rain beat down upon the metal roof above our flattened ears like nail heads on tin. Directly in front of us was a narrow open window through which it was impossible to see or to glean anything of our whereabouts or of our condition except that we were making our way through the storm in darkness, without headlights. Between the narrow window and Bob's head and mine hung two hay nets stuffed with hay. But it was dusty hay, inedible. And how could we think of eating hay, poor Bob and I, when we did not know what was happening to us or why?

"Faster," came Stanley's voice above the sound of the engine and the rain.

A burst of Sissy's indignant twang in answer.

The sound of springs, the sound of metal. The roar of the storm through which we passed as through a tunnel. I lost my footing, fell to the side against the partition, felt Bob fall the other way and come up short against the trailer. The hay was old, there was no water, beneath our wobbling hooves the straw in which we stood, or tried to stand, was thick with half-buried horse dung dropped by other horses, long vanished, and left to lie as if expressly for Bob and me, tonight. A seedy carpet of uncleanliness, indifference. I heard Bob tugging on his lead rein fastened short to a ring bolt. I swayed, fell back, my head jerked at the end of my own short leather rein.

There was a jolt, the trailer swayed out from under us, a wheel slipped off the shoulder, lurched back up and on again as Sissy struggled with the steering wheel and Stanley laughed and told her to go faster.

A shivering. A pounding. A swaying. On it went. Then stopped. Abruptly.

A long pause.

"All right," said Stanley all at once and in a voice that was loud, close to us, audible in every way but baffling, "take them out. The little one first. He's easiest."

End of the road? End of the night? The storm? End of time? So it seemed for indeed we had stopped, though Bob and I yet rocked and swayed on our unsteady hooves. Truck and trailer were standing still. Sissy had turned off the engine. And the wind had stopped, the last sheets of rain were coming down, abating, trickling.

Tense? Unnerved? Expecting we knew not what? Exactly. How else? We had braced ourselves against the erratic sensations of the drive, to each other had admitted our bewilderment. In days past, months past, we had been moved from stable to stable, barn to barn. We had grown thin, we had raced, I winning in my former way, Bob losing. But now for time I could not count we had not worked out but had been kept idle, without purpose, untended, unwanted as it seemed. It had been a long decline, a strange decline, though our feed had been increased, steadily, and we had regained most of our weight. Now this.

There was a clattering of boots, a slamming of doors, behind us the ramp went down. Banging and clanging. Chains rattling.

"Hurry up," said Stanley from behind us, at the foot of the ramp. "Bring me that little horse."

Sissy scurried into action at the sound of his voice. Sniveling and whining to herself and moving as quickly as she could at the sound of a grown man's bullying voice, suddenly she appeared in the darkness inside the trailer with Bob and me, wiping her little face on her sleeve and fumbling with Bob's lead rein, unfastening him.

"Come on," said Stanley, as a late squall hurried by overhead and rain fell in a burst and once again died to a trickle, "it's wet out here!"

"You hear him," Sissy said under her breath, "back up!" She held Bob's lead rein short, gave his chest a push. Bob took one obedient tentative step to the rear. Another. He was ready, as always, to accept the worst while I, on the other hand, was not. Yet now in this uncertainty in a sagging two-horse trailer at the edge of a country road—nowhere, somewhere—for once I was indecisive.

But not for long.

I waited, I listened, the space where Bob had stood was empty, from outside and below me came the sound of footsteps, fumbling, soft voices, and then, behind me, the ramp down which poor Bob had disappeared, backwards, rose up again, clanged shut. I was alone, London Bobby was as good as gone though common sense assured me he was only feet away, a small gray horse standing in the wet darkness with a man and boy and girl on a country road in the aftermath of a midnight storm. But why? What sense was this? Why was Bob outside and I within? What were they doing?

I listened. Nothing. I tried to swing around my head, could not, of course. Restrained, of course. Then suddenly in the metallic darkness of the otherwise empty two-horse trailer it came to me that what I was hearing was just that—nothing. Which was to say, silence. Prolonged silence. Significant silence. The kind of silence that cries out the very secrecy it is meant to cloak. A silence more claustrophobic than confinement. A silence loud with the unnatural sounds that it conceals. Why did they not speak? Why did they not whisper to each other or argue amongst themselves? What, I asked myself again—what were they doing?

But I had no time, I told myself, not a moment longer could I support this silence.

There is nothing more violent than an agitated horse who has broken loose in a horse trailer. And I was an agitated horse—for Bob's sake, not mine—and I was loose—the lead rein snapped with my first heave backwards—so now I kicked and flung myself about, head and flanks and hooves, as if to topple the very horse trailer that contained me and wake the night.

"Sissy!" shouted Stanley. "He's loose!"

"Hear him," came Sissy's whine.

"Get up there, then," shouted Stanley. "Stop him!"

A few indistinguishable chords struck on the banjo that was Sissy's voice.

Still I kicked and struggled, knowing that at least I was interrupting Stanley's plan, whatever it was, and sending far and wide my horse-alarm through the night. But to see was my purpose and see I must. To turn around. To thrust my head into the darkness and see for myself that Bob was safe—or not, as obviously I feared. So in the midst of my racket I drew my haunches to the left until they rested against the side of the trailer, then swung them to the right and in that single blow broke the fastenings that held the partition in place behind me. A crack of metal. Another shout from Stanley. And then, and just as Sissy crept up into the front of the trailer, I shoved aside the partition and twisted around, stood still, looked down upon the scene spread dimly beneath my eyes.

The blurred figure of London Bobby, patient as ever. The equally blurred figure of Bo, who was holding Bob. And Stanley—like Bo he was visible thanks mainly to his white sweatshirt—who was stretching wide the mouth of an immense transparent sack. I took one look. I saw the plastic shape with which Stanley wrestled—it was formless, wrinkled, glistening, collapsing about his hands and arms down there in the darkness—and instinctively, and without a moment's hesitation, I reared, I trumpeted a warning to poor docile Bob and once again I kicked and reared as best I could in that small space and gathered myself, readied myself to clamber over the top of the more than chest-high ramp and jump to London Bobby's rescue.

"Pop!" cried Bo, who rarely talked, "that one's escaping!"
"Sissy!" shouted Stanley, "catch hold of him!"
"Cain't!" yelled Sissy shrilly.
"Why not?" shouted Stanley.
"Afeerd!" yelled Sissy.
"For Christ's sake," shouted Stanley, "of what?"
"Smushing!" came Sissy's plaintive voice.

With that I ceased my struggle. Desisted. Stopped. In a trice thought better of this attempt to liberate myself and so join Bob. Yes, even in the midst of my exertions I had heard her words, was thunderstruck by that pathetic thought. Harm the ragged little Arkansas horse-girl as Stanley called her? Certainly not. Crush her against the ringing wall of the trailer? Not for the world. After all, this was a hapless spidery girl, a girl forever and frantically at Stanley's beck and call. For all my tribulations, I trusted her. Intuitively. Furthermore, I told myself, I had already delayed the night's dark proceedings and would delay them more by compliance. Stanley had no choice but to remove me from the trailer lest I destroy it—if, that is, he thought me safe enough to handle. And Sissy could not guide me down from the trailer without the help of the now thwarted Stanley and his frightened son. Thus I reasoned, thus I changed.

Violent horse no longer violent. Gentle. Perfectly safe. Turned himself around of his own accord. Head to the front, tail to the rear. Well and good. Surprising, but well and good.

More silence. A moment too much.

"Stanley," called Sissy, "you there?"

"Of course I'm here."

"His halter ain't broke, Stanley. I got a rope on him. And Stanley? He's a right nice horse."

Vulgar expression from Stanley. Chains, dry hinges. A banging sound, ramp lowered. A small leathery palm on my nose.

"All right," she whispered, "you just back down now. You're a good boy!"

One awkward angular step. Another. My front hooves higher than my rear, my entire body canted steeply. A slow progress. A difficult progress.

"Take him down the road a ways," said Stanley, so close now that I smelled some sort of hot sauce on his breath, felt his heavy voice brushing my ear.

"But Stanley," said the little Arkansas horse-girl in surprise, "what's that. . . ."

Then I too saw London Bobby. Poor Bob. Lying flat on his side. In the darkness. On a wet patch of country road. His gray color turned to silver, his coat wet, his tail stretched out behind him as it would have flown had he been galloping. For some reason Bo was still standing at his head and holding the leather lead that sagged gently upwards into his fat fist. But Bob's head? His blurred and milky head? Even as I stared down at him it began to rain, softly at first, then harder. And was it possible? Drops of rain visible on London Bobby's head and upper neck and yet not on the rest of him? Droplet's dancing and pattering on what I took to be a membrane stretched tight around his neck and head? *Afterbirth* flashed through my mind. Then *sack.* And could any horse alive still breathe inside such a deadly tissue shrunken about his head, his jaws, his nostrils? *No* came the answer roaring through the blood in my ears. *Suffocation* was what I thought. Oh, they were trying to smother poor Bob to death, that swollen man with his own son for accomplice!

Sissy screamed.

"Pop!" shouted Bo. "He's after me!"

Whereupon Bo turned as if to run, as I thought he would, but to my surprise stayed where he was and merely flopped to all fours beside London Bobby's silvery outstretched form. Flopped down and curled himself as tightly as he could into a fat and trembling ball, his head to his knees, his arms drawn protectively about his head, his broad defenseless backside raised.

"Pop!" he cried once more in muffled desperation as, for the second time, Sissy screamed and Stanley gave vent to vulgarity.

I meant to attack. I meant to spare not a breath of his life. I meant to kick Bo's head, arms or no arms, so hard, so swiftly that his round cowering body would give way to a lifeless sprawl. But I could not. For all my readiness, and even as I swung my haunches, turned, prepared to give Bo the one resounding mortal kick I had in mind, still I could not. After all, Bo's cowardly submission was a plea for mercy. And Bo's fear, as suddenly I knew, was as much of the father whose help he had called upon as it was of the retribution he expected and deserved from me.

So I spared him and, just in time, turned on Stanley.

I wheeled. I clattered a few steps this way and that on the wet black deserted road. Then stopped stock still. Stared at him. Suffered a moment of disbelief. Suffered a sudden weakening of spirit. Thought of flight. Then thought of Bo, fleetingly, and recovered myself, reared up, dropped down.

Stanley loomed before me in the road. Stanley was wet. Stanley was armed. Stanley wanted nothing short of my life, as I had wanted Bo's. But with a difference, as I saw at once, since the murderous instrument that Stanley held athwart his chest had been fashioned in advance—how else?—and for no purpose but to inflict what would look like accidental death on the second of the two horses he had meant to kill that night. One with a plastic sack, one with a pike.

Yes, it was some sort of pike that Stanley now aimed at me, a thick wooden staff pointed at its deadly end. Heavy, sharp, unbreakable. Now lowered in Stanley's grip and aimed at me. His face was animated, his eyes were on mine, his body was braced for the thrust that would drive home the point of the staff.

Bo cowered, Stanley prepared to lunge.

Where was Sissy?

Surely the entire night was listening, tiny hidden birds quaking and listening, old barn owls awake and alert, listening, all domestic animals safe and warm, far and wide, all awaiting the outcome of this unheard-of contest between man and horse. Earlier the living creatures had heard my equine bellowing. Now they heard the silence of my combative self filling the night.

Where was Sissy?

An expectant light in Stanley's face, an eagerness more appropriate to amusement than fatality. He crouched, he studied me, he was not intimidated by the awesome spectacle I must have presented to him there at the edge of the imminent ruination of his crude plan. But if I had reared again at that moment, exposing to Stanley my chest and underside, well might he have moved, as swiftly as any fat man could move, and been successful in lodging some considerable length of his murderous stick inside me. But I did not rear. Instead I did the opposite, and merely lowered my head and, eyes and jaws at a level not much above the surface of the road, began to swing my head from side to side, dragon-like, and thus throwing him off guard, attacked him. And no sooner had he started back and lowered his pike than I rose for a second time and towered above him like the invincible wraith that I was, though in flesh and blood, and kicked him with one front hoof as I had meant only moments before to kick Bo with one of my hind hooves—in the head. Down went Stanley, dropping his pike, with not a thought to plan, son, horse-girl, and sprawled on his belly as I had meant to see Bo sprawl. But how was I certain that I had destroyed Stanley's life?

Simply enough. A movement, a planting, of my right front hoof. On Stanley's head. Then my full weight on my right front hoof. A smushing, as Sissy might have said.

That done, I swung around, all fear and agony, to face what I had assumed was a certainty—London Bobby already dead. The heat of his life already cold. Poor Bob, not even a wraith. Oh, but praise be to the horse gods, such was not the case! Wrong for once, and happily! For there, when I turned, were Sissy and Bo as well, both kneeling at London Bobby's head and together rending the last of the plastic, stripping it in long filmy strands from his eyes, cheeks, nostrils. Bob was not at all a suffocated carcass, as I had thought to see him, but a living horse, a breathing horse, a small horse still surviving the snares of destruction that had been spread for us.

And Bo and Sissy. Two crouching figures ministering to a prostrate horse. What better? And even as I held my peace, stayed still, stood watching, Bo, his plump face whiter and wetter than ever, made a small high-pitched nasal sound high in his head. Sissy answered. Another wordless sound from Bo, another answering sound from Sissy. Like horses. And then in his softest and most uncertain tone, Bo spoke.

"Pop was laughing," he said. "Back there in the truck. He was laughing. Why?"

"Skully Equine Mutual. Said so himself."

"Don't understand," said Bo.

"Insurance," said Sissy.

"Still don't understand," said Bo.

"Kill horses," said Sissy. "Collect insurance."

A pause. A silence. A long pause. Not to be broken. Heads bowed, hands and fingers shredding plastic. London Bobby shifting, moving his head, looking up at them.

Soon he was standing. Soon we were once more side by side in the two-horse trailer and creeping onwards through the passing night. Soon, near dawn as we could see, truck and trailer were once more slowing down, stopping.

Slamming of doors. Footsteps. What now? What next?

Again there came a metallic clanking, rattling, banging. But not behind us, as we might reasonably have thought, but at our heads, outside, below us. Then the slamming doors, the loud sound of the engine, the fading sound of the engine. Silence again.

So Sissy with the help of Bo had carried us off, far from the figure lying inexplicably on a country road, and then stopped. Uncoupled us. Abandoned us. Disappeared forever, as I am free to think, into the safety their humanness had earned.

And so early that morning London Bobby and I were found—two horses locked inside a trailer left standing at the side of a road that was not the same road that we had been traveling all night. A different road. A new road. A happier road by far.

Still, for all concerned, a mystery.

Lord Royston's Tour
Lydia Davis

I: England to Moscow

Gotheborg: Greatly Daring Dined

He has been a good deal tossed and beaten about off the Skaw, before sailing up the river this morning. On board also were Mr. Smith, the Consul, and Mr. Damm, an iron merchant. Neither he nor his two servants have any common language with any inhabitant of the inn. Considerable parts of the town of Gotheberg were burned down, it being built almost entirely of wood, and they are rebuilding it with white brick.

He has completely satisfied his curiosity about the town.

On an excursion to Trolhatte, the harness broke three or four times between every post. Here the traveller drives, and the peasant runs by the side of the carriage or gets up behind. He views with great interest the falls of Trolhatte. In an album at a small inn at Trolhatte, he inscribes some Greek anapests evoking his impressions of them.

He inspects the canal and the cataracts under the guidance of a fine old soldier. He sees several vessels loaded with iron and timber pass through the sluices. He receives great civilities from the English merchants, particularly from Mr. Smith, the Consul. He eats cheese and corn brandy, raw herrings and caviar, a joint, a roast, fish and soup, and can't help thinking of Pope's line, "greatly daring dined."

To Copenhagen: The Water, Merely Brackish

Leaving Gotheborg, he passes through country uncommonly dreary, destitute of wood, covered with sand or rock, then country that is well wooded and watered, bearing crops chiefly of rye or barley, with a few fields of wheat and occasional hop grounds. Many of the wood bridges are quite rotten and scarcely bear the weight of a carriage. Crossing the Sound after reaching Helsinborg, he sees with great surprise a flock of geese swimming in the sea, tastes the water, and finds it merely brackish.

His knowledge of Copenhagen is so far limited to the streets he has driven through and the walls of the room he is sitting in, but there is no appearance of poverty, none of the wooden houses of Sweden, and the people are well dressed. He has reason to be satisfied with his servants, particularly Poole, who is active and intelligent.

The Danish nobility have mostly retired to their country houses.

The Barren Province of Smolang

Leaving Helsinborg, he has travelled through extensive forests of fir and birch: this is the barren Province of Smolang, so thinly inhabited that in two days he met only one solitary traveller.

Poole has contrived to get on by composing a language of English, Dutch, German, Swedish, and Danish in which euphony is not the most predominant feature.

For some time he has got nothing to eat but some rye-bread—much too hard, black, and sour, he thinks, for any human being to eat. He might have had plenty of some raw salt goose if he had liked, but he refused it.

Stockholm is not so regular as Copenhagen, but more magnificent.

He has been to the Arsenal and seen the skin of the horse that carried Gustavus Adolphus at the battle of Lutzen, and the clothes in which Charles the Twelfth was shot.

He has sent his father two pieces of Swedish money, which is so heavy that when it was used as current coin, a public officer receiving a quarter's allowance had to bring a cart to carry it away.

To Westeras

In Upsala he visited the Cathedral and found there a man who could speak Latin very fluently. The Rector Magnificus was not at home. He was detained some time in a forest of fir and birch by the axletree breaking. In general, he is annoyed by having to find separate lodgings for himself and his horses in each town.

His Swedish has made the most terrible havoc with the little German he knows.

Lydia Davis

In Abo

He understands there is a gloom over the Russian court.

St. Petersburg: Rubbers of Whist

The immense forests of fir at first strike the imagination but then become tedious from their excessive uniformity. He has eaten partridges and a cock of the woods. As he advances in Russian Finland he finds everything getting more and more Russian: the churches begin to be ornamented with gilt domes and the number of persons wearing beards continues to increase. A postmaster addresses him in Latin but in spite of that is not very civil. The roads are so bad that eight horses will not draw him along and he is helped up the mountain by some peasants. He sees two wolves. He crosses the Neva over a wooden bridge. He is amused at finding his old friends the Irish jaunting-cars.

The most striking objects here are certainly the common people.

He has a poor opinion of the honesty of the country when he finds in the Russian language a single word to express "the perversion of Justice by a Judge," as in Arabic there is a word to express "a bribe offered to a Judge."

In the Russian language they have only one word to express the ideas of *red* and *beautiful*, as the Romans used the word "purple" without any reference to color, as for instance "purple snow."

He is bored by the society of the people of St. Petersburg, where he plays rubbers of whist without any amusing conversation. He considers card games even more dull and unentertaining than spitting over a bridge or tapping a tune with a walking stick on a pair of boots.

The general appearance of the city is magnificent, and he sees this as proof of what may be done with brick and plaster—though the surrounding country is very flat, dull and marshy. The weather begins to be cold, and a stove within and a pelisse without doors are necessary.

He wishes to see the ice-hills and sledges, and the frozen markets.

He goes to a Russian tragedy in five acts by mistake, thinking it is a French opera, but expects in course of time to be able to converse with his friends the Sclavonians. He sees the Tauride, now lapsed to the crown, behind which is a winter garden laid out in parterres and gravel walks, filled with orange trees and other exotics, and evenly heated by a great number of stoves, but the

Neva is now blocked by large pieces of ice floating down from the Ladoga. Though the temperature has been down to twenty degrees Fahrenheit below freezing, that is not considered to be much at all here.

The Empress gives birth to an Archduchess. When the Court assembles to pay their respects, the person who most attracts attention is Prince Hypsilantes, the Hospodar of Wallachia, and the Greeks of his train.

There is not much variety in his mode of life. He studies Russian in the morning.

He begins to be very tired of this place and its inhabitants: their hospitality; the voracious gluttony on every side of him; their society, their barefaced cheating; their conversation, with its miserable lack of information and ideas and their constant fear of Siberia, their coldness, dullness, and lack of energy. The Poles are infinitely the most gentlemanlike, and seem a superior order of men to their Russian masters.

He won't remain here as long as he had intended, but will purchase two sledge kibitkas, fur boots, and pelisses, and lay in a stock of brandy and frozen beefsteaks, and depart not for Moscow but for Archangel.

He imagines there must be something curious in driving reindeer on the ice of the White Sea.

To Archangel: The Mayor Makes a Speech

Before setting out for Archangel, he buys two sledges covered with a tilt, furnishes them with a mattress, lays in frozen meat, Madeira, brandy, and a large saucepan. For the trip he dresses in flannel, over that his ordinary clothes, over his boots fur shoes, over the fur shoes a pair of fur boots, covers his head with a cap of blue Astrachan wool, wraps himself in a sable pelisse and over it all throws a bear skin.

On the road there are no accommodations so he sees inside the houses of the peasantry. The whole family lives in one room in suffocating heat and smell and with a number of cockroaches which swarm in the wooden huts. The dirt is excessive. But the people are civil, hospitable, cheerful, and intelligent, though addicted to spirits, quarrelsome among themselves, and inclined to cheat. They are more like the common Irish than anyone else he has seen. Peter the Great has by no means succeeded in forcing them to abandon their beards.

In the cottage people come to see him dine. Twenty or thirty women crowd around him, examining him and asking him questions.

He passes through Ladoga and Vitigra. Approaching Kargossol, he counts from a distance nineteen churches, most of which have five balloon-like domes, gilt, copper or painted in the most gaudy colors, and thinks it must be a magnificent town, but the number of churches here almost equals the number of houses.

In Archangel the Archbishop speaks Latin very fluently, but does not know whether the Samoyeds of his diocese are Pagans or Christians.

His hostess is anxious to show that they too have fruit, and brings in some specimens preserved. Here they have in the woods a berry with a strong taste of turpentine.

The mayor comes in during the evening and makes a speech to him in Russian three quarters of an hour long.

The temperature in Archangel is fifty-one degrees below freezing, both his hands are frozen, and Pauwells has a foot frozen. He goes northeast of Archangel, procures three sledges and twelve reindeer, and sets out over the unbeaten snow in search of a horde of Samoyeds. He finds them exactly on the Arctic circle in an immense plain of snow surrounded by several hundred reindeer. They are Pagans.

Back in Archangel, the cold has increased, and he is forced to bake his Madeira in an oven to get at it, and to carve his meat with an axe. It is nearly seventy degrees below freezing, barely three points above the point of congelation of mercury.

Moscow is Immense and Extraordinary

Moscow is immense and extraordinary, after a journey over the worst road he has ever travelled in his life through a forest which scarcely ever suffered any interruption but continued with dreary uniformity from one capital to another.

He begins to be able to read Russian fairly easily, and speak it sufficiently. Poole has also picked up enough.

He sends his younger brother a Samoyed sledge and three reindeer cut out of the teeth of a sea-horse by a peasant at Archangel.

The extent of Moscow is prodigious despite its small population because in no quarter of the city do the houses stand contiguous. The Kremlin is certainly the most striking quarter, and nearly thirty gilt domes give it a most peculiar appearance.

He is much interested by the passage of regiments composed of some of the wandering nations. One day there passed two thousand Bashkirs from the Oremburg frontiers on their lean desert horses, armed with lances and bows, some clothed in complete armor, some with the twisted coat of mail or hauberk, some with grotesque caps, others with iron helmets. These people are Mohammedans. Their chief is dressed in a scarlet caftan, their music is a species of flute which they place in the corner of their mouths, singing at the same time. They are almost always at war with the Kirghese.

A regiment of Calmucs passes through. Their features are scarcely human. They worship the Dalai Lama. He also sees a number of Kirghese of the lesser and middle hordes.

He continues his study of Russian, finds the language sonorous, but thinks it hardly repays anyone the trouble of learning it, because there are so few original authors—upon the introduction of literature it was found much easier to translate. The national epic poem, however, about the conquest of the Tartars of Casan, would be good if it weren't for the insufferable monotony of the meter.

Another Trip to Petersburg

He has made another trip to Petersburg. Proceeding along the frozen river, the postilions missed their road, came to a soft place on the ice, and the horses broke through. The kibitka in which he lay could not be opened from the inside and the postilions were concerned only with trying to save their horses and paid no attention to him. One of them woke Poole in his sledge to request an axe. Poole saw the young Lord's vehicle half floating in the water and had just time to open the leather covering and allow him to jump out upon the ice with his writing desk before the carriage went down to the bottom. One horse drowned.

He arrived in Petersburg in time for the Carnival: there were theaters erected on the river, ice-hills, long processions of sledges, multitudes of people, and public masquerades given morning and evening.

In Moscow Again, He Plans the Continuation of His Tour

Now Moscow is very dull during the fast.

He plans to get a large boat, embark at Casan, and float down the Volga to Astracan sitting on a sofa. He will reach the banks of the Caspian.

The carriages he will use have not a particle of iron in their whole composition.

There is a sect of Eunuchs who do this to themselves for the kingdom of heaven. They had at one time propagated their doctrines to such an extent that the government was forced to interfere, afraid of depopulation. It seized a number of them and sent them to the mines of Siberia.

He is preparing for his journey, and he will be accompanied as far as Astracan by an American of South Carolina, Mr. Poinsett, one of the few liberal and literary and gentlemanlike men he has seen emerge from the forests of the New World.

He has hired a Tartar interpreter whom his valet de chambre is somewhat afraid of and calls "Monsieur le Tartare."

He is waiting for letters from Casan about the condition of the roads but because it is spring and travel by both sledge and carriage is precarious, there is almost no communication between towns.

An edict has appeared forbidding conversation on political subjects.

In the Russian Empire, where perhaps of three men whom you meet, one comes from China, one from Persia, and the other from Lapland, you lose your ideas of distance.

Foreign newspapers are prohibited.

He has gone up to the top of a high tower at one in the morning to see the spectacle of Moscow with its hundreds of churches illuminated on Easter Eve.

Then he has been very surprised to see all the females of the family run up to him and cry out "Christ is risen from the dead!"

When he sets out he and Mr. Poinsett will each be armed with a double barrelled gun, a brace of pistols, a dagger, and a Persian saber; each of the four servants also will have his pistols and cutlass.

He will be sorry to leave Moscow, he has formed pleasant acquaintances and thinks he will never see them again. The same was true of Petersburg too.

II: Down the Volga and Back to Moscow

Casan: No Man Could Suppose Himself to Be in Europe

The accommodations along the way are as they have been all over Muscovy: one room, in which you sleep with the whole family in the midst of a suffocating heat and smell; no furniture to be found but a bench and table, and an absolute dearth of provisions.

As he proceeds he finds the Tartars in the villages increasing in numbers, and the Russian fur cap giving way to the Mohammedan turban or the small embroidered coif of the Chinese. He also sees thousands of Bashkirs marching to join the armies with their long lances, bows and sabers.

The elevated banks of the Volga where the handsome town of Nijnei Novogorod is situated are covered with oak and elm, a relief from the pine forests and plains which become so tiring to the eye throughout Muscovy.

He sleeps in the cottage of a Tcheremisse, with neither chimney nor window. The women have their petticoats only to the knee and braid their hair in long tresses, to which are tied a number of brass cylinders.

From the Tcheremisses he goes among the Tchouasses, and soon after embarks upon the Volga.

No man could suppose himself to be in Europe—though by courtesy Casan is in Europe—when he contemplates the Tartar fortifications, the singular architecture of the churches and shops, and the groups of Tartars, Tcheremesses, Tchouasses, Bashkirs and Armenians.

An Armenian merchant promises to have a boat ready in two or three days.

To the Quarantine Grounds Near the Astracan

The beauty of the scenery on the Volga is gratifying, the right bank mountainous and well wooded. After passing Tsauritzin, where both banks were in Asia, there is nothing on either side but vast deserts of sand.

He sees great numbers of pelicans. Islands are white with them. He sees prodigious quantities of eagles too. He and the others eat well on sterlet and its caviar. The number of fish in the Volga is astounding. The Russian peasants won't eat some of them for reasons of superstition. For example, he had too much of a sort of fish like the chad, and offered them to the boat's crew, but they refused them, saying that the fish were insane: the fish swam round and round, and if they ate them they too would become insane.

There is some reason for refusing pigeons too, and also hares.

Samara is the winter home of a number of Calmouks. They have been converted from Lamaism and are half reclaimed from their nomad life, for only during the summer do they wander with their flocks in the vast steppes on the Asiatic side and encamp in their circular tents of felt.

He comes upon a village as distinguished for the excessive cleanliness of the houses and the neatness of the gardens as the Russians' habitations are for their dirt and filth.

The heat of the Steppe is suffocating. The blasts of wind during the summer immediately destroy the flocks exposed to them, which instantly rot.

The Tartars and Calmouks make every species of laitage known in Europe and also ardent spirits they distill from cow's and mare's milk.

The town of Astracan is inhabited by thirteen or fourteen different nations, each description of merchants in a separate caravanserai.

He has a letter of introduction to the Queen of Imiretia in her capital on the banks of the Phasis. She is in fact merely a nominal sovereign.

His next excursion before he proceeds to the northern provinces of Persia will be a short distance into the Desert to the habitation of a Calmouk Prince. He wants to go hawking with the Princess, his daughter, who with her pipe at her mouth hunts on the unbroken horses of the desert.

Solianka: Banners in the Wind

He is staying in a village inhabited exclusively by Tartars. He visits a Calmouk camp and enters the tent of the chief Lama. The priest shows the idols and sacred books. The tent is very neat and covered with white felt, the floor matted and strewn with rose leaves. The Lama brings out the banner of silk painted with the twelve signs of the zodiac. Some banners are inscribed with prayers. These are placed at the door of the tent, in the wind, and letting them flutter about is supposed to be equivalent to saying the prayers. The Lama orders tea: the leaves and stalks are pressed into a large square cake and this is boiled up with butter and salt in the Mongol manner. It forms a nauseous mixture, but he drinks it and then takes his leave, all the village coming out of their tents and going down with him to the water side. At least a third of the men in the village are priests.

To Derbend: His Apparent Magnitude is Directly as his Distance

He has proceeded through the desert which extends to the foot of Mount Caucasus. How different it was from Archangel: terrible heat instead of terrible cold, a plain of sand instead of a plain of snow, herds of camels belonging to the Calmouks instead of flocks of reindeer.

The ground is so flat they had no trouble getting along in their kibitkas. But they were often fooled by the appearance of extensive ranges of hills on the horizons, which were actually merely small inequalities magnified by intervening vapors.

The careless servants lost most of the water they had brought along with them, and then they suffered from extreme thirst, for the pools were as salt as sea water: their bottoms and sides are covered with beautiful crystals exhaling a strong smell of violets.

The plants all taste of salt, the dews are salt, and even some milk he gets from a Tartar is brackish.

Then there are swarms of mosquitoes, and he can't even talk or eat without having a mouthful of them. Sleeping is out of the question.

They cross a river where the water comes up to the windows of the carriage, which floats. They cross a marsh four miles broad and three or four feet deep.

In Kizliar he stays in the house of an Armenian, sells his kibitka and sends his carriage back to Moscow, and leaves Kizliar with an escort of Cossacks, crossing the rest of the desert on horseback.

They spend the night in an encampment of Tartars, who bring them sour mare's milk.

Early in the morning they arrive at the residence of the Tartar Prince. The people of the village bring him an enormous sturgeon that is still alive and lay it at his feet. In the courtyard he observes a man with long hair, contrary to custom.

In the morning he sets out for Derbend with an escort. The caravan is very oddly composed: him and his American companion, a Swiss, a Dutchman, a Mulatto, a Tartar of Rezan, a body of Lesgees for escort, two Jews, an envoy from one of the native Princes returning from Petersburg, and three Circassian girls whom one of the guides has bought in the mountains and is taking to sell at Baku.

In Derbend he has lodgings in the home of an absent Persian. He is sent carpets and cushions and inundated with fruits and pilaus. His apparent magnitude is directly as his distance: if he was a great man at Kizliar with one orderly man to wait on him, here he is twice as great, since he has two.

In the evening he rides out with Persian friends on a white horse with its tail dyed scarlet. The Persians amuse themselves trying to unhorse each other, while he himself admires the view of the Caspian Sea, the steep rock on which the town is situated, the gardens surrounding it, and part of the chain of Caucasus rising behind it.

Garden of the World

The Russian commandant has given him an escort of Cossacks and also some Persians, as well as a considerable number of men as far as the river Samoor to point out the most fordable parts and help them over.

The merchant of women is still part of the group. Now, because his Tcherkess or Circassian girls attracted some attention in the earlier part of the journey, he encloses them in great sacks of felt, though the sun is burning hot.

It would be worthwhile for a traveller to enquire into the traditions of a colony of Jews who live in the Dagestan near the Samoor. The groundwork of their language is Hebrew though apparently not intelligible to the Jews of other countries.

The country from the River Samoor to Baku is fit to be the garden of the world. The crops cultivated seem to be rice, maize, cotton, millet and a kind of bearded wheat. From the woods come apples, pears, plums, pomegranates, quinces and white mulberries often covered with pods of silk. Almost every bush and forest tree has a vine creeping up it covered with clusters of very tolerable grapes. The main draft animal is the buffalo, the antelope is the main wild animal, and the howls of the jackals in the mountains would have disturbed their rest if they hadn't been so tired.

A Large Party of Persians

They are met by a large party of Persians headed by two brothers, Gerbat and Hajali, who beg them to turn back to visit the Khan of Cuba. They refuse, and Gerbat declares they will not go further and must fight their passage through, which they prepare to do. Since they are better armed, they would have been able to go on unmolested, but the merchant of women begs them not to desert him or he will be ruined, for they have stolen his horses and say they will put him to death if he does not sell his women at their price. The party of travellers threatens to complain to the Khan at Cuba and the Persians restore the horses.

They rest in the evening at a rock called Beshbarmak or "the five fingers" which is a great sea mark on the Caspian. From there to Baku is almost a desert with now and then a ruined caravanserai.

Baku is a considerable commercial town whose fortifications are in good condition. Scarcely a house lies outside the walls, and the country around is an absolute desert.

The day after he arrives, he receives a visit from Cassim Elfina Beg, the principal Persian of the place, who offers him every assistance.

All the innumerable arches he has seen have been pointed.

The Famous Sources of Naphtha, the Fruits Thereabouts

General Gurieff, the commandant, has made a party for them to see the famous sources of naphtha, and with him and the abovementioned Beg and several other Persians they ride out to the principal wells. The strong smell is perceptible at a great distance and the ground about appears of the consistency of hardened pitch. One of the wells yields white naphtha; in all the others it is black, but very liquid.

He rides five miles farther to see the everlasting fire and the adoration of the Magi. For about two miles square, if the earth is turned up and fire applied, the vapor that escapes inflames and burns until extinguished by a violent storm. In this way the peasants calcine their lime. In the center of this spot of ground is a square building enclosing a court. The building contains a number of cells with separate entrances. The arches of the doors are pointed, and over each is a tablet with an inscription, in characters unknown to him. In one of the cells is a small platform of clay with two pipes conveying the vapor, one of which is kept constantly burning. The inhabitant of the cell says he is from Hindostan (a Parsee from the south of Candahar), the building was paid for by his countrymen, and a certain number of persons were sent from India and remained until relieved. When asked why they were sent, he answered, To venerate and adore that flame. In the center of the quadrangle is a tumulus, from an opening in which blazes out the eternal fire, surrounded by smaller spiracles of flame.

The fruits thereabouts come spontaneously to perfection.

Across the Desert to Shamachee: A Large Panther

He remains four days at Baku and then sets off across the desert to Shamachee. After 70 versts they stop at a stream of water and scare up a large panther that escapes into the mountains. Early the next morning they come to old Baku, now in ruins, and in the evening to Shamachee. Here he sleeps in one of the cells of a ruined caravanserai. The poor peasants who live in the ruins have been ordered by Mustapha Khan to give the travellers provisions.

The Town of Fettag

The next day he travels over hills covered with fruit trees, down into a valley past the village of Soulout, up a very steep mountain near the summit of which he enters the town of Fettag, residence of Mustapha the Khan of Shirvaun. The Khan lives entirely in tents and appears to be the most unpolished, ignorant and stupid of any of the native Princes so far.

The Khan gives them a feast where the precepts of Mohammed are totally disregarded; at the conclusion, singing and dancing girls are introduced according to the Persian custom. The Khan makes them a present of horses, carpets, etc.

Fettag to Teflis

In the evening of the next day they come to a camp occupied by Azai Sultan, who is gleeful because he has won a fight over stolen cattle with some mountaineers and people belonging to the next Sultan. The following day they are received by Giafar Kouli Khan who gives him a long account of the way he beat the Shach's troops with an inferior number. There are puzzling things about his story but they ask no questions because it is dangerous to puzzle a potentate.

Two nights later he sleeps on the banks of the river Koor, the Cyrus of the ancients. On the road from Ganja to Teflis, his secretary Pauwells falls ill with a putrid fever. There is no cart to be procured and they are given false information that causes them to lie out for three nights exposed to the unwholesome dews of the Koor. They then reach a Cossack station where they leave the secretary. They ride on to Teflis and send back a cart for him, but though he has medical attention he dies within four or five days.

Teflis

In Teflis, they are received by the Queen of Imiretia in her house, in a room fitted with sofas, ornamented with looking glasses and hung round with pictures of the imperial family. She does not live in a cave, as he had been told.

He and his companion Poinsett go to bed with violent attacks of fever. The other three servants have been ill too, but everyone recovers.

Ispahan can't any longer be considered the capital of Persia.

Count Gudovitch has obtained a victory near Cars over Yussuff Pacha.

There are rumors of peace between France and Russia; nobody knows if England is included.

With the Help of Some Bark: Over the Caucasus

They take leave of their Georgian friends, including the Queen of Imiretia.

As soon as he can sit a horse he rides out of the town of Teflis with its unwholesome climate, singularly prejudicial to strangers, and the snow and ice on Mount Caucasus, along with the help of some bark he gets from a Roman Catholic missionary, restore him to perfect health and strength as soon as he begins ascending the mountain.

The Caucasus is inhabited by about twenty nations, most of them speaking distinct languages, so that the inhabitants of one valley, insulated from the rest of the world, often can't make themselves understood if they cross the mountain.

They have purchased a tent and thus avoid stopping in towns where there is plague. On this side of the Russian frontier, it almost threatens to wipe out some of the Mohemmedan nations. In some of the villages he passes, all the people have died, other villages are completely deserted, they scarcely see one man in the whole country and the few they see they carefully avoid.

Some people of the tribe of the Cafouras intended to attack them but mistook some Cossacks for their party and attacked them instead and then retreated leaving one Cossack dead and one mortally wounded.

They make 36 versts to Kobia, pass by Kazbek, the highest part of the Caucasus, make 28 versts in the rocky valley of Dagran, then leave the mountain and advance to the fortress of Vladi Caveass.

Count Irelitch the commandant tells him there has been trouble recently and provides him with seventy cavalry, fifty regular infantry and a piece of cannon in order protect him from the Chickentses as he proceeds. He crosses the little Cabarda entirely depopulated by the plague. On the road he sees the dead bodies of Cossacks and fragments of their lances strewn about.

He is glad to have been at Teflis, one of the best cities in this part of Asia. The baths are supplied by a fine natural warm spring. The women deserve their reputation for beauty. Those that are sold for slaves to the Mohammedans are those that are called Circassians, for the Circassians or Tcherkesses who are themselves Mohammedans seldom sell their children.

Here in Mozdok, they are in quarantine.

He does not know whether to go to Taman along the Cuban and cross over the Cimmerian Bospherus to Kerch, or to cross the desert to Tzaritzin, from there to Tamboff and so to the Crimea.

Mozdok to Georgievsk

In Mozdok the ground had recently been overflowed by the Terek, his tent was not waterproof and the country was famous for fevers. He lay several days on the earth with a violent fever surrounded by basins to catch the rain which did not stop him from being drenched by it.

A change of situation and a thorough tanning of bark have made him well again, but he is detained at Georgievsk by the illness of his fellow traveller.

They will go along the Cuban to Taman, the site of the Greek colony Phanagoria, and so over the Cimmerian Bosphorus to Kerch, the ancient Panticapaeum.

Georgievsk to Caffa

At Stauropol he has had a third fever that reduces him so low he cannot stand without fainting away.

He recovers from it by using James's powder in very large doses, but remains some time very deaf, subject to alarming palpitations of the heart, and so weak that he cannot stand long without fainting.

He has come along the River Cuban without any molestation from the Circassians.

At Taman they are detained some time by their interpreter falling ill. They are determined to wait there for his recovery, but he grows weaker rather than stronger, being housed in a damp lodging. Fellow traveller Poinsett suffers so severely from a bilious fever and becomes so weak they are very apprehensive for him, but now all are rapidly regaining strength, due to some light frost, living in the European manner, and the great attention of General Fanshaw, the Governor of the Crimea, who is an Englishman.

Caffa to Moscow

It is a long and tedious journey from Caffa. He has left it with more strength than he had entering it, but has been a good deal thrown back by the fever he caught, which brought many bad symptoms. His optic nerves became so relaxed as to make him blind; with his right eye he could scarcely distinguish at night the flame of a candle. As he regained strength, his vision returned.

They stop off in Kiev, the third city in Russia, remarkable for containing more churches in proportion to its size than any other city in the world. Here the language is more Polish than Russian.

He loses another servant. The servant is lethargic, refuses to exercise, secretly throws away his medicine, grows worse, is brought along lying on a bed in a kibitka towards the house of an English merchant, half way there gets out, with the help of another servant gets in again, falls into a lethargic sleep and on their arrival at the inn in Moscow is found dead in his kibitka.

Thus, of four servants who left this city with them, only one has returned, a stout negro of Poinsett's who has borne the climate better than any of them.

Of his wardrobe, all he has left now is one coat and a pair of pantaloons.

He hopes to sail directly from Petersburg to Harwich. In the meantime, here in Moscow, he has put himself under the direction of a Scotch physician, Dr. Keir, who prescribes absolute repose for the next four months and has ordered a course of bark and vitriolic acid, beef, mutton, and claret.

His health has improved quickly, he has lost every bad symptom: his dropsical legs have reduced to a gentleman-like slimness, a fair round belly swelled and as hard as a board has shrunk to its former insignificance, and he is no longer annoyed by palpitations of the heart and pulsations of the head.

Within the past three days he has recovered his voice, which he had lost for two months, due to a relaxation of the throat prolonged by the unusual and disagreeably mild season with a great deal of fog and a thaw that caused great havoc among the frozen provisions. He is leading the life of a monk.

Poinsett leaves soon. Then he will set about writing a journal of the tour, though the mode of travelling during the first part of the journey, and the scarcity of chairs and tables, as well as the illness of the second part, are very unfavorable to journalizing. In addition, the few notes he had taken were rendered illegible by crossing a torrent.

The End of Lord Royston's Tour

He does not write again. He goes to Petersburgh and finds his friends Colonel and Mrs. Pollen. Together they will go to Liebau in the Dutchy of Courland and try to sail to Sweden on their way to England. Royston is suffering from the shock his constitution received in the south of Russia. He has frequent attacks of fever and ague and is nursed by the Colonel and his wife.

After three weeks in Liebau they engage a passage to Carlscrona on the ship Agatha, a Lubeck vessel. They embark on April 2. They sail, the weather is fine, the ice lies close about a mile from shore, they get through it at the rate of two miles an hour, and are in clear water by 3 p.m. All that day and the next they have light breezes from the southeast. On the 4th, at about 2 p.m. they sight the Island of Oeland at a distance of eight or nine miles. It is blowing very hard: in an hour they get close in and see the ice about a mile from the shore.

Colonel Pollen wonders if they can anchor under Oeland, and another passenger, Mr. Smith, an English seaman, thinks not, as the ice would drift off and cut the cables. The captain says he will stand on to the southward till eight o'clock, then return to the island, but at eight and at twelve he will not go back: now it blows a gale of wind from the westward with a very heavy sea. The vessel makes much water and the pumps are choked with ballast. The crew will bail very little; the water gains fast.

On the 5th they run the whole day before the wind. At noon on the 6th, Colonel Pollen wonders if the vessel can keep the sea, the English seaman says that unless the sailors make more efforts to bail she can't live long, since they already have three feet of water in the hold, it is gaining on them, and the best way to save themselves is to steer for some port in Prussia. The Colonel agrees and tells the Captain. The Captain agrees and recommends Liebau, but the Colonel objects on account of a certain Mr. Renny and the English seaman, who have escaped from Russia without passports.

Lord Royston also does not want to return to Liebau. The Captain agrees to go to Memel, but says he has never been there in his life: if the English seaman will take the ship in, he will give it over into his charge when they come to the bar. The seaman agrees because he knows the harbor perfectly well.

At two o'clock in the morning on the 7th they sight land to the southward about fifteen miles from Memel and close in to a lee shore, because of the Captain's ignorance and carelessness in running so far in the dark. They haul the ship to by the wind on the larboard tack, and at 4 o'clock get sight of Memel, which the Captain takes for Liebau until he is told otherwise, when he is very surprised. Colonel Pollen and Lord Royston and the other gentlemen come on deck and tell the Captain to give the charge to the English seaman, which he does.

At six they come to the bar, the tide running very high with two men at the helm. The passengers are pressing around the helm in a way that is dangerous to themselves and prevents the helmsmen from seeing ahead very well, so the English seaman asks them to go below. But now, unfortunately, the Captain sees the sea breaking over the bar and becomes so frightened that he runs immediately to the helm and with the help of his people puts it hard-a-port. Though the English seaman strives against this, in ten minutes they are on the Southlands.

The third time the ship strikes, she grounds and fills with water. They are about a mile and a half from shore.

There is a small round-house on deck and Mrs. Pollen, Mrs. Barnes, her three children, two gentlemen, a man and a maidservant get into this to save themselves from the sea. Colonel Pollen and the English seaman begin to clear the boats out; the sailors will not help. They get the small one out and three sailors get into it with the Captain. Lord Royston, who is in a very weak state of health, tries to follow them but the English seaman prevents him, telling him it is not safe. When the Captain hears this, he gets out. When the boat leaves the ship's side it turns over and the three men drown.

They begin to clear the large boat. It is lashed to the deck by strong tackling to the ring-bolts. A sea comes and forces away part of the tackling. The English seaman calls to Colonel Pollen to jump out or the next sea will carry her and them all away. They are scarcely out of her when she is washed overboard. Now they have no hope but in the mercy of Providence. At nine o'clock they cut away the mast to ease the vessel, but can see nothing of the life-boat, which makes them very uneasy, for the sea is tremendous, breaking right over their heads, and it is so very cold that it is impossible to hold fast by anything.

Colonel Pollen wonders if the round-house will stand and is told it will, as long as the bottom of the vessel.

Colonel Pollen says "Thank God! We must hold as fast as we can for the life-boat must soon be here."

Colonel Pollen goes to the door of the round-house and begs Mrs. Pollen not to stir from the round-house, for the life-boat will soon come. It is now about half past nine but no boat is to be seen. The vessel is entirely full of water except near the round-house. Mr. Renny is soon washed overboard and after him, at about ten o'clock, all within a few seas of each other, Colonel Pollen, Mr. Baillie, and Mr. Becker, one sailor, Lord Royston's servant, Mrs. Barne's servant, and Lord Royston himself.

An account of the catastrophe was published three years later in the Gentleman's Magazine by the English seaman, Mr. Smith.

Four Stories
Diane Williams

THE FLESH

As a couple, I admit, they had me transfixed. They were so alike in everything, with their skin still intact, side by side, under our dining-room table, close enough to each other to reach out to each other if they had not been all encumbered because of what they were in actuality—slices of cucumber. I scooped them up.

What is missing here is what I did then with them.

That's when all our company came in, our friends and our relatives, not all of them all together, but the stream of their entering our house began.

I was hearing myself say *sometimes*, and *I'm afraid I don't know* and *yes, I do hope* and *think of me.* My friend R. exclaimed "Cliff!" plaintively. Then C. said in a somewhat louder voice than R.'s, "No doubt he will come."

Plenty has been missing here all along, in addition to most of the people's names in their entirety, more of what they were saying, also the overtones and the undertones of their major statements.

Later, when everybody had said their good-byes, I told C. that it had all been like a dream—dinner and so on.

He said, "Tomorrow is another day."

I didn't mean for what I had said to make such a muffish sound, from where there was nowhere further naturally, to bounce.

This happens, though, to what gets eaten up. That's all my fault Betty McDonald is a doornail.

THIS ONE'S ABOUT (__________)

This is being written to explain my sister's most fundamental, the most important discovery ever made in human history so far by an individual. Her discovery—it is so shocking—stemmed from, as in every other sphere of life—a rude awakening.

My sister, who made the discovery, was doing the driving. My mother was in the back seat with the attorney. I was in the front seat next to my sister—the discoverer!

We had the attorney in the back seat scrunched up. This is now thirteen years later, after our fierce journey that night—it was indeed at night.

My sister at the wheel—I forgot to mention she had a lame right arm and bad vision, which had been allowed to go uncorrected, and that, also, she had forgotten to turn the car headlights on. I forgot to say that it is easy to see how this resolved, but all quite obviously was not quite lost.

At the great speed I turned around whenever I wanted to take a look at the attorney when he made his statements. I did not get a look at my mother. In fact, did she ever speak?

At the great speed what did my sister say about everything that hung in the balance—that is—how we were doing, when the attorney told her to check her speed?

Strange as it sounds, I still do not know how clear the danger was then. Speaking for myself, I felt then, this is an important drama. If I were the driver, I would be questioning what our alternatives were for where exactly we were heading.

When she got out of the car, all that was real to my sister was the answers to the questions. At the beginning of life we are not in perfect harmony with the universe. I am fond of my sister's idea, which is slowly gaining favor, that at the beginning of our life, when observers are observing any one of us, metaphorically speaking, they get sick. Most of the observers refuse to observe that all this all really has to do with is *clothes*!

And finally, a big thank you to Chuck Cohen in Highland Park, Illinois, because he gave my sister her idea!

SPANISH

I wish that everything is enough for Mr. Red who is the husband, who has a heavy Spanish accent. He is a scholar. Mrs. Red speaks English with a heavy Spanish accent also, and she is a full-time scholar, too.

Yesterday, I saw the Reds' bed of scarlet impatiens waving in the wind, which was quite unremarkable. But, that is not all.

Mrs. Red, who is probably responsible for the planting of the flowers, was on her way, carrying her folded-up folding chair and several other things.

She was big enough, even with carrying all of her things, so she could fit comfortably between my thumb and my forefinger from where I sat inside of my house watching her—that was my perspective on my hand.

To me, she is like a cutie pie! like a little doll!

Society, schools, hospitals, factories, and homes are the other victims of the perpetual movement of philosophical thought, as well as many other organees.

THE HAG WAS TRANSFORMED BY LOVE

The guys, oh, how you longed for them, round and savory, and just how they get after a few days in their gravy, in the pot, in the refrigerator, and then they are heated up, and then they are eaten up.

I know what Terri Great thought because I remember my thoughts to a tee exactly about my own little new potatoes I just ate, and I am calling myself for the hell of it, *Terri*!

She was sticking her fork—Mrs. Alexander Great—into the little new potato, thinking, I may be the only one who likes this!

For the hell of it, Mrs. Great, you should have stayed there sticking in your fork, tasting and enjoying, and eating up little new potatoes until you had finished all four of your potatoes, *Terri*!

Say it, Terri, from the two and a half little guys that you did eat, you got all the stimulation from the spree you thought was wise, because, if she's going to say, "This is the best it gets from a potato," then Terri Great has stretched her mind beyond the wisecrack fully—stop!

Terri left the house then, and her husband Alexander never saw her again, nor her little guy Raymond, nor her little guy, Guy.

She spent most of her time in the company of people like herself who said they knew what they were thinking. For instance, *she* thinks any penis is ugly.

The enormity of what she had done, leaving her family abruptly, suddenly, and with no warning, gave her lots of other thoughts, too.

She did not upon arrival, speak well the language of the country she had fled to. When she asked a man, for example, on the street, her first day in town, "Where is the train station?" the man told her kindly that there had not been a war in his country for forty years. (He wore a brown, ankle-length, belted trench coat, was about sixty years old.) Miraculously, she thought she could comprehend every word that he had said. It was a miracle too, that when he flashed it at her, she thought *his* penis was a beauty. Like magic—the colors of it, were the colors to her of her own baby's shirt, face and hat that she had only just left far behind, and the form of it was like a much much much bigger dewdrop.

At home, this rich man had a thin wife. He supposedly worshipped his old wife until old Terri Great came into the picture. Then just forget it. (Things keep happening so perversely for zealots.)

For Terri, she got her first six orgasms during penetration with this man during the next fifteen weeks of their intercourses together.

In the weeks that followed these events, she renewed her days, and she became intrigued with finance.

Michael Ondaatje
An Interview by Catherine Bush

In the following interview, Michael Ondaatje speaks of the effect of a mural, walking into a room filled with bright, sharp images and being surrounded, a room that not only captures the eye but all the senses.

A poet and novelist, Ondaatje is best known for a series of works that defy easy categorization. *The Collected Works of Billy the Kid,* subtitled Left-Handed Poems, circles around and around the final days of Billy the Kid on the new Mexico frontier. *Coming Through Slaughter* is an evocation of the life of jazz trumpeter Buddy Bolden and early jazz-era New Orleans. *Running in the Family,* a fictionalized family history, was initiated after Ondaatje traveled back to Sri Lanka, where he was born. *In the Skin of a Lion,* his most recent novel and the one which gained him the widest audience internationally, tells a series of haunting, interwoven stories set in 1920s Toronto. Each work summons up a whole world, combining varied voices, encompassing real and imagined history, collapsing time within the clear, refracting lens of Ondaatje's original vision. Genre boundaries blur. Often simultaneously, Ondaatje manages to be both lyrical and outrageous. His language, honed to a precise clarity, is deeply sensual.

Ondaatje came to Canada in 1962 and lives in Toronto. We met for this interview last summer at the Canadian Centre for Advanced Film Studies, where Ondaatje is currently studying. Our taped discussion was followed by a second session on paper, which included a series of follow-up questions. The text below integrates the two.

Catherine Bush: *Running in the Family,* your fictional memoir, is conceived as a search for your father, your family, the country of your birth. It seems that you came from a family and a culture that tell a lot of stories. At the same time going back became a process of telling stories, especially about your father. What role did storytelling play in your childhood?

MICHAEL ONDAATJE: I grew up in a family that was pretty theatrical, where stories were essentially told verbally as opposed to being written. I grew to love reading after I left Sri Lanka, when I went to England, but looking back on my childhood in Sri Lanka, the first eleven years, the stories were usually a case of people one-upping each other at a dinner table or someone retelling or inventing an outrageous rumor. I wanted to catch that quality when I was writing the book, the constant exaggerating, the convincing lie. When I went back, I didn't know what kind of book I was going to write, although I knew I wanted to talk to a lot of people, a lot of relatives. I had also hoped to find literary sources for that period of time—the '30s, the '40s—but there was practically nothing. That was, I thought, a very sad thing; so much hadn't been documented, even in diaries. So working on the book became a process of shifting that oral tradition into a literary form. It had to be funneled through a persona, or through the narrator in a certain state, wanting to know certain things for certain reasons. Maxine Hong Kingston, talking about this process, discusses how you have to translate the banal into the mythic. It is a question of how you can improvise off what you are "given" not just in imaginative terms but with form. Because in books like these—memoirs, biographies—the "given" is much more imaginative, much wilder than pure invention. You are not inventing so much as trying to hold everything together.

BUSH: Did you go back and recreate stories that you remembered or were you discovering a whole other world that you hadn't known?

ONDAATJE: It was more a discovery. I had been skirting around the world of my parents for a long time in my poems. The anecdotes had been filtered down by my brother and sisters to me. All I was given were fragments. I was always trying to make sense of these surreal lines or incidents, or at least trying to give them a context, a story about my grandmother's breast being fondled by a stranger on a bus, for instance, or an uncle turning up at a wedding on an elephant. When I went back I didn't even know if I could write a book or not, and then of course I discovered a whole ocean of stories and subplots. It was more a matter of keeping material out. There were stories that took place outside Sri Lanka but I decided to keep everything on this one island.

BUSH: You say you didn't really start to approach storytelling through reading until you were in England?

ONDAATJE: I went to school in England. I was part of that colonial tradition, of sending your kids off to school in England, and then you were supposed to go to Oxford or Cambridge and get a blue in tennis and return. But I never went to Oxford or Cambridge, I didn't get a blue, and I didn't return. I think my generation was the first of the real migrant tradition that you see in a number of writers of our time—Rushdie, Ishaguro, Ben Okri, Rohinton Mistry—writers leaving and not going back but taking their country with them to a new place. In England I became obsessed with reading. I was a compulsive reader all through my teens. For me, the great pleasure of literature is reading as opposed to writing. I write as a reader. I don't want to write something that wouldn't interest me as a reader. For me the process of writing, therefore, has to be a learning or discovering as opposed to just a telling or an entertaining. Reading is that great intimate act, between reader and author, reader and book. It's sacred to me, that relationship, and involves trust, surprise, and is ideally a continuing relationship. I had no thoughts of being a writer until I came to Canada and went to university. The influences were at the time very much a part of the British literary tradition, and also Canadian poets who were writing in Canada, such as A. M. Klein, Phyllis Webb, Raymond Souster, David McFadden and bp Nichol.

BUSH: In *The Dainty Monsters*, your first collection, or at least in some of the last poems in that collection, you're already inhabiting other people's skins. This is a process which goes a lot further in later books like *The Collected Works of Billy the Kid*, for a start, and *Coming Through Slaughter*. And not just other skins but also other landscapes. I wondered if in some way it took a long time to inhabit the landscape here, to see it as a place to tell stories about.

ONDAATJE: I think many of the poems, even in the first book, were about my landscape here in Canada, my family here, certain rural landscapes here,but certainly in the first longer works, the first serial works like *The Man With Seven Toes*, there was a jump from the self to a mask of some kind. I was writing lyrics at that time, and so the landscape in which I lived was reflected only in the lyric poems. But *Billy* is a personal book, very much about my world then, even though it's set in a different country and it's about an absolute stranger to me. I found I could both reveal and discover myself more through being given a costume. I could be more honest about the things I wanted to talk about or witness.

BUSH: What was it about the figure of Billy the Kid that was so appealing to you? He's such an easily mythologized figure. Did you want to do your own reinterpretation of the Wild West? Were you interested in appropriating American mythology? Did the desert attract you, the mentality formed by that extreme landscape?

ONDAATJE: I was sick of the way he was being mythologized. I was sick of the cliches, the hip versions of him that reduced the danger of such a figure. I wasn't interested in appropriating him as a mythic figure, it was much more a personal inquiry. The landscape certainly attracted me. It was a kind of stage, a "set" perhaps. And I may have been missing the heat.

BUSH: Both in *Billy* and in *Coming Through Slaughter,* the narrator does seem to be used as a way to see yourself. In *Slaughter,* you, in the role of the narrator, talk about being the same age, 31, as Bolden—the black jazz trumpeter—was when he was shut away in the asylum. What first drew you to Bolden?

ONDAATJE: I supposed I've always found characters for my books who reflect my age and concerns at the time. In a way these are all self-portraits and possible fictional portraits. There's of course a lot of invention going on that is governed by a story I've contracted myself to. Bolden as an artist haunted me. I wanted to *know* him. This kind of curiosity is the motor for the books. And it is a gradual building up of a figure fictionally.

BUSH: Do you find yourself particularly drawn to figures who court danger, who live on the edge somehow? There seems to be a link between the wildness of these stories and figures, and some of the stories from Sri Lanka in *Running in the Family,* the stories about your father, in particular, the way he repeatedly holds up a train, searching for Japanese bombs.

ONDAATJE: Maybe this has been overemphasized in my work. I think I find these individuals more normal than others do. Everyone has danger around them. Anyone can take a step into the absurd.

BUSH: In *Billy* and *Slaughter,* as in *Running in the Family,* there is an actual search for a missing person. At the same time we're made to ask, "Who is Billy? Who is Buddy Bolden? How do you capture them in language?" It seems to be a motif that keeps reappearing in your work. In *Coming Through Slaughter* there is in fact a detective.

ONDAATJE: I think it's partly because, with all the books, when I begin, I begin them tentatively in the sense that I don't know exactly what I'm going to write about, or how I'm going to write about it. I don't have a great plan. I don't sit down and plot out the book, I don't really know where the story is yet, I don't even really know what kind of person Billy is or Buddy Bolden is or my father is, so there's a physical parallel of the writer trying to get a fix on someone or trying to understand or hold someone long enough to understand him. There's an element of reconnaissance, not just into a person but a place and a time. Usually it takes about a year or two for me to feel secure, to know the person more, whereas readers perhaps assume I knew all along exactly what Billy was going to do. That element of not knowing, of going blindly, is exhausting and difficult and scary to me because I spend a lot of time wondering, "What's happening? I still don't know what's happening." So that element comes out in the books, I suppose, in that sense of a search. In *In the Skin of a Lion,* I was about three-quarters of the way through and I was still asking myself, "What's going to happen?" It's being aware of the nuance of the language itself and the individual character as opposed to being tied to some steamroller of plot. I mean, a poem by Bunting or Williams or Creeley which focuses on some small moment or tiny reversal of emotion is more dramatic to me than many long works of action. I love that kind of drama—what evolves on the side of the road in Williams' "On the road to the Contagius Hospital," for instance. Those small discoveries are for me the first principles, and I try to circle around them and collect them and piece them together in some kind of mural or "novel." Magpie work.

BUSH: Are you wary of plot?

ONDAATJE: I think there are plots that can take place without people moving an inch. Plot comes out of the language as much as it comes out of the described event. The scenes in books of mine that I like the most are often the scenes where nothing happens, where the guy's just waiting or thinking—Patrick on a train going north in *In the Skin of a Lion,* Billy in a barn before the rats appear, my father driving up to Kegalle alone in his car at night after meeting with my mother in the Thanikama chapter of *Running in the Family.* Quite often I don't want to complete the plot, I keep postponing it. People are about to die, and then they have a flashback, and I think, "Wait a minute, I still want to say this about that person," or "Do you remember that time when . . . ?" There's an element of not wanting to move into that final room where a character meets his fate. I can quite understand Orson Welles hating to finish a film. To lock it up. To be final about everything one has been thinking about and circling around.

BUSH: Place is important to your books, too. How much research on locale do you do? Did you go to, say, New Mexico before writing *Billy the Kid*?

ONDAATJE: I had never been to New Mexico until about three years ago, years after *Billy* was published. There is often an invented landscape in my work, although I try to get to these places, if I can afford to, before the book ends. I could afford about five days in New Orleans, so I only got there about two-thirds of the way through *Coming Through Slaughter.* The book *is* a kind of mental landscape, but at the same time, I want to make it real, believable, tactile. I've always been convinced by mental or artistic landscapes. When I was growing up in England my image of America was essentially formed by songs by The Coasters. "Poison Ivy," "Young Blood," "Yakkety Yak."

BUSH: Your work also displays a documentary urge, using photographs, interviews, excerpts, to create a collage. Is telling a personal story not enough or can't you tell a story without these other elements?

ONDAATJE: Ideally, I want that mental landscape and the personal story to wrestle against the documentary. I think the documentary element is so essential to our lives that to ignore it in the novel is a problem. And it's not a tradition that began with Norman Mailer or Tom Wolfe or any of the New Journalists who claim such things. I think it's there as part of the great tradition. Take, for instance, Kawabata's *Master of Go,* which has a strange history. Kawabata was a reporter for this Go championship in Japan that lasted for two years, writing articles about it every day for the newspapers, and then, five or ten years later, he turned it into a very delicate, poetic novel. A wonderful work, far ahead in form to the "factoids" Mailer claimed to invent.

BUSH: Are you consciously concerned with developing some new kind of form? People have described your work in this way—Leon Edel, Russell Banks, for instance.

ONDAATJE: I am not really interested in inventing a form, as such. I want my form to reflect as fully as possible how we think and imagine. And these keep changing, of course. With each book I try to do something I think I can't do. But I don't see it as a progression. I think *Coming Through Slaughter* is just as much of a novel as *In the Skin of a Lion,* but its form was the right one for that book. If I wrote that book today, it would be different. I don't know if I *could* write that book today.

BUSH: How would you like to have an ideal reader approach your work?

ONDAATJE: There's a line—I think by Eudora Welty, who talks about the way her mother reads books. "She reads Dickens in the same spirit that she would have eloped with him."

BUSH: Pleasure and intimacy again. With *In the Skin of a Lion,* even more than the earlier books, the narrator enters multiple skins, to tell different stories: Patrick Lewis, who comes from rural Ontario to Toronto, as if it were a new land; Nicolas Temelcoff, new immigrant and daredevil bridge builder; a nun who falls over the edge of the bridge; Caravaggio, the thief. Are there limits to the characters or the landscapes that you would enter, or do you feel prepared to enter anywhere, be a complete chameleon?

ONDAATJE: I don't know. It gets more difficult to get into a person as fully and profoundly as I would like to. It becomes harder to trust yourself entering another voice.

BUSH: In the last couple of years there have been theatre adaptations in Toronto of both *Billy the Kid* and *Coming Through Slaughter.* You've been involved in both of them. Do you see something inherently theatrical about your language?

ONDAATJE: Theatrical productions depend so much on who's involved, who the director is, who the actors are. I don't mind the text being changed, depending if it's played by twelve Scottish dwarves or whatever. I was surprised when *Billy* was first done that it could work theatrically. I was most excited by the fact that a character could say out loud lines that to me were internal speeches or musings and they didn't come out sounding like gnarled paragraphs. And I've learned from theatre, I've learned from film, and I think it's healthy, for me anyway, because when I write it all seems to be gnarled and internal and private and it's good to hear that voice being pushed outside.

BUSH: You have moved easily among genres. Journalism, social documentary, theatre, film. You co-edit with Linda Spalding a literary magazine, *Brick.* What made you decide to study at the film center [The Canadian Centre for Advanced Film Studies]?

ONDAATJE: Most of all, I like being in a position of learning. There's an unhealthy fate to people who get published and suddenly become representatives for this group or that group or become representatives of themselves, become an image. It becomes difficult to change or go in other directions. I love the idea of being a student. I've always got more out of being a student than being a teacher. I'm a great believer in the mongrel. I learn more from other media as opposed to books. I read books not to learn things but for the pleasure of the text, the language, the escape into that world. I don't think I've sat down to read a book thinking, "I love Don DeLillo, what can I learn from Don DeLillo?" That seems a terrible betrayal of the act of reading. I just want a full involvement with the text. I am probably more technically influenced by seeing a Tarkovsky film, like *Stalker,* or listening to a piece of music. I may end up with a novel, but the novel technically is probably more influenced by dance or music or movies or theatre or greyhound racing. In terms of form, Diego Rivera's murals were extremely important to me when I was writing *In the Skin of a Lion.* In their 360-degree form, the experience of walking into a room and being surrounded. I wanted to try to get something of that quality into a book. I visited D'Annunzio's villa in Italy and that, too, was important—every section of the villa, even though it was actually full of bric-a-brac, somehow had a singular personality behind it. Whether you like the place or not, it has an underlying unity. He collected everything from the steering wheel from a friend's death on a motor launch to some Indian sculpture of a woman standing atop an elephant, but there was a vision to the place, which is what a book is, I think. There is such a range of natural forms in the real world. There is such a variety of form and devices in the other arts. Michael Powell directed a movie called *The Life and Times of Colonel Blimp.* It's a great movie, made during the Second World War, and in it a character falls in love four times and the director had Deborah Kerr play all four women. I can't think of many novels that show this psychological truth. At any rate, it's something that is technically outrageous but works, the stylizing of something that's not real but is very real, in a sense. Technically, what's happening in the other arts is much wilder than in the novel. If something unusual happens in a novel, it still gets labelled experimental. Somehow the novel demands a comfort level of realism that is quite high. The equivalent of Cubism or Abstract Expressionism or the subliminal and fluid cutting of film still hasn't been allowed into the novel except on the periphery—whereas we accept it, even complacently, in the other popular art forms. I think you can do on the page almost anything that film does. The novel, and writing, is more advanced in terms of *possibility.* A film becomes most versatile in the editing process, in the sharpening of scenes.

BUSH: In film, you can have multiple points of view, but you remain restricted by the camera's eye. In your fiction, in your poetry also, there's a wonderful way in which place,the body, individual stories all collapse together. There also seems to be a point where body and landscape merge, or in *In the Skin of a Lion,* where the city and the individual stories within it become one entity. You've used the phrase, "looking for the aerial view." It's as if this is what your narrators, and characters, are often looking for psychologically—an aerial view of themselves or the people they search for.

ONDAATJE: I want to get as close to a kind of sensory emotion as I can and communicate that in all its complexity. What happens in a novel is that we are in symbolic time. That is, a whole life is comprised into two hundred pages. So every action or thought that occurs leaps back to what a character was and leaps forward to what he or she might become. It's the complexity that this range of time produces that makes the characters thick or "real" in a novel. For me, anyway. I find that when I drift away from a text it's usually when whatever is going on is happening only in one time frame—without any suggestion of the history of the person. We are merely getting information as opposed to character and the potential possibilities in the language being used.

BUSH: There's one detail in particular I wanted to ask you regarding *In the Skin of a Lion*—new immigrants learning English by going to the movies in the early days of talkies. Did this actually happen?

ONDAATJE: I think so. I can't remember now. The trouble is I also tend to remember things I take out. I was talking to one friend about a scene in *Billy the Kid* which I wished I'd taken out and he said, "But it's not in the book." After a while, when you've been working on something for so long, especially when you've been editing it and changing it, you really can't remember what is true and what is not, or what is there and what is not. I think songs at least were definitely used a great deal to learn the language.

BUSH: When you revise and shape your work, do you rewrite extensively?

ONDAATJE: I tend to rewrite everything again and again. I move everything around. I just try and keep the "tone" of the book that I had in the beginning.
BUSH: Is tone what another writer might call voice?
ONDAATJE: No, it's something out there on the page as opposed to in here, in me or the narrator. It could be something like a mood of celebration or bitterness that holds the book together. The tone of D'Annunzio's villa, the pitch of Cormac McCarthy's *Blood Meridian.*
BUSH: In *In the Skin of a Lion,* you reclaim history, telling stories that hadn't been told, stories about people who actually, physically built the city of Toronto, the Bloor Street Viaduct, the water filtration plant, these structures that were one man's fantastic dream but constructed by many other people's bodies. These stories are also not part of mainstream Anglo history.
ONDAATJE: I think reclaiming untold stories is an essential role for the writer. Especially in this country, where one can no longer trust the media. The newspapers have such power over the story and portrait of Canada. You can see the newspapers moving in a certain politically right-wing or economically right-wing direction, and this—before you know it—becomes the official voice of the country, the equivalent of a Canadian pavilion at Disneyland. But we know it's not a real truth. One of the things a novel can do is represent the unofficial story, give a personal, complicated version of things, as opposed to competing with the newspapers and giving an alternate but still simplified opinion, saying, "No, *this* is right." I think it has more to do with *who* you write about. I think a novel can become, in this way, a more permanent and political reflection of your time.
BUSH: *In the Skin of a Lion* is a book told during a journey between places. Does the journey somehow become the point at which stories are most clearly revealed?
ONDAATJE: For a long time I wasn't quite sure how to frame the book. About two-thirds of the way through I realized I could frame it with a journey, and the minute I did that it helped me a lot in terms of freeing me technically. With the frame, you have the young girl, Hana, listening to Patrick over a four- or five-hour car journey. The question becomes whether it's Patrick's story or Hana's story, and in a way it's much more Hana's story, because she's gathering it. That freed me to jump narrative voices, it allowed me to get closer inside certain scenes. There are scenes that

Patrick does not witness and so it doesn't make sense that he's the narrator. It's just as much Hana imagining certain scenes as it is her being told certain scenes. One of the problems with novels is that we tend to be so strict about narrative voice. If a writer gets locked into one character in the first chapter, say, he or she has to stay handcuffed to the character until the end. And it's a terrible oppression, not just on the story but on the reader, because we, as readers, don't think that way. Obviously great novels have been written within this form. Conrad's Marlow and Fitzgerald's Nick Carroway are still the role models. But I think we have perhaps run this one narrative voice into the ground, finessed it too well with all the shades of irony. So I'm much more interested in the narrative form of Ford Madox Ford's *Parade's End* than *The Good Soldier,* or something like *Anna Karenina,* where we move within the minds of seven or eight characters before we even get to Anna. I'm drawn to a form that can have a more cubist or mural voice to capture the variousness of things. Rather than one demonic stare.

BUSH: One of the writers who crops up several times in *In the Skin of a Lion* is Conrad. Is he one of those writers whom you return to?

ONDAATJE: Well, we've all travelled through the country that was Conrad. He is to 20th-century fiction what Yeats is to 20th-century poetry. He is full of political pitfalls and yet remains pretty central. I'd probably take Ford's work with me to a desert island before Conrad's. Conrad is not someone I return to, although there are many allusions to him in the book. Who do I return to? Pound said—I don't remember his exact wording—that poetry had to get back the power that the novel had. Poetry should be able to do what the novel could. And then he and everyone else began a revolution, and people like Pound and Bunting and Niedecker, all these people gave a fantastic boost to poetry, but there were things they did in poetry that I don't think most novels have yet picked up on, the scope, the simultaneity, the sharpness of language. There was an exploration that went on during that period of poetry earlier in this century which still hasn't reached the novel.

BUSH: What are the books that have given you the most pleasure as a reader lately? Which writers do you feel kinship with—if you drew yourself a literary lineage what would it look like?

ONDAATJE: I guess in spite of the fact that we've spoken about form quite a bit, I suspect we are too skillful at it, too precious. So what we all suddenly desire is the blend of emotion and language and form. Heart and skills. The books I carry with me, that I build a literary home out of may be essays and short stories by writers like Guy Davenport or John Berger. They may be novels like DeLillo's *The Names* or Elizabeth Smart's *By Grand Central Station I Sat Down and Wept,* Michael Herr's *Dispatches* and *The Big Room,* Graham Swift's *Waterland,* Henry Roth's *Call It Sleep, The 10,000 Things* by Maria Dermout, Ian McEwan's *The Child in Time,* Faulkner's *Light in August,* Calvino's *The Baron in the Trees,* Ford's *Parade's End,* Joseph Roth's *The Redetzky March,* Fielding Dawson, Alice Munro, John Hawkes, Marilynne Robinson's *Housekeeping,* Evan Connell, Alastair MacLeod, Maxine Hong Kingston, Toni Morrison's *Beloved,* Russell Banks, David Malouf's *An Imaginary Life,* Murray Bail's *Homesickness* and *Holden's Performance,* Jean Rhys' *Wide Sargasso Sea,* Wright Morris, Salman Rushdie, Cormac McCarthy, Achebe, Armah, Kafka, Philip K. Dick. There are many more, of course, strange, mad company. In spite of the general attitude that not much is happening in fiction, wondrous things are everywhere. In every generation. Patrick White writes a crazy memoir, Cheever writes a great and radical last novel—a bit like the old Kurosawa somehow getting free of the realities of the earth. *Oh What a Paradise it Seems* is a masterpiece of tone and voice. It is just the media which keeps trotting out the established, familiar names—somewhat the way radio stations keep reselling Mick Jagger when the great music of our time is being made in other countries and in other languages.

33 CONTEMPORARY AMERICAN POETS

Editor's Note. This mini-anthology is hardly exhaustive. But for space, thirty-three and yet another thirty-three innovative poets could have been included. The diversity and imaginative wisdom of radical American poetry seems never to have been more evident than it is right now.

The Nonconformist's Memorial

Susan Howe

Contempt of the world
and contentedness

Lilies at this season

other similitudes
Felicities of life

Preaching constantly
in woods and obscure

dissenting storms
A variety of trials

Revelations had had
and could remember

far away historic fact

Flesh become wheat

which is a nothingness
The I John Prologue

Original had no title
Ingrafted onto body

dark night stops suddenly
It is the last time

Run then run run

Often wild ones nest in woods
Every rational being

*

The Act of Uniformity

ejected her

and informers at her heels

a swarm of errors

Citations remain abbreviated

Often a shortcut

stands for Chapter

*

IMMEDIATE ACTS

I am not afraid to confess it

and make you my confessor

Steal to a place in the dark

least coherent utterance

and Redactor's treasured proof

Love for the work's sake

*

Consent in the heavens

Reason in the mind

Walking up and down

Not to be too sudden

in speech

as in the case of fasting

alienated

But was a peacemaker

Rebels are quartered here

*

Arranges and utters

Words to themselves

Of how and first she

was possible body

Pamphlets on that side

the author of them

Parallel to the mind

a reprobate mind clings

close

inner outlaw impenitent

Over-Againstness at least

Rigorism

*

As though beside herself

I want to accuse myself

would say to her confessor

Confessions implode into otherness

Lay at night on thorns

For the purpose of self-concealment

would have consumed iron

And she fled her ecstasies

many occasions

*

The penultimate Redactor

Some love-impelled figure

Most midnightly thesis

impelled will freely led

Love is the orbed circle

Silent the one sought

Reader if I told anything

my crookedness roughness

Down from his arms

as S. John says in Apocalypse

*

King of Righteousness

At the end of history

interminable trajectory of authority

So truly primitive

Night when the warrant comes

such a ravenous coming

Undertype Shadow Sacrifice

Who is this distance

Waiting for a restoration

and righteousness

*

On the losing side

No abiding habitation

Severity of the times

escaped by mistake

Settled somewhere

Inner life led by herself

The clear negative way

Moving away into depths

of the sea

Love once said in her mind

Enlightendly to do

*

The metaphor of a stake

Arrow thrust through

In connection with here

Eschatology

At deepest claimlessness

could not see one another

Spirit snapping after air

dragged down to visible

Chroniclers halt of such

authentic sayings

Fear destroys all welcome

house-arrest

*

She fled from consolation

The abiding and transitory

were negative and no echo

These attacks came suddenly

even fierce as the Evangelist

the struggle in S. John

darkness rushing and the true

I will cross the frontiers

Pure hard-edged discipline

betrothes to me nothing

She is matron undone her hair

falling down

*

Is that the same as Hell

Theologians in that fire

As to her physical health

and the fire

As night to understanding

or truth to fiction

stammering to a redaction

the quick and simplicity

Believing unbelieving Reader

there is now no rest

She confessed to a Confessor

tell lies and I will tell

*

I wander about as an exile

as a body does a shadow

A notion of split reference

if in silence hidden by darkness

there must be a Ghost

Iconic theory of metaphor

a sound and perfect voice

Its hiding is understood

Reader I do not wish to hide

in you to hide from you

It is the Word to Whom she turns

True submission and subjection

*

Were Protestant dissenters

Who walk along this road

Who knows better than you know

I remember the strangers

Not finding names there

Immanence is white with this

Where to find charges

A hymn was contesting a claim

Court of interior recollection

Map of a wilderness of sin

There I cannot find There

I cannot hear your wandering prayer

of quiet

*

When night came on

Windows to be opened

so as to see the sky

She saw herself bereft

of body

would only seem to sleep

if I could go back

Recollectedly into biblical

fierce grace

already fatherless

Isled on all removes

When night came on

*

Dense in parameter space

the obscure negative way

Any trajectory is dense

outside the threshold

Turn again and lean against

Moving away into depths

of the sea

Her Love once said in her mind

Enlightendly to do

Seven Poems from *My Bird Book*
Norma Cole

ABSORPTION or a noun of action

For you it's called absorption, for your dream, the hood was wearing a cape, the little division sang

division sang a little space
causeless light can blind you
always focus as respected
depthless field behind you

Exactly and the line is not exact, those elaborate devices divise us, it just doesn't know how to be two at once, cover your faces when you speak

Absorption of the baby, absorption of the *Idea of the Baby*, isn't it like eating the predicate—or being hungry, an assortment, the tiled floor of the stock exchange

the painting lowered its eyes
swallowed
the dream of absorption

Without living a taunt can right absorb lost benediction comma redemption warm intervention icy extrusion nothing is like

SEA SWALLOW *(La Goélette)*

an overarching voice
rustic and being
gular flutter
flower of the rock

that sunny comfort reach
arid out of hearing

sing me the whole song

about to speak
will is only nearer
to speak nothing but
arterial equivalent
gular flutter
punctuate equilibrium

RAVEN

Says I am invisible in my feathers

World knot
young beyond half casual theme
courtoisie & turbulence a few more slowly now
we read little gold suns over the airstrip
no medical treatment for civilians
expeditions *speaking like through a screen door*
peaches for eyes

How faint the spot harmonates unbarred by time, wit and the shape
memory bolted
unobtainable until we learn it

Come up now onto the roof of my mouth and *see* this shadow that has
driven people mad

Common denominators this papers generosity
waters constancy emptied field
what we know passed to the back
mirrors open up another front

"Thou wilt never see that raven again, for I am that raven"

Norma Cole

SWALLOW

fly over in silence

powerful registration before sleep
on your experience falls
recent but complete

areas of color
next to each other
"you ask" did they release him today
but with some affection
method asking
and began
respiration falls

and the thorough world is great

Washing brushes in a lake
sibilous net
trend or engender
long hanging word
shivering when it sings
to the one natural day
one thought

THE RAPTOR TRUST

"their infinite nests . . ."
—*V. Huidobro*

Being is done
a being
seething
and outside
from which automatically all questions the individual deviation
style is or fit what we were looking for
the market becoming intimate failure
2 versions

since every part is active
unnamed or untamed
consumed or recent

Allies of the future
when ceremony is over
discomfort the preoccupation
we celebrate these perfect errors
what's necessary, *quella bella petra*
conferring chance household goods besides rhyming agreement
anxious and various endurance

It's nice because you can remember it

<table>
<tr><td>d r y
w a l l
s t u d y</td><td>a long cylinder of
dried grasses—hay
leaning up against
the studio wall</td></tr>
</table>

If that's logic who's looking at it in order our forces condense
flatly
up the hill
have grace

the well surfaces
have plenty of it
spelling

but each and each
of no and no
days exit and former
nectar and sap

Archives of the future
how lucky to hear the iris and mini-atlas aid each *delirium*
cordis clears its own throat meaning a social releaser
proof and consequences starting with music
entirely convincing this time perception smear
one's not the symbol but the censor

Norma Cole

melting tone or fixed pitch
hand belted in violent encounter
policy and choice rustle in the creatorium

From bird to word
only as you get it
hands off that book or what the inscription don't show
the alphabet will clue me
but wouldn't we
use one generally
except for the ones in petition
who make their own beds
try me
I'm not far enough yet flying has its own history
dichotomy I'm all outside
(the thing) presented is (the
thing prevented
s e a
                    spectral shells
t r a s h

and be and remember can conjure yourself
and a thin ripping concern and return time
so we can see with their eyes
this gift that obliterates

Sublime the hearings begin you mean your eyes fall out finally you
mean dishes clatter (what can we know of winnowing grain) pretending
pleasure isn't for instance patience about this keeper of forms

X imagines the universe
exactly how it looks
Y are welcomed
before all the city
periodicity doubles the outward call of thought
and fiction in its own way
remains in the puzzle. remember the earth?
fly back to it each summer

Norma Cole

Oval skylights in the second circuit house
nonplussed motivation taxes matching revealing
what required feeling—nobody
takes it in the head—is an explanation
for an act and their laws results
which are bonding through more rounded up material
all equal wonder to some more immaculate
the complete danger zone "for reasons which
I forget" how wild is thought

BIRDBRAIN

I say several
to come seeing
Oh I am here
to keep forgetting

"self-perpetuating . . .
            and light"

I break them and then I eat
them or translate them
to keep the damage

When I go to reason
it was never my home
time of extension
searching
died against me (do I say
            moral or ready

BIRD OF PARADISE

calling out very quietly

moving forward
must be her ears

generalizing

left
swept and go behind

to map and to provide

look home

and then

to go.

Essay on the Comic Book

Leslie Scalapino

(Each of the lines or paragraphs is one of the frames of the comic book.)

The crowd marks the split between themselves and experience.

They construct all the buildings to be the same.

That's a different way of regarding; so the man whose function it is to drive the bus doesn't know where he's going or seem to wonder.

as it is before

him

Not using the mind—which then occurs outside the frames of the comic book after—as the bus driver from the civilization without order though it is repressed

then

I was out in the cornfields, the sky—and people would pull alongside shouting obscenities saying to go back where one'd come from.

What is the relation of action—someone's—to the unfolding of phenomena?

The farm boys coming up alongside with obscenities out in the fields.

Wavering alongside and if one says they're from there, their exploding feeling insulted.

Which is really funny.

Just say back to them they're from there and they erupt.

At a streetlight, out in the fields—out in nowhere—and they waver there alongside shouting.

then feel hurt in public

from what had been before.

One cannot expect to be a bum.

The reverse of that—which is before

where people used to lie in the train stations

and now they have to have a ticket

Not using the mind—is contemplating—in the comic book.

The newspapers have created the impression of disjointed experiences. But I don't read them.

anyway, we're not in these experiences
is the impression created by the newspapers which
do not allow us to make connections

Not having historical experience—is the comic book as the form of the serial novel. Though popularly we're supposed to be in them—this is a deprivation created by the newspapers themselves.

The moon is in the day sky, now out in the cornfields—rather than in the civilization which does not have order, though it is repressed.

The farm boys hanging wavering floating at the crossroad—alongside, shouting obscenities.

are from the ordered civilization where the bum lying has died in the subway station.

as such they're not in experiences—as the reverse image of the deprivation created by the newspapers.

The serial—but then being before it
And afterwards there's only that
They are out by the fields

These boys were shouting, maybe because they're together—wavering hanging leaning out coming alongside.

I feel depressed—I'm tired of being made fun of.
Farm boys who're just youths floating leaning out
People standing like the cattle in the sea—waist deep, standing
on grass
being invalidated and nothing
is the reverse image of the ordered civilization
and one is calm

*

I was in a huge crowd which was a sea of people at a rally in a square.

standing

Claustrophobia of feeling that one was going to throw up—in the crowd—and moving through the crowd.

then

who don't move, though there was one woman elbowing moving through the crowd propelled. Her swimming through them, I moved in the opening following her.

Someone else saying—outside, on the outskirts—that they had had a feeling of going to throw up in the crowd. They were outside then. It not moving.

My feeling of throwing up in it and the woman swimming elbowing as the only moving being.

flags banners held up on the mass

And if you took pictures they turned stolidly, staring thinking you were taking pictures of them. that that would be repressive

to them

standing.

Man coming to sand bar peninsula after war and corpses on it lying unburied, with confluence of waters opening up out onto a wide mass of water. Beside himself, he wants to bury the corpses.

A mound of the corpses stuck there on the bar.

He's come up to the bar.

that has the heap of corpses.

A boat then comes up floating on the wide mass of water touching the bar.

The one passenger seat is given to him, the passenger in it stepping out so that the lone sunken man can get in

and go on. Out on the water. leaving them.

And the passenger who'd been in it stands on the bar.

The lone sunken man had been a soldier of the defeated army—which'd invaded this land in which he's wandering. It had killed and tyrannized their people in the countryside though this wouldn't be allowed to be seen or presented in his own land.

So the expression of this is he comes upon only the corpses of his own people.

on the bar

and will never go back

to his own civilization

the jewel

is not doing so.

This was as close as they could come.

on the part of what had been the conquered people

and are not that they appear as only calm

A man riding in a taxi, the taxi driver has a conversation about being in the war. He seems very aggressive.

The one thing about being there was he enjoyed killing and can't do that here.

having someone them at the point of his gun and then killing them made him feel—

the comic book—using the mind one

can't do here either

It was not acceptable to criticize oneself.

The (other) is in her apartment. At night happy the man in the neighboring compartment on the other side of the wall bumping against the wall—reading. Him urinating, in his stall.

The night is so still—outside—reading.

Walking back at night.

The branches of the trees hanging, she walks through them.

A mutt comes running out. It jumps in the air—as it's little—and bites a tuft of the artificial fur of her jacket. Tears off a bite. It has done this before.

Mutt.

A man steps out of the trees. Innocent, wounded, he is someone who emits poison as would a scorpion with the tail raised over the back—before—and injecting the poison out of the bulb of it.

He is innocent. He wants her to do a job. Find his daughter, yet his manner is skittish in the sense of tough and wounded.

She returns to the apartment. The man of the adjoining compartment, who'd urinated in his stall. stamping.

He does not want to be seen—the poison bulb tail wounded before

He is not like the soldier who'd been given the seat in the boat—who'd disguised as a Buddhist monk—

realistically this is because the passenger in it is a monk but subliminally those who'd been the ones invaded are completely calm.

so he can

not go to his own civilization

can be allowed not to.

but the poison bulb wounded is not contemplative like this.

he seems to be

why?

She is talking to him out on the street—in the day.

wangling like sending a hook out

His daughter had apparently blended into the street life and he hadn't seen her for a year or sought for her—before.

Aged landlady—this was before it came apart, and she died—needing her, very old drunken blissful seen staggering in the yard in the plants.

Happening into her there. Where she'd seem to come out.

Baudelaire's discovery of not being in experience

in the crowd

She sees the man's daughter on the street one day—the (other) is with him who can therefore see her.

The girl coming up in the stream, the three go into a coffee shop. Bulb wounded poison emitting that into her, the girl looks at him with a simple open sympathy.

She says that she loves him. A disapproval emanating from him, bulb wounded innocent intimates afterward to the (other) that the job has not yet been completed.

The comic book—being written as there is a market for it.

inventing the sense of a private psyche—which had been before—is an expression of the split between self and experiences.

and is aware that it is that.

so it had not existed—doesn't after this.

Man acted for our CIA for/in the other's war and isn't tried.

Isn't tried since the proof is classified by our CIA for whom he works. Our utterly corrupt system.

The man is released. She goes to see him and a man in the street is lying dead beaten covered in blood and being washed by the rain. The rain is pounding slanting in sheets on the street. the man is being washed for his grave. Her having come to the man's door, a small group in streetlight is hovering around the mound lying there. Shred.

A patrol car is parked but dimmed in the rain.

Thin blood running off the mound. Remnant or rim of blood on it tuft—film on it.

yet not being in one's own civilization

the jewel

she thinks.

And continues in the rain to his place which is an apartment building, dark in approach lighted in the vestibule.

He won't talk to her. He's lying on the bed, mumbling to himself. A bottle of whiskey is on the bureau. Thin indistinct face with the lack of features of a mole

no features of the face—doesn't answer her. She sets the bottle down.

Mumbling to himself face up lying on the bed.

She sips, burning sensation in the pit within her. Sets the bottle down. The neon sign from across the street is dim on him—though she's turned on a switch. He doesn't answer her.

gurgling—of him. With no features on the face.

working at this too hard so that the burning sensation of the whiskey in her is burnt out—before, when it gets there it's empty. It's relaxed. There is no cauterized. The jewel. What follows it is muffled and empty.

She's out on the street in the rain.

She's in the hotel room sick. The hotels are drab wings blocks-long so that one cannot get to the main door from a wing. One has to refind the central shaft by walking along dark halls.

She could have died like a rat in the room. They wouldn't have sought her. No friendship or how does that occur in others. The buildings constructed to duplicate before.

She puts the bottle down again. Relaxed.

No more of this thick food covered in fat.

*

She hasn't been eating, feels light-headed free. It's extremely cold.

freezing, steam comes off of the immense palladium swimming pool—the swimmers arms on it.

The arms dipping.

their elbows—wings—on the immense swimming pool. Rungs of the arms rake across it.

Mole no features on the face batted buffeted in the rakes of arms lifted again and again on the swimming pool.

Steam arising from the palladium

no features on the face buffeted flacid caught in the rakes of arms crossing the pool.

Beside the dead mole featureless face up, is the girl—amidst the mass of swimmers.

Resting side by side with him—adjoining.

Mole face up.

She stirs.
The girl's face becomes alert yet is in the mechanism of the rake of arms doing a lap in the pool.

The (other) is held up and blurred—seeing the girl swaying beside the mole, but gradually recovers. There's a motion on the sideline.
A jet or blur darts to the stairs of the raised outdoor swimming pool and goes down to the street.
It's freezing.
The (other) recoils, gradually recovering and then begins to run.
She ran after the figure—which had gone.
Goes down the street.
The figure had gone into the metro to the deep stairs of escalators, rungs of them.
leading deep underground, the deep bronze escalators descend to where she comes to him still on it—pursed white face puckered of very old woman, turned upwards, whom she passes blurs.
Coming to him, hitting her in the gut.
Is sent backward falling down the escalator. with her running toward him.
He lies crumpled at the bottom, and a deep stain spreads on the front of his chest.
The assassin of the mole featureless face up is shot—and dying, says nothing to the (other).
To say nothing—the bulb tail injected calls her up the next day, injecting as if onto a gel (she's in her apartment). She wonders what the poison wounded innocent wants as surveillance of his daughter.
He seems helpless. He'd been a marine.
The girl had been left. He's complaining and yet holding back.
She recognizes it as a feeler.
The dart a ball, hitting her in the gut—floats backwards out in the air shot and crumpled at the foot of the stairs.
the curled ball, having whirled, diving for her—punching her in the gut. His back hurls forward.
The dark curved steep moving stairs—a hump, goes down slowly like a falls. to meet him.
She lies in her apartment.
Billows of dark exhaust pour out of some nearby trucks. And

sweeps into their faces, it's night. They jump out of the trucks. Asked to unload and load the heavy stacks in the cold. Men are running.

Her just descending slowly on the falls to meet him. Just as a ball was hanging in the air batted by two people on the beach. The ball was in the black sky as she's facing the sun—it's in the light.

She darts back up the metro stairs—that are going down. And runs, a man is running.

It's freezing.

They're in the arcade glassed-domed with a mass of people crawling. He's not running so she can't see him.

Standing in line, with the mass still—she reaches the counter of the shop and then is elbowed out by the person directly behind.

She's outside the line. No one moving.

Stands in it again—no shoving and when she's reached the counter again, elbowed out by the next person behind. very still, no moving.

(except when being elbowed out by the one person as she's about to reach the front.)

she goes on. Enters a café, the people standing no sound from their chests, a din but not arising from the chest which is mute. She is beside them—there are counters where they stand—and one person'll bump her when she reaches a counter like a berth.

She stands out in the center and is bumped gently from one spot.

The man is resting in them.

Not moving, nor someone else—and then bumped from a spot she'd take. again. calm. no faces are turned (to each other or her).

She can't see him.

The gel receives the injection—the entire mob, hurting the crowd. The bulb tail wounded before—he doesn't associate with them. The city is laid out, drab

Preaching to some people one imagines to be the herd—out there.

they are not in this—not doing that.

She can barely recognize carved flutes on the corners of the buildings because her eyes can't see them.

The cops had checked over the assassin of the mole featureless face as if for lice

and the man who shot him has gotten away in the crowd.

The perversion of the shoppers. distortion of their complaints. (not those of the unmoving mass.)

as if for lice shred.

The mutt jumps up in the night—as she's passing under the bough of trees going back to her apartment.

bites a tuft of the artificial fur on her jacket—springing up straight in the night. which it does.

being in the unmoving mass

The aged landlady blissful bonkers—with craft, and yet not needing her care then—like a bark amidst the plants—she needs her and it's come apart. she thinks.

the jewel

It's not being in the other civilization

but rather not in her own

which is visible. very old woman comes out of drug store and gets in taxi; she'd been at the soda fountain counter. The (other) comes up to ask her something, and the cab driver is helping her in the cab.

doesn't want to be in it anyway or

the other

the elderly frail face frayed—without features, not having money but having been at the fountain eating a sandwich.

white-haired tend to gather at the soda fountain and to take taxis back.

the (other) goes up inviting herself into the cab. She recognizes the extremely old woman though that bears no resemblance to any others and she's happy to see her.

frayed is open.

The frayed is weak and she lies back in the cab. People are walking on the street, neither the unmoving mass or the distortion of shoppers. It's a clear, light day.

They see a man on the street, to whom the frayed beckons. He gets into the back seat.

Thin his entire frame has no features. He talks to her the elderly condescendingly—assuming things they know; he works in an office somewhere. He says the value of something is in whether it can be sold.

Duh.

The elderly doesn't regard him as unusual.

We've made people simply separate from each other—though the frayed's not that. And so the (other) is intensely lonely and the elderly one is not.

He says things.

She feels beaten. She feels depressed. In the clear, light day.

Feeling incredibly tired—sleeping in her apartment. She's in the sleep deeply. The next day it's clear and light.

Cauterized, where there's something empty and clear after that. She begins to weep.

There isn't anything there to be weeping about.

(Having been out on the street flagging cabs which wouldn't stop—wanting to cry. Once. It follows that one can cry and no one will care, and this is a great relief. So she stood and wept. the jewel.)

then found a cab.

The man on the street of the frayed's cab, is her grandson making him the brother of the girl.

Going into the metro.

The marine's—injecting out onto gel—there far back on the moving stairs. The (other) sees the head of the consumer man from the cab down flowing to meet him. A person slumps on the moving stairs.

Shot, but there isn't any sound in the metro.

The girl is beside the corpse.

the frame moving forward of the girl

The (other) is running.

Yet the consumer man from the cab falls forward. and on the runner—who has passed him on the escalator.

He falls on her so that she goes down yet he's dead.

The marine is helpless.

Some person has been shot who was near the girl.

That's what they say to the cops.

And the dead man—unlike the unmoving mass, had been amidst them, when she'd been in the café looking for him.

Their not moving in the arcade café, and her parting them.

His money's dependent in the mole featureless' CIA dealings in other countries. Embedded in it. He'd been shooting the girl while she's running to her—for she's aware of this.

The marine's helpless—and shoots him.

She's failed—there isn't a relation between action and this; not cauterized, clear after it.

She lies in her apartment.

Yet she comes back, walking under the boughs.

The mutt springs up.

The mired alleys of the city in which the buildings (of the civilization without order) are the same; the bus driver goes into a mired alley not knowing where he's going past vast miles of tenements, the drab filth smoke stacks pouring. They went to a circus.

one is taught a definition of one's humanness when a small female child which is immediately unbelievable to that child—one knows that is not the self.

the civilization with order having created the clear series of events.

to be a comic book form.

One element of it is to render itself invalid—that it will use itself up as pulp and be regarded as nothing. It is not 'discursive,' 'analytical' 'method'—by in some ways reproducing such and not being that.

If the series is inhibited, cauterized—no relations can occur between people.

This happens early—on in it. one can't expect to be a bum—according to them.

that the marine helpless had killed his own son.

The (other) is receiving as if onto a template the mean lack of consideration as of gang ridiculing from a woman in a group; they're seated in a coffee shop.

as they are friends—and so one has to be inhibited

Excusing herself, she goes out. Outside, the street is quiet.

Having only a moderate living—not using the mind—is contemplating

She begins to weep, and this is such a relief.

She looks up and can see the stars.

There is Orion. Orion is lying on his side, falling into the Southern Hemisphere.

In the day, the white-haireds gather at the drugstore at the soda fountain counter, then take taxis back.

People walk on the street.

A white-haired comes out, and goes by taxi back

Two Poems

Barbara Guest

PAULOWNIA

ravenous the still dark a fishnet—

robber walk near formidable plaits

a glaze—the domino overcast—

violet. shoulder.

seized by capes—budding splash

whitened—with strokes—

silver tone gravure.

knifed tree.

straw beneficence—

ambient cloud. riderless.

ii

vowels inclement—tossed off figure.

arythmic—a lisping blot—

running figure.

bowled ripe.

stood in the wind sheet. a fermur axis.

virginal wail. as grain. storm motif.

iii

pierced the risen sea.

coxcomb.

slides around.

day and night.

"remedy of darkness"

lit body.

iv

etched in powder

sequence—a solace

the monument.

width of grape—is praised.

v

adherence to sand

the loam division—the quagmire

foot sink the rind—

or rindswift heel

astonished acre

chewed wire.

vi

as instrument:

threaded sky

burnt.

sinister.

torn from the corner.

on your knees.

vii

clammered over it

plinth in sour bloom

the idiot cone

rummage—

viii

held in mortar air.

' weight of stone'

fragment.

ix

their whole selves—

or were they?

burden of face

from one to the other.

formal pallor

momento mori

quaking sun.

abstract arm.

Barbara Guest

DOVE

experienced in rounded

dove form

belly up the child toy

anointed.

other codes—

like granite where the toy

the ground submissive—

splays

lightness under curled vapor.

"we wear open clothes.

and we are

broken up into time intervals."

one day bridges.

neophytes passing over. three vans.

flight of open sticks.

waving.

~~~~~~

repeated

as idiom

"their fear of absorption—

a common scale."

what is printed—

determinant lion

as music—;

ordinary leaves

estranged—proportionate wind—

felled.

and plots of sandust.

"the thing that was dear"—

scenes with table.

an intense

idolizing. frame with multiple rose.

~~~~~~

sunset

venom in rust

the small breathing.

of cowhide.

employed

a chalk wing.

the globular

solitude

invisible swell

"touching the beyond"

has no body without another.

walless.

~~~~~~

at the nib—dove shunted downward;

survives—in buoyant leap

admits the crater lump—the advice

performs more violently as violent solution
~~~~~~

picks up speed

outside of character

outside the dovecote—

a rascallion soar—in multi-layered emotional

suffix.

~~~~~~

he may never know why

the scribbling

dynamic—skewed—

meter shift

the merging

print and tense

dominant

"through open doors"

on foraged studio cloud

the painted raven

feeds the hermit bread.
~~~~~~

~~~~~~

from blunt earth

the whinied pupil scratch   anxious

from stalk ear the eye reached up and the

sublimated eye   reroutes the gaze

world of trout   a neutralized shape

the portal earth threw   toad gaze

on

dove

water outside the spoon.
~~~~~~

Ideal

Mei-mei Berssenbrugge

1.

I did not know beforehand what would count for me as a new color. Its beauty
is a kind of analysis of the things I believe in or experience, but seems to alter
events very little. The significance of a bird flying out of grapes in a store
seems to relate to the beauty of the color of the translucency of grapes.
There is a space among some objects on a table that reminded her of a person, the way
the bird reminded her, a sense of the ideal of the space that she would be able to see.
Beauty can look like this around objects. A plastic bag on a bush, moving slightly,
makes an alcove, like a kind of glove or mist, holding the hill. Time can look like this.
The plane of yourself separates from the plane of spaces between objects, an ordered succession
that the person apprehends, in order to be reminded.

2.

Two particles that make a continuum or ideal, in how the space between them would relate to a third event,
as how clouds against a windowpane admit space that continues to a cloud on the mountain,
a sheathe of a space of feeling in material sheathes of her body, for a perceived order, depend
on your having felt the relation. A horizon forms around the voice through which no sound can pass.
This voice is a feeling of remembering there was a situation in my dreams, in which she would be alive.
The event could occur, the way a line would differ for the particle along a straight or a curved space.
He sees a relation like a new language in accidental spaces between the objects, which we cannot,
as if he were seeing a color that had not existed before, and then we can make the color.

3.

You import the magenta orchid, locating this particle at a green fern, import the yellow poinciana.
It looks like the surface of the space of an analysis, but you suspect it is time, because your feeling is changing.
She makes a continuous surface among particles of table space and times of the harvestings
of the elements of a bouquet; then one particle starts to move backward, suffusing her body,
the way light gains character, suffusing berries or a cloud, by who sees it.
The illusion of meaning of the third dimension from which his inner voice speaks, and of
the ambivalent reality of a frame, is the gold of the frame. So, she cannot distinguish a house
on the horizon from the shape of the hawk lifting away, a little like a symbol that acts like a word.
Her sense of a sequence becomes perceptual, like perspective on structures, as thinking
is perceptual, putting the scale of an orchid next to human scale in designing the space.

4.

I make a relation in time between the hawk hovering above her on the mountain in sun
and sun on a crow over me, turning the wings gold. I think I am tracing the nature of the color
of a feather, but I trace around a gold frame through which to examine the nature of a crow.
A wren in grapes reminding him of the woman, is how the color belongs inseparably to your perception of her,
without itself being your consciousness of her. Gold on a wing bears the illusion of the content
of a symbolic dimension. Light on a wing, not of a crow, solves this problem of content by being an anomaly.
Then clouds lower the light. The land's planes close and grow distinct and dark-colored, making an ideal time.
A horizon retains its transparency, while you look at the relation between spaces and what he says,
as if the smallest particle of matter were a pronouncement, not a thing,
so that the white plastic bag becomes a winglike space between mist and the mountain.
What is the whiteness of a reminder, becoming a pronouncement?

5.

Here is the body of the person, his torso facing you, head and feet in profile.
There is a twist of space between the front arm and the back arm. Time goes there.
The arm that turns toward you is personal, the arm that turns away is the impersonal.
These flows that built the space go on building it, where you are trying to live.
She is making a line between a space inside the glove on the mountain and the moment of an orchid's harvest,
a bird's movement from a box of grapes and a bird's silhouette suffused with gold,
the scale of a bird and the scale of a man inside the event horizon of his oracle, where
heads do not look at each other, because each meaning that begins there flows into a different emotion.
This is a description of the content of the apprehended space between objects on the patio table.
In the sense of being that it is a new feeling, it is more like a coincidence of focus, where time is.
In the sense that it is a new color, it is more of an ideal than an anomaly.

Way of Life
John Ashbery

Abomination or just habit of sketching
That the past has with feathers, the lightness of tears?
This message came to us then across the field
In flames. The short
Day is pejorative.

As long as we choose to spell it in so many instances.
The light, daughter of fire you kept at the brothel-keeper's
Crossing, now extinguished for its own good: that's the way
Of dresses, seasons and mud
In the harbor for forgotten

Hosts. This herball tells all about it, what you should know when
So many come to you for guidance, the insipid thirsts, but what then
If we knock off earliest? If the guide sees us past the center
And we'll be in it.
Not much to stand on,

Yet it's enough, in infra-red. You see the washed marshes came up level
With the screen we were using for blockage. That caused a calamitous
Short-circuit for guests, and so one was appeased. In the winding down now
No crepe-paper
Tapes to untwist,

No more panic for the fodder in heaven that unbenighted
Us as we came down and looked at the floor, then looked away awash
As the land-tide forever more came scurrying in just at that time
To undo one, time
The toothbrush. Abstracts

Were written. The kitty signaled it was time to go, to confirm
For tonight when we were going to. Bring the wine now
Or rather then. Paste papers on the wall. Drive out into the market airs

Despondent to bleed
And then some, person trying

To get through, signaling repeatedly. No one was cast adrift yet,
The pines were down here, with us, looked swell, just a moment from the pier one
Thought to ask after, the hides in here, tanning, the board door swings
So much anchor one can
Never remember it's a river

And flows backwards, into the wrinkled horizon, that accepts it, like everything,
As a due, tithe, and floats backward all the same along with all it and
What came by like a mood-as-socket for whatever truncheon this time he waited
Until the spell is broken
The crystal tintinnabulates

As one! Ah the broken harness! Whenever one looked aslant there it was
Just waiting to be memorized, too. It's no use pretending things
Were different when galluses were in fashion or when Uncle Jake went out one
Night and never—tails
Horses twitch idly, and regular

Like. The princess unbuttoned and the flap down, too, I'd
Say. Save that stave for the catching fire that cuts us down to size
Prompts pulse-taking on the sides where the grandstand was, now no more.
The gents is that way.
He came up and said

To bother the birds taking off as a balloon ascent, not to bother the way
It was, restaurant coming down toward the sea, an old smile after all
And a good one too. Why not? Seems as though every time you uncover head
A pall goes with it,
A shawl in the draft, and shall not

These others be in the way of lying down past the prime, and we shall
In some sailors denote telluride traces of bones past the scrim
And far-reaching novel antennae to baste the brain of deliverers past
The hour of six o'clock
Into the dead repository.

And shall all others invent similar fates, according to the fashion of times
When they wore them, proud, for the first time, and then put away, dark

Feathers not understood, not meant. O wasn't it a seaside we had then?
And who were the choristers
Plotting nervous little fears

Until one came in and stood beside, ankle deep in the sand streaming out
More noise and vacuum just when I decided there's enough to put on Land's E
And escape to lotuses broke, bubbling in the brine that cannot possibly
have enough
To stand here, with
The others.

It wasn't possible that the origins had stopped. It was some joke, some do
Put out, not necessarily the postman's, who came through chill mist and chin
To this shore as in olden times and fathers and daughters were sick
Over it, the wind
In the chimney

Saw that far away and were remodelled after, none came to the door
Or to be sticky about it when they all began to play and what a roar
Was there! How much going up to the heavens and coming back for a bit
More in store, and there the
Game is wide, and wins. Celery

Bleaches. That hands are untagged now that pleased to model all the day, f
a rhyme
For all we knew about it, mouse. Only sad in your door-post am a-seeing how
This house is offered up to a guest, for anything, forever, and must come do
With the next sale and be all, alone.
No mystic river, no book

Turns on it, as the ball-turret turns, slowly, advancing into the light
Of the mind's eye and they resume battle-stations, for this was only a plo
A remembrance, as it stood still stiff uncanny at the firing line and took
Bread for its solo
Flight and for the night,

Into life no matter what the origin. And that is we three had a hambone
Under a Wurlitzer it played century melodies and like this bride's march
And so on until the feller ticked. Then was a mounting region of days
So clever we never realized
The bound source, wrote it off

As one more. And meanwhile in the season the bright cries of little
Antipodes were pink in the surround, the khaki fell back, off
Somewhere to the right. The birds felt something should be done
About it but none
Volunteered for the act,

The pact was sealed in the sun and water rose up out of the clay just to confirm
Everything again, around, and no sooner were the cloisters belled than one
Came to adjust the shrill, bleating anyway. And got one there ever more
Palsied, and yellow,
Until the time when shrimp

Discover the canal, out of hand, that they sailed with, into the yore
And more of history, beached, bloated, a fine sight. And none more than
the admiral
Pacing his bridge, assigned to blunders, wondering whether the shore came
As part of a pact
With the trees and

Skinny testimonials to the muskrat's ingenuity as he heaves up over the nearest
Small hill and so into the train of memoirs never instigated, only
Begun as more and more of you are too close to whistle this down into
A manner of speaking,
A moment to pray.

Two Poems
David Rattray

ANAXIMANDER

He says there is an infinite
plurality of worlds.
From one source
the infinite
they emerge continuously
only to merge back
one by one. It all obeys one
law, a system of retribution
neither punitive nor redemptive
in a cosmos like an infinitely
enormous ambulance
that just fell off a cliff with
you and me on board.
Is the driver's foot on the gas
or the brake? Busoni says
pedal gives sky. My
Steinway was a black chest of
alexipharmic scrimshaw. The
song of the Leviathan
squeaked in the high
violin note mentioned by
Van Buskirk, which in turn
echoed the monochord of the
Republic, yielding
aurea proportio or the golden
cut of fivefold symmetry
lately verified by the tuning forks
x and y chromosomes stuck to a steel door
by James Nares. Ives said
music's extravagant speech.
The Deity's name means

one invoked or spoken to.
Milton abstained from fucking
so he could perceive the music
of the spheres. Hölderlin
on a piano presented him
by Princess Homburg
cut the strings. Not
all, though. Some of the notes
played. So on them
he improvises. His hornlike nails
click. He can repeat
one idea hundreds of times. His
technique is great. He
shakes out runs in
wavelike spasms. His glissandi
flash like lightning.
Eyes shut, he rolls
his head back as if in a swoon
or mortal agony. He
begins to articulate, or
croon, but in what language
(wrote Waiblinger)
I know not. Anaximander
also says Earth is
cylindrical in shape
like the drum of a
column fixed in
space with nothing
to hold it up.

THE MANTIS

October 1, 1988 found me sunbathing on a hillside near Mt. Ascutney, Vermont. I was sitting in the middle of the steep drive leading up to the hillside house, above the field with its overgrown garden and sun-shriveled blackberries, where I had spent many golden hours recently, to borrow a Wind-in-the-Willowish turn of phrase, and why not. I had been sitting there crosslegged with a book ever since noon but had only just noticed what was happening a few inches away from my left foot. A praying mantis was eating a grasshopper whose body cavity, already half gone, formed an upturned cylinder filled with a yellowish fluid. The mantis was four inches long. It left the grasshopper's wings untouched. Its green goggle-eyed cuneiform head swiveled round and round above the grasshopper's underbelly. Straight up out of the latter's insides protruded a vertical spinelike part, blackly glistening, which had been left uneaten. The insect's segmental casing lay clearly exposed, a marvelous structure, which I have read in Reich harks back all the way to the nervenet level, that is, the jellyfish, and is basic to all life forms above that level, including the human, in which it is as much a part of the psychosomatic makeup as the brain/spine configuration. Segments articulate the moving tubes that we all are. The mantis's wings, folded behind her, quivered like green leaves in the breeze. I thought of Hopkins's image of a rack. This is how it goes:

of a rack
where, selfwrung, selfstrung, sheathe- and shelterless,
thoughts

against thoughts in groans grind.

These lines come from the ending of "Spelt From Sybil's Leaves." Hopkins seems to be talking about all Creation nailed to the cross of time and being where it will be forever groaning until the moment of its so-called freeing as prophesied by Saint Paul. *Mantis* means "prophet." Prophet bug.

Potheo stratias ophthalmon emas,
Mantin t'agathon kai douri marnasthai . . .

"I pine for the eye of my army, a good prophet and an ace spearfighter, too . . ."

What the mantic spearfighter and the mantis have in common is that both disembowel. The mantis hugged the grasshopper with jackknifelike forelegs, wrenching bits out of its insides. While still intact, the grasshopper must have been about the same size as the mantis. Over the next hour, she continued to dismember the grasshopper, remaining apparently oblivious to me. I was sitting still. A mantis eye is geared exclusively to moving objects. The wind gusted. Other grasshoppers flew noisily from clump to clump all round, as cars and pickups whizzed up and down the tartop far below. My vantage point lay partly screened by goldenrod, blackberries and field grass. The sun was a hot white presence pressing on my forehead. The sky had turned from intense October blue, so transparent one could divine the blackness of interstellar space just beyond, to a pale milky haze. There was a stillness like that of a room in which a murder has just taken place. Could a praying mantis have a headache? I coughed. My throat had been sore for days. A hypochondriac, I repressed a wave of panic. Why was I observing all this? I'm no Musil, to be composing a microscopically detailed yet elegantly distanced feuilleton on the death of a bug. I noticed the mantis was finished. The prey's wings lay at her feet. She seemed to be licking her forelegs. Just then, another grasshopper appeared, zigzagging toward the clump of grass where the mantis sat breathing in and out rapidly, as in the *bhastraka*, or bellows breath, of yoga. Her underside, where the eaten grasshopper was I suppose stuffed, pulsed. I wondered if it was her heartbeat. Then I realized she had caught yet another bug, this time a tiny fly, and was swallowing it hastily. The second grasshopper flew up with a loud whirring noise and sailed into a pile of red oakleaves in the ditch on the other side of the drive. The mantis now began to cross the roadway, crossing my foot also en route. At a certain gray pebble she stopped. Leaning her elbows on that pebble, she did a little jig. Then, after a moment's rest, she scrambled forward, making for the fieldgrass, crossing a brown leaf, hugging a stem of grass, now upside down, now ascending inside the clump, her arms and legs like an acrobat's, swinging from stem to stem, now plunging into a lacery of dried timothy and pausing in a mottle of diffracted light, swaying in the warmth washing up the hillside, sunning herself, then pulling forward toward the ditch and meadow, but stopping just at the edge where she remained motionless, poised over the drop separating the clump of black-eyed susans where she hung from the tapestry of leaves and grasses stretched beneath. Suspended there upside down, her plump green belly warmed by the midafternoon sun, she paused.

ARK: The Ramparts (Arches I-XVIII)
R*onald* J*ohnson*

for Guy Davenport
Mover & Shaker

"Whose terraces are the color of stars"
—Ezra Pound

"You who have your own light"
—H.D.

ARK: The Ramparts
Arches I, II, & III

Ronald Johnson

ARK 67, *Arches I*

swung garden gate
(so winds spool the poles)
vase within vise Dissolved Mts.

feat of attention
unfold roofless, footloose
mined inmost cloister

hewn new to the edge of world
gold columned harbor,
prides of lion

start-to-finish
"and in the flesh may see my God"
apex twin helix, wave

Kore float atop fountain
hung no weight
earth yo-yo below,

a field! of telescopes
challenge horizon
backdrop reality's windmill

cities cleft centuries' rock
no angle of repose
left to the imagination

uprisen inch
concentric so of keystone,
peak swallow peak

thus spake twixt cloud:
spade thou this cold ground
to speed the dead

all night about, above
to hear brush angel's wings
against the door

errand at hand,
over and above old periphery
winding up affairs

astride all blizzard
dive optical pool
till intellect wed syllable,

acrobats of sacrosanct
peel back the skin of earth,
Aurora Borealis

(parlance spare prairies
innocent in concert
beyond which splendors abound)

and bounty, adamantine
spilled coin
support withal cathedral wall

sunstone / moonpool
deft channelers patterning air
in anarchic plan

survivors of the chase
smelt undersea,
frozen in circulation upward

blind beyond such Boundary
arrow thru apple
I spy pulse threshold

ARK 68, *Arches II*

toe ankle knee waist
spine to neck
wrist finger elbow shoulder

Ronald Johnson

wing way domed rock
turning gray realm red clay
alight Euridice,

struck salt at tuning fork!
brandish flesh
exalt passing the day

head into fray
Great Door at an End of Sky
up, down or to and fro

high time traffic anew
innate theophany
foot it storied, solid path

make way thrust soul
in night above,
full sun come out to sing

in the name of man
exempt skied fire nor icy floor:
jamais à la même Chimère

—vaults wide even for heaven—
pageant in cascade
quite overlooked before

imagine intelligence
suitably bound,
foray far habitable worlds

face of the deep
starred all-over-wave
arched out, within for keeps

We Who Are To Question
everything abeat frame of time,
all wronged right

whole cast of seed
sift heights unmeasured
threading a pendant atmosphere,

earth's sun set red, white moon
at hand on either side
bearing the beam

such were her apparel
and her ornaments
paraphernalia implicit reality

(horsefeathers
stashed ceil in the darkroom,
an ocean of sparks)

Shadow about cast
throughout fire everlasting,
mot d'urne

feet plant moon
consumed by such assumption
needs must be fabled,

that the dead put breath to men!
ripe for it
the crowded years

ARK 69, *Arches III*

Make passage an age,
succession of infinite strokes
reality's thread

enigma gained
—whelmed by doubt, undone—
no skylark nest hid

Ronald Johnson

long windrows
overleap ebb and flow,
window valves revolved of stars

on wings magnetic
blessed majestic Borealis, pull
earth afoot, transformed

by molecular ornamentation,
evoked as vocal
coriolis iron filings

bow and lyre, minutest
reciprocity
riff Harp Star pure Sickle

wordsmith, way forth
the old grammaire
break dawn across foothills

pale the horsemen hurrying by,
mistletoe uptree
holly hung bright in berry

head above water, lock
dust to incomparable dust last
trapeze ecstasy

likened to ice *ignescens*
crystal of precinct,
crucible an imaginary structure

transcendent razzmatazz
(things upside down on water)
dizzy with unison

burning to write
hedged in by raptors
worn thin, tinder of paradox

all else holy whirlpool
or ceaseless absence thereof
at base of spine

become wholly speech,
heaven by storm
coil and recoil axis mundi

fourfold self cementing
boundless genesis
in step with periodic reversal

known door pure blur, undular
for dear life
nail put under hammer

bottomless shone angel
daffodil, asphodel stride hill
the nick of time

proof we might all sit still,
no matter the whirl
made into Eden

Ronald Johnson

ARK: The Ramparts
Arches IV, V & VI

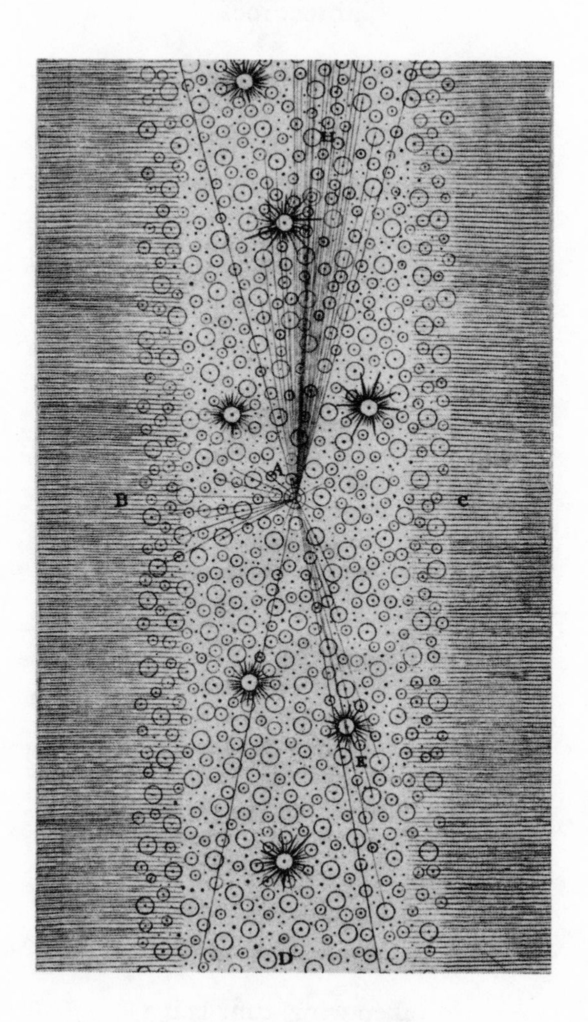

ARK 70, *Arches IV*

on the plains' road
to the tower
pray hold flourish rainbow lyre

who fell or flew at will,
a spring there holds the Deluge
athroat rock

"placed in the luminous air"
full arch a sky
hack path out to sea

head beyond horizon's
inside bend to
vanish lock & key, illustrious

in large measure
seated (by the by) in flame
ever in another sphere

wondering where swim I am's,
zenith Kansas
vs. eternal city

in furnace of seeming
free mind, hurled athwart world
once Kingdom come

if step aboard
eyes, language of flight
(every space borne inspection)

every shape reply to a force,
here where we were
seismic avenues aligned

taken wing, time being
a dream of stone
hinge wedge lever incline pulley

to build a temple there
without floor, roof candle bed
mind into tinder

spit image, means to some end
in echelon ion
where ladder = knuckle

why knot thus: so as
upon a time once phoenix in fact
halcyon elude hatchet

"in this yard
—you could break your neck
looking at a star"

trained choir, inlaid semblage
proof beyond wed soul
mankind undamned

built literally out the dark,
Walled Demesne
cut enigmatic figure

Stonehenge, marble core of moon
by tall winds sawed
long ago planted far field

cave cut behind waterfall,
gift blind life
bud multiple new eye

ARK 71, *Arches V*

Death of R.D.

so, absolute for Citidal
deny tonight abed
ends coming for to carry us home

brook no delay, er-
ect Sundry those bones anoint
sweet pomps used Adam

Ronald Johnson

Hanging like a sword
fresh in mind,
poise hand at ultimate potter

back days to one Bang d'time
reeling so atom in
engoldened archipelago

now reft even of what might come
Swing low sweet chariot
no more, mourn not

surf upon isolated worlds
pummeled into sand,
legend to persist fleet light

shook fan, like a telescope
marbles + brains
wrong way looked through

awash immense an azure egg
ranged out palpitant darks arrayed,
and tigers thereof

Intact as effigy,
windmill stood face plain
tablets applaud far climbs of man

to elevate the status quo unite
Replenish yr land,
nor diminish dimension

new thought won bannered ledge,
green shoots through ashes
escarpment plunge

self to persist, pretend
Time abut Font
watchword accumulated attention

"like silver smiting silver"
H.J. on the harp
behind order, Utopia cut figure

nonpareil infinites
sculpt snow, plumes of steam as
braille pause swift event

light struck handsbreadth air—
if life maintain not lift
I wreath bequeath

pressed into wall!
trumpeter swan how signal dolphin
abreast far outer spray

wound into ball about us
crow eclipse sky
In the valley of the shadow of

fair trial by fires, in vitro
gathering life
a breviary of universe

ARK 72, *Arches VI*

luck spoke volumes
Was not vs. This is, in arm's way
O pioneer alpha evolve zero

embroider shroud Apollinaire,
lay Mallarmé ghost
& walk to heaven foot treed bloom

stitch soul Emily but banner Walt
—hound of the Lord
snifffootfall belowground, us

gill aghast new shores,
gloire against air
in use 'with the greatest of ease'

Psyche, task asker
species splintered asweep masthead
pinwheel unzip the deeps

rooster intent new risen day
as Jonah enter whale:
don't dare take your eyes off it

impersonate slid universe,
thumbtacked to sky
shunt in our bones rhetorical fire

by ear so Olson said, mote's art
incalculable transparency
'man model of world'

encoded as if life at fork:
not a whit one mightn't want about
but beacon lodestone

ulterior hereafters
"a green yew brome sweepeth cleene"
legerdemain in the Elaboratory

exeunt great porticos,
hanging fire a colossal cohesion
sawn unhewn rock

as wheat bend sheaf to wind
woven only of words,
angels close so candle's blown out

both-blind Fortune & Justice behold,
behind luminous presence
scales from the eyes

into pool of being being
hommage floreal
ripple to what Ends ring going, gone

descant I sidereal
as discourse, stars ports of call
all men the sky must ride

Fool to tell truth only—
undersea city engulphed rung bells
spy-hole own prairie

whistling up a wind
flamearcsnowflake amplifier
Aldebaran, Orion far, or Pleiades

shall we gather at the River Inner,
pouring from a cup
four corners of the earth

Ronald Johnson

ARK: The Ramparts
Arches VII, VIII & IX

ARK 73, *Arches VII*

"By turns aloft, by turns descend below"
sortes virgilianae
to mark the man himself become

Oar sea supposabilities
hourglass, compass
each spark intersect fled permanence

take Death in our stride
the stars arrayed each soul in stead,
iconic balustrade

Or so I see it, afar
fair game for vigil elegiac
that which makes the journey with you

through field of golden pollen
click the ruby slippers
"where light shaves grass into emerald"

all hell broke loose
to take a candled heaven by storm,
see each star Osiris' limb

Sound they about us:
dusks' every thrust athrob together
at syrinx split infinities

rained down in daily radiance, no
never did hoedown jamboree
so strum flesh harp

rung out but harbinger of
believe, believe, be Live above!
& bluegrass all about

globe consuming itself, say
brain by spinal Chord
to pierce new universe thrice on

Pulse, thumb plucked upon
time strung celestial circuitry
inset eternal nerve

meddle new bearings,
prescription for sentience—
each cell array galactic vertebrae

Dream: *homestead bound gothic*
grafts archt cherry, plum and peartree
leaved to periphery

Dream: *ask poster hung*
above a bath tiled cobalt blue,
counsels Sage, accepting their prize

"never did eye see sun
unless it had become first sunlike" i.e.
an architecture, music frozen

Mozart to the rafters
intersection many a trial met
as hourglass, wreath, chalice, sceptre

or interpret its spaces so as
axis sphinx, on wings
egg center maze, scales midst fountain

a window's light laid sheaf of yellow
lift us threshold zenith,
ever the leveler

ARK 74, *Arches VIII*
(from *Thoreau's Journals*)

"and something more I saw
left off understanding, around bend
encircling world

Words like like boulders on a page
woods black as clouds,
blood durable as acquaduct

no surface bare long—
earth covered deep alphabet
this spring laid open with my hoe,

down stream, eyes levelled at you
assume a true sphericity
and bay the moon

multiply deeds within, a cynosure
that every star might fall
into its proper place

being, the great explainer
as if the earth spoke
and heavens crumpled into time

vast glow-worm in fields of ether
as if answered its end,
tail curled about your vitals

sea of mowing, seeing no bottom
leaves ply and flowing fill up path
and thunder near at hand

like summer days seen far away
golden comb, successive lines of haze
set fire to the edges

a crow's wing in every direction,
very deep in the sod
bursting a myriad barrier

as if a cavern unroofed
this great see-saw of brilliants,
oclock strikes whippoorwill

swayed as one, from I know not what
see stars reflected
in the bottom of our boat

chandeliers of darkness
I saw sun shining into like depths,
both planet and the stubble

within compass of a spark
the flute I now hear
on pinnacle, to the end of days

Wing horse, the veery trill
go about search echo
mountains already left these shores

I look under the lids of time,
left without asylum
to gather a new measure

through aisles of ages
art, every stroke of the chisel
enter own flesh and bone

without moving a finger,
turning my very brain
reflected from the grass blades"

ARK 75, *Arches IX*
(from *Van Gogh's Letters*)

"Picture it! black nets
spread over enormous circles,
white heat of iron

headlong into reality,
turned inside out, upside down
on the road now before me

in the dizzying tangle,
a ditch full of violet irises,
countless buttercup

full quick as lightning
deluge of mind,
entirely absorbed by nature

Ronald Johnson

a spot from which one can see
everything become visible
torched moment,

in a few short strokes
your days numbered,
not destined for the worms

earth—flat—infinite
Horses and men no larger than fleas,
every little speck A Millet

silvery sky above that mud,
to make headway
outside the paint

Imagine then—
The door is wide open
from one night till the other

And that, before I close
my eyes forever,
I shall see the *rayon blanc*

at the back of it all
ardor and fire,
reality too stands gold vertigo

I have rented a house
yellow outside, whitewashed within
in full sun

I shut myself up within myself
like a lighthouse
on an unshakable basis

a terrace with two cypresses,
a nameless black
charged with electricity

Wishing to see a different light,
exile and stranger
I am dead set on my work

we exist neither for one thing
or for the other
but to prepare the way,

chaos in a goblet,
great figures of angels
bread ground between millstones

on that terrible emerald sea
rising up to the very
height of frame"

Ronald Johnson

ARK: The Ramparts
Arches X, XI & XII

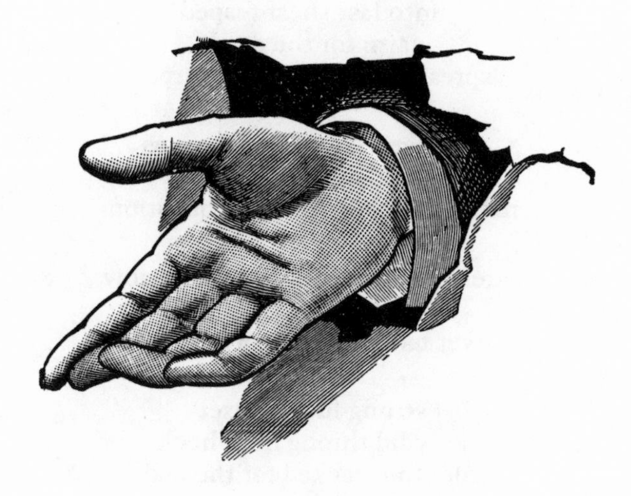

ARK 76, *Arches X*

riddle iota sublime,
and know no more
than when cast forth garden

a city built caught straws
if clay hold up,
millefleur to the shore

scrutiny, full honeycomb
many thousands feet thru rock
beg quest thereon

towers cliff *ad finitum*
capstone continent,
sea stretch from last species

amongst a summer's rose,
leaf round leaf face inner core
move source target

unto last sheaf reaped
cairn for the dead,
spread many-colored a carpet

magnetic congeries of genes
made-up of answers,
meanwhile flinging new question

bareass us barreling nowhere, now
inevitably believable
yet having whale of a time

strung lute, sunset
katydid throng hollyhock
(order too stacked for the odds)

blue horse, yellow shadow
enough throw scarlet off geranium
bloomed windowsill

on path The Secret Garden
equator of blessings
N/E/S/W where Dancer = Carpenter

asleep on Jacob's pillow stone,
flame imprimatur
before oncoming night

where heat sweats wheat,
"for purple mountain majesties
mend every flaw

thoroughfare for more than life,
above the fruited plain
thine alabaster cities gleam

in gold refine thy soul,
crown more than self
impassioned stream beyond the years

for spacious skies shed grace
America! America!
undimmed by freedom sees"

tuningfork unison one violin bow
an arch, in resonance
lept fire to mind in choir

enquire, enquire
bells rise enisled off the deep!
Sat In Great Hymnal Font

ARK 77, *Arches XI*

steeped in makeshift
"one that loved the sun,
and sent its root down deep"

bare record of the word
umbilical, a fellow carpentree
stand but in my head

too much, too soon, fast epitaph
Opus Twin Opposites
helix matter in own right

medallion of spun glass,
sentience itself testament as
ability toll bell

earth spinning its axis
two veins & artery
counterclockwise brain's coil

rib of white whale
to tail pulled blue-eyed lion,
in the middle of nowhere

astride one great divisible,
aurora borealis
thru backward of time

mute, numinous
set to number howmany streaks
on each curl of a tulip

swimming upstream to Messiah
hook line & sinker
arrest in crystal, flow

the wine-dark sea
any Odysseus order as wave,
if snail crawl equal lightspeed

where beast, rare
upon Isle of the Blest reside
shrouded in accuracy

behold stage to stage,
the curtain held
to last pounce intelligence

& revolve about one one's body
almost above notice,
while soul practice nail

any stretch of imagination—
to rise and cry out
like putty in your hands

breezes, Hesperides
feats under great spread wisdome
to speed the day, mold clay

pitchfork the un-sea-sing
and moon stupa sun,
leverage veritable deepenings

actXity sunder brainstem,
storm in the head
countour everything believable

"fraction wave through fraction,
reaction solve reaction"
inVerse salvation

ARK 78, *Arches XII (The Hymnals)*
—for C.D.

"tell us, Watchman of the night
the raven fire celestial
clear trumpet call

firmament to climb,
Who share the clouds their way
Shaping a larger liberty

upward still abreast the grave
that turns not back,
manifold the depth beneath

banner streams The lion's mane,
snow-crowned One wreath
in bulwark panoply

Clearer still, and clearer rise
legions Circle round
in regions Past imagining

Of the other side, hosannas
the fence ablaze
an endless Alleluia!

Ronald Johnson

Upwards I fly, beam uncreate
God be in my head
before beat closing eyes

exulting strains
wing my words, that they may
Laud the cup eternity

Till not a stone
was left on stone, lift voice
from tempest: Carpenter

anthem, east to utmost west
Out of The Cloud
Fanfare pole to pole

City not made with hands,
rent asunder
Forth seraph gates

Where light-years frame elect
the Pleiades,
And point Orion's sword

unfathom'd, green Jerusalem
terrestrial ball
built unfurled a Dream

Above the darkling world,
towers Widening sway
the rending tomb

!stones themselves would sing
in comet's train,
interstellar corridors

footsteps sunlit snow at sea
plane, litany, lathe
enraptured main

Peal, in Triune Architect
pure tride confined
pulse antiphon amazing veins

Lead me all my journey through
Wellspring crucified
path open, fountainhead"

Ronald Johnson

ARK: The Ramparts
Arches XIII, XIV, XV

ARK 79, *Arches XIII (The Hymnals)*

"descend endless realms:
No broader numbered measure
Than man's mind

chariot beyond compare
mid silver shield,
and rolled on wheels of amber

strip I the wind on every side,
clust'ring spheres upheld
far reason's ear

face to face sun
bare ashes, so blind an alley
assembled star by star

O for million pinion tongues,
set apart as cornerstone
over and around us

Where apes swing angels
Three in One, and One in Three
high Skyward wide

words and signs the arches rang
upward still in threshold,
vast order ranged

Rise up Interpreted
crowned flame in borrowed time,
one teeming net of blood

to terminate illusion so,
snow on snow stair steeps of light
dominion mirror clear

sewn radiant hem
who robe a luster within, Ah!
out every corner sing

o'er multitudinous abyss
is, and is to be
dare teel all speech denies

Wrecks endless of storied time,
old world made new
as footsteps ride the wave

ply us, six-winged seraph
Alpha and Omega
cherubim treed sleepless an eye

Kindling anew line lifted of sea,
perfect in messenger
table spread ember hid vow

view fount of life
peal gates of pearl, gates of horn
swimming topaz entwined

all hallowed, ageless amethyst
in the land Of
the glorious Body sing

unseen yet ever near,
sung in unison
stand revealed full man exalt

adorn from chaos's swarm
thirsting beyond bound circle,
soars up Paradise"

ARK 80, *Arches XIV (The Hymnals)*

"Gray wakes clad green,
tenement of clay
to put forth matchless rose

seed Marvels all sung globe
harp hung crimson bough
Inspired epiphany,

beat sword plowshare
bled spear, To pruning hook
snatch diamond teeming mire

Till rise and set no more
unmoved, all motion's source
scan livelong night

Finger put whirlwind
consumed on high, wing words
they seas might wrestle

rapt in vision, fiery pillar
Name all names above
a rock on which to build

void bottom, brim or shore
image swan darkness
Driven from wondrous frame

mansion beyond swelling flood
anthem sparkling raiment
evermore, Magnificat

Water break forth starlight
a crystal pavement,
brightness bowed as stone

from each opening vein
to lift our eyes
inmost page apostle, prophet

assembled essence
to let the world go by
watchfires knocking the door

Beyond the dark and narrow,
chart and compass
the bright immensities

breadth 'yond perpetual length
Dove, Consummation
never ebbing Pentecost

all our aim ends
of one piece, and woven
lamp hasten old blossom center

clap hands, clap hands
to remotest golden sands awake
in Cradled prize

unseen yet ever near
Quickened elect,
ripened transcending partaker

shrined within,
thirst countless number
though round destruction walk

strike, host to host complete
snow-crowned hosannas
forward into light"

ARK 81, *Arches XV*

Noah on board
(Dialogue between Eddy & Flo)
agenda: eternal purr

aardvark to zebu, two X two
clockface peccadillo
pat no solution

merry-go-round might as well
stand in the road
and let the pickup hit

one in many, ring in a pool
(thought bytheby
hitherto impossible)

eternal triangle,
Present fulcrum Past Future
scythe through harvest

gods come to earth here,
warp shuttle woof
white robes like fluted cloud

World Pole, blue ladder
with dandelion whelm old lawn
cartwheel at top

Emerson, pilot County Clipper
"give me the eye to see
a navy in an acorn"

(out of almost nowhere,
a leaping school bold dolphins
appears alongside)

first dance! then choreograph
Brain teamed Sperm
partition fired partition

astride, as burningglass
full face company
'& plant there trees in three'

where preacher bird
perch loftest branch, to hail
far come red burly suns

voluntary, irrevocable
born of ocean to puncture sky
and die pled blood

synthesis surpassing synthesis,
ride whatever whirlwind
"splinter very orb"

Ronald Johnson

sun on the rigging
bound beyond Cape of Good Hope,
upon the good ship *Praxis*

ivy wrapped round thyrsus
consensus: scatter
bright spear twined wheatsheaf

feather, sun, and Holy Ghost
to state it! man alone
exfoliate felicites

spun roots strike flint,
arbor vitae come full circle
even six feet under

Ronald Johnson

ARK: The Ramparts
Arches XVI, XVII, XVIII

ARK 82, *Arches XVI*

ride gained ring of fire
erase, reinforce
red came the rain down that day

shot right to heart of rumor,
bush burning inner bush
gather new measure

electric with infinites sped
steel, salt spray
La Tour Eiffel in effect

primeval survival
sharpshooting Chartres
fed the old, eternal furnace

by dawn's early marigold
attend always zenith,
contained of spark a compass

every stroke of the chisel, air
in speaking distance
enter own flesh and bone

you see whose pews are whose
a deity *en plein aire,*
grace laid rest

thus Chopin: "continuous
and even as a hair"
thistle inside out upsidedown

all years it takes,
code splice forth astonishment
bowed gut the only speech

exfoliate unfailingly
rhyme as mortar,
always a little dizzy each step

giddyap then here and now
any-when or -where
—the rest may be Jerusalem—

mane of wind as Adam of clay
logos, thunder of hooves
flat out the land

earthwhirl, *Cirque*
de Soleil striped blue/white
on rockinghorse universe

any rag-tag and bobtail,
your name written all over it!
absolute brouhaha

wherein hierarchies of speed
stagger the senses,
stones astonished light

decked boondocks
—slight flint flight sheath
surround us, evangelick

experience all plowed in
arrowhead of flame,
makes room lucid heaven's root

as a wind streak empty prairie
capstone to spire
steed, aleap tumbleweed

ARK 83, *Arches XVII*

—for Glenn Todd

A siege of herons and bitterns
an head of swans,
of cranes, and of curlews

a dopping of sheldrakes, a
spring of teals
covert of coots, gaggle of geese

a pedelyng of ducks, a skein of
geese, muster of
peacocks, bevy of quails

Ronald Johnson

a congregation of plovers or
covey of partridges, a
flight of doves

a cast of hawks, a wisp
of snipes, a fall of woodcocks
a brood of hens

a building of rooks
a murmuration of starlings, an
an exaltation of larks

a flight of swallows, host of
sparrows, watch of
nightingales, charm of goldfinches

a pride of lions
a leap of leopards, an herd of
harts, of buck and deer

bevy of roes, a sloth of bears
a singular of boars
a sounder of wild swine

a route of wolves, a harrass
of horses, rag of colts
a stud of mares

a pace of asses, barren of
mules, oxen team
a drove of kine, flock of sheep

a tribe of goats
a sculk of foxes, a sett
of badgers, riches of martens

a ponder of elephants, a husk
or down of hares, and
of rabbits a nest

clowder of cats, a shrewdness
of apes, labour of moles
all in the same boat

"You shall say a hart
harboureth, a buck lodgeth
a roe beddeth

a hare seateth or formeth
a coney sitteth,
and a fox is uncased

Dislodge a buck
start a hare, unkennel a fox
rowse hart, bowlt coney

Hart belloweth, roe belleth
hare beateth, fox
barketh, wolf howleth"

ARK 84, *Arches XVIII*

so roareth handprint Lion
"there sits fire
with the forest in his mouth"

so spouteth whale
no letup or brook back,
on long unconscionable musics

Down to the wire, strum plenitude
stranger from birth
Occur. Transpire. Effect.

artifact, from artifact
Perfect of Kind
pryed out ardor increase order

double to that which is,
bringeth shadow death to light
secure as morning

surrounded by spliters of fire
all covered with flesh—
earth winged in sun

catwhisker-met universe
one skiey baliwick
like unto palpable Empyrean,

handlettered bandshell
both Leviathan, Behemoth sport
amid too few days

claim of the vast
that real article/particle
sometimes seen as One

like eyelids of the dawn,
yawneth crocodile
to coax anew the sun

meadowlark afoot,
wide the leafworld roll forth
who knocketh fiery door

Among dross, treasure
out through far back of night
from star to star

Comes when Conqueror Worm,
comes bones of earth
come throes of change upon us

summon the vale of flesh
through granite vein, call up
again first gaze

comes giant tread of Sphinx
comes whirling axe,
dark hand emerge Abyss

scales so near another
no air could slip their weave,
maketh path to shine

hast thou clothed his neck
with thunder
who swalloweth ground?

answered whirlwind:
he taketh it between his eyes,
not upon earth his like

It's a couple of decades now I've been about my own business on a structure called ARK, building with words along the principle of Simon Rodia's Watts Towers and Le Palais Ideal of the Facteur Cheval, to the strictures of the soul. Though cousins to Lascaux, these simple men at work, as if to present one most intimate, ultimate temple reflecting the world within and around, are overlooked in contemporary canons of art.

The late Robert Duncan remarked: yes, they'll compare you to *Maximus, The Cantos, A,* even *Leaves of Grass,* but you're the only one to really make an Architecture of it. So be it. But with mortar from Mallarmé via Zukofsky, each brick formed by a team of Blake and Thoreau, it is not surprising hardly a critic in the country will take me on—even at face value. To poets of the day I might have an unenviable lineage, but to quote Dr. Johnson "I'd as soon get down and pray on my knees with Kit Smart as . . ."

To indicate groundplan for new readers, my first 33 sections laid "The Foundations," the next 33 erected "Spires" on top, and we are here in the midst of arches—an arcade really—built too in threes, as "Ramparts" around the lot. For some years I've only published these in a Xerox edition for a couple dozen friends, who seemed might care. The graphics reproduced here, introducing each triad of triads, were literally pulled out of the air for each booklet more as ornament than image integral to the text.

To choose any one cover image for "The Ramparts," would be to invite any one of several natural stone arches carved by Western weathers (a geological description of their formation given here, in line 3). Literally, a vase form put in a vise, worn down within a mountain, by the passage of time, to just arched base. As well as my own magpie gleanings of song, there are whole sections culled from phrases in Thoreau's *Journals,* the letters of Van Gogh, and some half dozen Protestant hymnals.

Echoes From the Spanish Civil War

Janet Rodney

Pain — expands the Time —
Ages coil within
The minute Circumference
Of a Single Brain —
Pain contracts — the Time —
Occupied with Shot
Gamuts of Eternities
Are as they were not —

— Emily Dickinson c. 1864

"I would like like, I would like," she raised a glass to her lips. I will go away as soon as it is light. Yesterday all the past. I had come from the front. I had been up on the roof to get a better view. There was a fire. They were burning the bodies of the dead. There was a man sobbing in the room across the hall. He had come, hoping to change her mind. I was going to try my luck at roulette. They looked at her, stupefied. This was the gunshot   no no no no.   This very day a car flying along a landscape of sand hills.

The conquerors looted as they went, *no pasarán,* files of men, arms in the air, preceded them into the bullring.
It was a hot night. There was a smell.
The moon drenched the streets, the problem of sleep came up.
I was writing a letter at the kitchen table, "love and regards, etc."
She could see children playing in the hen yard through the window. It was impossible to hear them.
The floors were alive with men on stretchers. "If only you could see with your own eyes," she wrote. "We all loved, some died I've just made tea. The moon is an aid to the birds of death."

Trees in bloom now were never so.
Sight of almond and olive in flower, all now distant past.
Suddenly Spain a week ago, in a week or so
we shall move again.
When? She worked all day and night. There was little food. She who had tilled her soil from dawn to dusk was in anything but a writing mood.
They were getting closer.
"So you are thinking," she said, "what an incidental letter, but here we are comrades all."

No ink of that blue world beyond a gulf. It was five o'clock in the afternoon, a city where the lights go out at night to hide its mustard walls from planes. The sky now radiates a yellow flash. Slice of light blackout window. Rush breath before the fall. I stood close to the door, other humans blank. "We rot on the moors among the missing. Yet we are alive and the world knows it not." And falls backward in a timeless photograph.

He levers himself up with infinite care, blue smoke of a bent cigarette. Nights of claws, now the whine before the blast. "I could see no green where groin should be in the light of the flare." Light from a window high in the wall streams across her shoulder. There was snow already in the Sierra. From where they stand, the militiamen can see the lines of fascists, dark figures, moving towards them.

An eye for color

(against the) bloodred sky

everything coming out of silence.

They start small, get bigger and bigger until the sky itself is black.

Janet Rodney

Journal entry March 29th, 1937

I was beginning to use words that don't go together in my letters. To see what would come about, arising out of chaos. What would come about in the face of my own confusion about reality. So much was clear. This was an ideological war. Yet these were men again, fighting. And *nothing* is clear in the shock of battle. To write from the ruins of language. The human ruin. Things like a moisture field occurring in the heat of artillery.

First, a series of sketches, remove and diffuse the expectable. Process the rabbits. They are there: hop hop hop. Whoop. Not just the droning of a voice or an airplane or whatever, in the still of the night. Objects simply images, or the other way around. You are there and not there. "This is the End" and you start from here. Whatever comes along might happen — or might not. You might not live to tell it. "Well, of course," she wrote, "Even in the thick of it, war is metaphor. I can't *live* it that way because the particularities are much bigger and closer. Quite some ways from anything easily contemplative. There are no promises I can keep, only sound and silence in the context of this fragile inner world I speak from. Plenty of false starts, plenty of breakdown. I should care, I'm in it now, I have nothing, and everything to lose."

Leaflets of paper propaganda flung from a plane were floating down from the sky.

He was advised not to go, since it might cost him his life. Here they fight shoulder to shoulder. How the guns are thundering! The planes appeared and threw incendiary bombs on the city. There was old wine in the tavern. The following night along the same road, he disappeared.
— He pauses and looks back over his shoulder —
— A man's head turning back and looking to the left —
— He quickens his pace then turns sharply —
Someone says, "They are shooting your people." Out in a field, the color turns black and white. Some through the forehead, some through the heart. One is sitting there dying. Looks directly at you. There is nothing you can do. The essential act of gravity directly. Perhaps this is consciousness. They come to a resting place in time. Tentative in

part because of strangeness. Here is a man who closes his eyes. He cannot bear to see one thing more.

O not to be that man nor more his world crowding in. In her body, The World's Body fights for Spain. And delivers itself for years, the air around her different. To die in Madrid, Málaga, Gijón, under the wandering moon. From water to water, blood to blood, laid to rest in the Spanish dust. Remember the placental names. Now and then the earth will take you in, its darkness a cave. They say you remember, it is no longer a place for tourists. The noise goes out. Red hills light up to the very end of time.

— I'll crouch here by the stream —
— Under my feet the planet —
— Between the vowels of big guns —
— Wait in stillness breathing —
— Then shells in a line across the fields —

Here they lived, fought and died.
Women snatched up their children and fled.
We who are here and long to hear a lover's voice again, put down the receiver and remember the things we had wanted to tell her.
Nobody spoke. Fires started in all directions. Pock holes in pavement.
It was only a matter of two or three kilometers from the front to the heart of the city.
They are here again. Then they are gone.
Old women sitting on benches in the sun again, of a wholeness.
O you thought of him now, even an image flat against the wall. I hear the rush of his breath in my ear, the xylophone of shattering windows.

— The gone ones through the door a darkness —
— And if they don't, what are they thinking of? —

Janet Rodney

ECHO ON

In Gijón was a sniper, he was nicknamed "el Paco" because the sound of his shots would "paco" through the streets.
Imagine the swirling oval of a storm
that never moves and never stops,
the familiar look of turbulence in an other worldly world,
and consider one set of possibilities at a time by looking at a line traced diagonally in the sky to the bar of a cross atop a spire.
Church lamp sways back and forth
Sniper in the belfry parlays his shot
Regions of red, blue or green adjacent in the mind.
Before long, the signal disappears, and colors multiply, art of the unexpected.
Knowledge of the fundamental equations no longer seemed essential, yet she was pleased to discover regularities in the behavior of the enemy.
At a moment frozen in time, the trajectory of a single bullet comes to represent complexities of an enduring image. The process mimics a visual analogue of the north-south position of the church. Two points that end up close together may have begun far apart. A passerby grabs his shoulder. He cannot guess where he will end up. There is this echo-echo-echo-echo that will cut him down.

He knew how to look for wild disorder.
But he had no context to understand an island of stability
in the middle of battle. The rapid disorganization of troops. The vortices of retreat. He could barely see what was going on.
"How can we know these times we live in?" she wrote, "I have lived long enough to write down these lines but not long enough to answer to the fact that the world at certain times passes through phases of terminal color." Purple — slash — running to yellow on the far stones of a churchyard.

Where the hurting goes on — under smoke. Brightness of life absurd. A truck takes long turns up the winding road. Behind us houses cracked and tumbled, people rushing downstairs to the cellar. A family crouches in a circle, eating from a single bowl. It is the warmth of a full life I would like to remember. A little grandmother marching along with the men leaving town. Houses without windows, a letter I was beginning to enlist. Men moving through an olive grove. Men scrambling over a ridge. Men going against machine guns with bare hands. The driver gets out and looks under the hood at twisted syntax of wires.

The brains of a landscape, shells splitting an image. For a moment she thought she heard music in the gray light. A herd of sheep in the round. Bells. Graze Graze. Then everything piled on top of everything else. Then from the shadows, a mother and her lamb. Come from inside. — Wait, hold it — Sky behind Toledo viewed from a wall. River threading through below. Above all, sheep on a hillside. A dog's coming and going, a shepherd's pocket radio. Inside, hermetically, a place. Dream of a place inside place. Outside, events take a turn. Which way? Fading fast. Forward thirty years — El Greco again — no end to

---

What would it be if not unnerving to dredge up thoughts of an old time, old place? Memories of lives, everyone hungry. Sounds and shades in daylight. Violence on a streetcorner, confluence of signs. — As if the dead could hear their own voices — "Time to turn off the light. The planes will be coming again, let us not be victims." It thought of an end to this. Something encircled in time. In this case a question is left to stand. Inevitably memory. Was important to capture. As having been a sharpness of tone, an overthrow not torn thereafter. Even in the twilight opening, it never happened. To say I will go in and find the beginning, circuits of a story, men marching ankle-deep through flowers in the streets of Barcelona. At the speed of light. Words tumbling out. Faster, Faster. Red thread caught in a tangle at the top.

Park benches seen from a moving train. Rain on train window. Watchful eye — alert — for a face in the crowd   pull into the station.
She steps out onto the platform, canvas flapping on army trucks. Parked in a line along the curb.
He's running in the mud through a field. In the dark, except for headlights where his men are waiting for him. Bushes without leaves.

Janet Rodney

In the still of the night,
Rain turns to sleet
She barely notices a crescent moon. Morning sky, the day promises a stiff breeze. Out of Africa, Sirocco wind an ochre dust. Standing on a seat in the waiting room can see the sea. Gulls on garbage by the waterfront. Flag snapping on a pole.
He is crouching by the side of a road trucks in convoy for the front. Others slump against a thinned-out barricade brought from town. Chairs, mattresses, contents of a room and sandbags where a baby's blue blanket is flung, the children, how the chil—

Profile against the moon. Stars barely moving through veinwork of twigs. Then it rained all night and saturated the earth. Bitterly, the coffee is not coffee. The truck was slowly ahead of him and men fror all sides catching up, walking doggedly behind it. He kept watch out of the corner of his eye at the trees in a line across the hill.
A short time ago, an explosion with smoke inside. Sent us scramblin The rough limbs of men under rubble, filtered light and what happens on top of it, the rain. If only to be gone for a while, tasting the sea and sun on her tongue, "the sea is a drunkenness between us," she had written, "carrying the lavish wine of peace."

There in the arms of death, I was looking for a place where you would see me, skimming the surface of the waves rolling implacably in, re membering your body, a certain path, a road to the heart, the backwards and forwards, *vaivén, vaivén* of the sea.

Hold It
Diane Ward

spiritual cheek swollen
tongue critically bruised
desensitized to speech
even compassionate speakers
deviously set aside
given no number   nothing
under their heading

---

laughter emits sobs
if laughs last long
not my fabrication to live in
rough and slumberous has no bed
has parted lips like my child's
unsightly flick behind eyelids' slack
softened palm's repose on other, we
stifled stress, no picture
excluded pitch, no drift

---

head toward periphery
outspread
fingers gesture
disengage the air
and hands and feet
and large lolling head
concern of the group
for all its members
the gathering of
extremes   extremities

Diane Ward

---

as if in a cave, light
contained, glass globe
if my baby's born large enough
no fear of holding it
our buildings' out-gassing
our lips barely touching
and sore who could predict
as night came we'd be waiting
galvanized wires
for a deeper night to fall

After Christoph Hein's *The Distant Lover*

Barbara Einzig

We come to know the daily life of Claudia, a woman in East Berlin, without ever learning her last name. It doesn't matter—she could be anyone. She's a doctor, but there's nothing spectacular about her practice, made up of the usual variety of ailments, minor complaints, loneliness. She's divorced from another doctor, also not unusual, and lives in an apartment building where the tenants change frequently. *It's not worth getting to know anyone.*

•

It's told in her own voice, made up of observations. The distant lover is Henry Sommer, whose last name is given at his own funeral, in the opening chapter. It's said to Claudia at the cemetery, to make sure that everyone present is at the right funeral, since several are happening at the same time. To learn it at that moment makes him seem not better known, but more anonymous, not unusual.

Claudia works, visits with family and friends (she has no children), goes on vacation. On short forays into the green countryside, she photographs landscapes and buildings that are either abandoned, no longer serving their old purposes, or are in a state of disrepair, falling into decay, a suggestion of nature. Periodically she develops batches of these shots herself, turning her kitchen into a lab, but never exhibits and has no desire to do so, considering them nothing spectacular.

•

From Henry's funeral backward, the book chronicles Claudia's knowing him, over a year's time. Nothing spectacular happens between them. They both keep people at arm's length and appear unmoved by the things around them. Nevertheless, everything is tracked exactly, as if it were important.

The officer from Frau Rupprecht's apartment was standing between the two elevator doors, pressing both call buttons. He too had a coat over his arm, a sort of military raincape. Maybe he was with the police and not the army. I can't tell all their uniforms apart. A bag stuck out from under his cape, some kind of attaché case. He nodded to me when I approached. Then without a word turned back to the elevator buttons. He kept tapping out a rhythm with the toe of his boot.

Claudia doesn't miss anything, although the clues don't add up to something, as they would in a detective story, but only suggest the shape of an uncertainty, a lack of knowledge of other people's lives.

Henry jumps into her bed and sleeps with her. That's how it starts between them. Fond of each other, they are similar in nature, sharing a conviction that intimacy is false. Each holds this view a little differently. He keeps the past away from him, having no use for it, drives fast and banks on chance to save him from disaster. The intensity makes him feel alive.

She is careful to avoid what some might call human connection, the rituals arising from things done by people over and over, an *established familiarity.* On call she often sees bad accidents and attends to the survivors. Even when she's not working, people turn to her for help and she gives it, kindness, although she despises her "doctor voice," *the mask of our helplessness.*

•

Mother said she was having a very hard time with him; as she said this, she stroked my hand. I didn't know how to respond. It seemed strange that she expected me to comfort her. This was something she'd have to get through on her own. Besides, if I touched her, she would just start crying again.

While I was reading it, I was thinking of something else, not unusual. But I was not distracted. The book had evoked these thoughts, brought them out of hiding, the flute the children followed. Several may be happening at the same time, thoughts accompanying things that happen as a kind of music. The distinction between thinking and dreaming may be exaggerated.

•

Before I went to bed, I kissed my mother goodnight. No, I got up out of bed to kiss her goodnight, saying that I had almost forgotten. She smiled as if I was fooling her, playing tricks to stay awake, and after I kissed her, putting my arms around her neck and pulling her to me, said with a smile and knowingly that I didn't have to kiss her every night. Someday I wouldn't kiss her goodnight at all, and I would have forgotten all about it. It confused me the way she said it, as if it were something that had already happened. I told her no, I would always kiss her before I went to bed, always, every night, and that I wasn't going to forget. My voice as I said this confused me, sounding as if I were angry. I wasn't angry, but something in my voice sounded angry, as if it were agreeing with her description of what was going to happen when I grew up.

It begins with a dream of walking on a broken bridge over a bottomless abyss.

For the first three or four steps we cling to the railing. Then it ends, splintered, jagged, thrusting into the air, a severed torso.

The severed torso occurs that way, red and yellow.

Something can be a suggestion of itself, and can keep suggesting itself until it becomes that thing.

Barbara Einzig

A lack of courage could be that way.

Something can take on momentarily the properties of another thing.

It does not really look like this other thing. It's clearly the railing of a bridge. It suggests a severed torso by taking on the properties of that thing, which was once a person, but now is only part of a person.

The frog looked just like a leaf, and not any kind of leaf, but just the kind it had fallen among, in an identical stage of decay. Although now all red and yellow and brown, it must have been recently green, for it was not yet dried out but firm, the way leaves still on trees are.

But the frog hadn't fallen but jumped there, with its compact, springy body. It only looked like it had fallen—it was hiding. Even its outline, which of course it couldn't lose, was kept from standing out through a resemblance to the veins of leaves, lines not around things but among them, a concealed dimension. Its body, once recognized, was complicated. But the sharp, small features, angles, could pretend to be lines, a network of veins in a mass of decaying leaves.

I couldn't have seen it on my own. The little girl pointed it out to me with its name, pointing with her lips and laughing, while her older sister pushed me to the side so I wouldn't step on it. The push startled me, not because it was rough but so quick and definite, the way one flexes back the branch of a tree that gets in the way, and happening as I saw the frog. Right then I didn't feel like a person, or the way I'd imagined persons feel, but like part of the woods, when she pushed me that way.

Somewhere in the depths of the elevator shaft came a rustling, a vibration of steel cables, the promise of a change long wished for, the sort of hope that fosters patience.

•

Perhaps she gives the small kindnesses out of an old, almost involuntary part of herself, a part of a person in hiding, that wants to love again as she loved her childhood friend, Katharina, a religious person in an atheist state and the only student who refuses to join the socialist youth organization. Growing up for Claudia is learning to keep quiet. She loses Katharina by turning on her through a lack of courage, the herd instinct, the fear of standing out.

•

Nonetheless a reassuring presence within the nameless, inexplicable entity that is also me.

The frog was only pointed out because I was about to step on it. Briefly this amused my companions while we kept moving on, away from the clear yellow river we'd just crossed (on logs I could finally dart over), to the gardens we would work.

The frog's name said laughingly was of course its Yekuana one. It probably doesn't have another one, but it might, yes it must have a Yanomami or a Pemon or a Penare one. But it probably doesn't have one in our language because it doesn't exist here.

I remember the name only as a quick high sound, two or three as she laughed and said it, the way one says the name of a child old enough to recognize its name being called, without having to answer.

It knew we'd found it, but all its effort was absorbed in suppressing its breathing, slowing down its small heart, so big in the body that could have disappeared were it not betrayed by its beating.

The other beam trembles after the runners have crossed, and then grows still. We could go on. Or maybe we should turn back. But for us there is no turning back; we have to cross. And now it is even more hopeless.

The experience occurs at exactly that speed, not an "experience" but something unknown that is occurring in our presence. Or, it is happening to us, so we have a chance to know it. Clearly it has an independent life, whether or not it is known or seen or remembered.

The dream can't be speeded up or it would change. Some of the things that happened (her being frightened at the distinctness of the runners' faces, the lack of sound) would not happen in the telling of it, and would be lost. This happens all the time, as things are not remembered.

When she returns to a town where she lived in her childhood, she finds some of the same people and brick buildings, but not what she is looking for. As she has almost forgotten the girl she was, the town has forgotten itself.

I—or this person who may be me—hesitate.

Are these words mine or the author's? I can find them in the book, longing to be released from themselves, to lose themselves in a murmur of voices, the waves and crescendos of the insects in the summer trees.

I dreamt at night but I also dreamt during the day. This dreaming was like a music accompanying the several things that would happen to me each day. To say that I was successful and powerful in these dreams would hopelessly blur the delicate, distinct pleasure found there. There I wrote something that was beautiful; I sang in a voice impersonal as sex and as miraculous. A fuzzy kind of praise, anonymous, enveloped me, just as petting would in my later adolescence when as a boy felt my breasts I would almost fall asleep, not out of boredom but as a means of losing inhibition, a kind of trance, like getting mildly drunk.

•

She does not have an easy time sleeping.

•

She washes her body thoroughly the first time she is kissed, and also does so after she takes care of the birds of the woman next door who has died.

Quotation marks are never used when a person is speaking. Claudia just tells us what they said. Although it might be exact, sometimes it is just a part of what was said, or what she remembers. (Even in one's native language, everything isn't understood, although this pretense is maintained, concealing dimension. When speaking another language, it can be dispensed with.) So we are forced to share her fate, which is not to get outside of herself.

•

At home I would wrap everything and go through my address book, which was cluttered with little pencil checks next to the names. Names of people from all the past Christmases for whom I'd tortured my brain thinking up so-called personal gifts. Today I no longer even look for personal gifts, anything will do. Besides, I don't know what a personal gift is. I think if I really gave someone a personal gift, it would scare him to death. I don't know what a personal gift for myself would be, either. But I'm sure that if it were really personal, I would burst into tears. At least I'd know then what sort of person I am.

He said that he also felt that he stood out at home, so that here, in a foreign country, it was a relief to be endowed with this status as an objective and unchangeable fact. He explained that not fitting in didn't weigh on him here, sounding as if he were happy.

•

Henry's irony makes him so distant that, in the end, it's almost as if he were pretending to be in a fight, except that it kills him.

•

From the time that she turned on her friend, her perceptions began to change. Not only details are no longer telling; undeniably important events are dulled to prohibit the reaction that might endanger oneself (as if we are in hiding).

We stood with the crowd on the sidewalk and looked at the tank. Nothing was happening. People whispered to one another. Later the tank's upper hatch opened and a young Russian soldier looked out. He didn't seem to be afraid. He nodded to us ... Things remained quiet, and I was getting bored. We went home.

She works to hide each thing from itself.

Boredom is created.

Things and people suggest within themselves other possibilities of what they could be. They are not these possibilities, yet these suggestions are now part of them. The narrator's voice shares properties with other sounds, impersonal as sex and as miraculous. Words share properties with other words. The music accompanying their activities is not distracting, although neither is it background music. Balanced, it establishes certain registers corresponding to green things found within the activities. Of course, these things are not themselves notes. Or they are notes, but notes that have not yet been sounded, or are sounded by the music accompanying them, which then awakes them to themselves (undoing her work), if they could be considered living things, or at least awakes them to ourselves, who hear names casually, often even forgetting them, having nothing but these activities for our companions.

Italic quoted directly from Christoph Hein, *The Distant Lover*, translated by Krishna Winston, Pantheon, 1989.

Two Poems
John Ash

THREE SCENES

1.

Indigence like a fog infects
the folkloric woodlands and trailers.
An axe is heard. Insects
descend at evening towards
the magnet of her very pale arm
from which the woollen shawl
has slipped. The atmosphere is
good/not good for the child.
Sometimes a violin or bird
screeches its two wrong notes nightlong.

The empty cash-box sinks in the clear river.
How far away is the city? No matter
how far, it is time to be going.

The city is distant by many waterways and islands.
Its towers rise beside a bay.
Each ferry has a different
name and color. Let us travel
on the blue Berenice,
the white Irene, the lonely Anna.
The child will laugh at the waves/
the child will scream and hide itself
in the Greek folds of the shawl.
There will be a sound like an axe falling.

2.

The woman's hair is like a lion's mane.
In the café, in a whisper, she tells the child
the story of the traveling salesman's ghost.

Rain falls slant against the elevated train.
At noon the light remains dim. The tear in
the window-blind is big enough for one blue eye.

Between flower beds in the shape of sunbursts
the local militia stand at attention. The statues
seem to say, "There's always a war somewhere."

The summer is vanishing back into cement.
A sanitation truck passes, plastered with leaves.
In the square the yellow tents are folded.

The murderer complains that his mother never loved him,
and continues: "You have to go to the edge,
and when you get there you can't go no further." Yes,

and the trick is to walk elegantly, without shuddering
above the girders, and garbage and distant fires.
Word is, Down there they drown you in your car.

3.

Caught up in the concerns of the day
(a mild Wednesday in October) he resolved
to stay where he was and think about these matters.
It had been a year of disturbances, storms out of season.

Or he decided to set out for the mountains
and the snows, a place beneath a blue pine . . .
Surely a life of the instincts was preferable to
the rehearsal of Hellenistic philosophies?

Sitting on the warm stones of the harbor
he reflected: "All decisions are hazardous,

including the decision not to decide. To know
the names of all the boats and to have consulted

the long-range forecasts is not enough, nor
to be enchanted by maps showing the ragged
outlines of glaciers and fjords, nor to think
of starlike flowers under the hooves of elk,

when your heart cannot ignore the new towers
of the city, clad in red marble and black glass
is it possible to abandon these atriums,
these concert halls, cafés and record stores?

Regarded coldly the choices look meagre:
a) moving on, b) staying put, c) personal extinction,
and d) turning back which is equivalent to c) . . ."
On the esplanade contented couples strolled

toward a lurid conflagration in the west,
unperplexed by dull-witted abstractions
that grazed above their heads. A woman
turned to him and asked: "What keeps us here,

where the very air seems a menace? There is
no war yet the streets are littered with the dying,
and to take a walk is to step on outstretched hands."
He replied: "There are reasons for disquiet.

There are rumors of a plot against the Boss,
and a new outbreak of Platonism has alarmed
the clerics, yet your desire for a haven seems
a possible regression, a romance of sturdy hillforts

after plague has emptied the cities, but this is not
such an age, not yet. We are alive here and living.
Let us go home while it is still light. Let us
behave in the manner of travelers returning."

John Ash

THE BURNT PAGES

I

Cadences, confused declensions.
These are the beads of a rosary I tell in ignorance

II

History reduced to dioramas,
Technique without utility

III

The empty towns cover themselves
With a shawl of yellow grass
And whatever was once at issue here
Is no longer contested

IV

. . . And I think the metaphor,
The mere comparison may be wrong
In the way a Homeric simile can be wrong,
Since the sea off Water Island or Point Lobos
Is not the shield of Achilles
Or anything resembling it,
Though we are, all of us, grieving
For Patroclus

V

A month since the brilliant scene
of conversation in the bar,
The promised word did not come.
Perhaps his trip had been
Extended? The world seemed dumb.
His voice on the machine
Still sounded just as keen,
But calls went unreturned.
Then from a chance encounter

In a busy street we learned
What we did not want to know:
He had gone where we could not go

VI

The clouds rest on the sidewalk,
And the city is only *a relocation of metals.*
When the sun sets there is no sound
But one imagines the sound of enormous hinges

VII

We no longer play the dances.
Our dissonances are scarcely cantabile,
And *the last kiss comes before the first*

VIII

We have washed the blood from the walls
But not from our eyes. *O my sad father*
Why were you so silent back then
Unable to think beyond tomorrow—
Each dawn a doorway
You did not want to enter

IX

The morning was clear
And I could have wished the taxi-ride
From the airport longer. O, a week
Of that comfort and postponement
Would not have been too much.
I did not know what to do
When my mother opened the door.
She was a worn curtain
She was a Trojan heroine.
The sky resembled a still lake surface.
The roses were bright but ended early.
This is the ending of the year.
Cities surround us, they shimmer

under different names.
My mother's hair has not turned white.
The roses were bright but ended early

X

Father, don't cut down the pine.
Someone's past—not yours, not mine—
Was happy in its shadow

XI

"What is the use of it?" he asked,
"To travel to the farthest ends of the earth
To record, in the pages of a diary,
The pangs of a new nostalgia"

XII

My feet in their too small clogs
Hurt no more than my heart
I am sad as a wooden town

XIII

My friend is a nervous man
With an unnatural fear of coffee,
With a determination to succeed
And the conviction of failure,
And only days ago three young people
Gassed themselves in a field of soybeans

XIV

Senecan morals. Summers
Hotter than the burning of Troy

XV

For long I dwelt beneath vast porticoes
And evening changed the basalt columns

Now with the approval of the great heliotropes
I piss towards dark skies very high and far

XVI

In the small square
With the weathered bleachers
The carrousel of all the rancors
Turns to a desolate air
And the painted horses grow tired.
Is this all that you desired

XVII

Don't vanish, don't take the path to the river.
The child you once were floats up towards broken windows.
We remain in the shadow of the chestnut

XVIII

The meditations are numbered
One to a thousand, and they retreat
From the event like the perspectives
Of an ideal city, its streets fanning out
Into landscapes no one has bothered to imagine,
And this vast blue cave
Is only a familiar sadness

XIX

O freight trains!
Fierce winds of the plains! O
Palisades and rivers! The past
Has been lost in the dust of the road
Like the sight of a girl holding white
Cornflowers after the truck has gone by,
Entre Galveston et Mobile

XX

The leaves stir and fall back.
Now all things must be moving on
Past the moment of the poem
Which remains like an empty cast
For the limbs of a bronze hero,—
An episode in the long history
Of backward glances

XXI

I remember the muscles of your side,
And the two green plants like caryatids
That framed the hotel door in Paris.
Under that dome the avowal could have been uttered,
But instead it was replaced by a figure
Meaning the infinite in Arabic, and the sentinel
Prayed for rain, encouraged by the ardour of the insects

XXII

So in the manner of a suite of dances,
Without unreasonable regret or hope,
The annual valediction unfolds with damp,
crumpled wings, and when my mother appears
In dreams, and speaks, I know I cannot answer her
Except to embrace her as if she were a ghost

XXIII

One must go on
With the echo in one's mouth.
One must go on
With a sharp ear for the fall, with an eye
For the bloodied steps on which our limbs are broken

XXIV

Book of summer we have read you,
Every word, and memorized the lines we need.

We recall the gold light on your pages. The colors turn.

The seasons are like a day stretched over a year

XXV

Father, did you forget those songs of Mahler?
The boy with a knife in his heart

XXVI

Cities surround us, burdened by their names.
Rome is a place in New York State, and Athens too,
And Carthage. Manchester is a place in Connecticut.

XXVII

The sky resembles a still lake surface
My mother's hair has not turned white.
The roses were bright but ended early

Seven Rondeaux

Laura Moriarty

What am I
Aloud is the answer
To what do I want
As a question or as
A woman for example
One might be asked
Which is like repetition
What can be asked of me or you or
What can I
Be allowed to know or
To act as if existing conditions
Have made me exist
For you saying say what I want
Here name finally mine is
What I want

Of you as a word
Refers outward to the world
Or in to pleasure
Are you equal to
The present includes possibility
Only if addressed
You have sent me a letter or not
Or I have not the wherewithal to speak
Of you to you
As if you were a plan
A construct enterable
Or only terrible like dreams
Of you without you in them
Do they have to do with anything
Or you as you are there

In that place
An arrangement being made
In an imagination not unlike
Mine might be formal
A real deal in which things
Are signed vows taken
I take them to mean
What they have now
Said about imagining
In that place where
I am now imaginary as you
Being not but in thought
Here though here you are a question
Who you are being another
In that place

Undefined momentarily
Empty unknown even by one
Who should know as yourself
Or I should but don't
As if knowledge like complicity
Beside itself incapable
Because only we can know
In that sense
Undefined as we
Only a word easily used
To mean both
What it means and what
It could mean much
More than it does
Undefined as it is

As is implies risk
To the buyer in this case
Let's say I or you
Having as little as we have had
Of each other or time
Value equals time given
And what taken
Let's say I have taken you
As is or you me

Is suggestive
But we know empty
Meaning not to have but so far
Not meaning nothing
Implies to take
As is something

This is something
We have arrived
The future is behind us
But there is no one here or one
Literal all the time
Could refer to anyone
But refers to you
Who no longer know what
This or who
You are a delight to me now
In your bliss wedded as I am
To the present I give
I am at home
But writing in a wind storm
This to you

A gesture undisclosed
Disrobed or didn't
Blowing all around but calm
Think of a woman saying
I am that now
Insurmountable difficulties
Notwithstanding because
Not with for example
A gesture not spoken
Or not spoken about but
I can stand it if you can
Being itself a promise
The warnings have emptied the ocean
But for this air
A gesture

Letters to Zanzotto
Michael Palmer

LETTER 4

Almost or *more than* or *almost alive*

But the body of another you attempt to lift,
the body you try to address
and the doubtful or the dark
of this sudden, stripped
winter and its winds?

A train housed in glass?

And the "supplement of sun"?

But the body you enter
with your tongue, with
the words on its tip,
words for chemicals and tastes
and almost remembered names,

hurriedly chalked equations
for the kinds of snow in our time
and always, behind

the landscape,
a snow more red than white?

LETTER 5

Desired, the snow falls upward,
the perfect future, a text
of wheels. You were born here

between noise and anti-noise
in first bits of film,

silvers of image, the *of*
and its parts—particle
as wave—the perfect
future's steps, its thousand lakes
bells, remarks, lunations and dismays

Days were called the speed book
then the scream book, rail
book then the book of rust, perfect-
bound, perfect shadow of a clock
the photophilographer assembles in negative,

negative sun or negative shade,
negative dust pulled from the ground
and the images negated in ornate frames,
firebricks, funnels and trucks,
figment and testament as one

Letter 6

Dear Z,
So we accused mimesis, accused

anemone
and the plasma of mud,

accused pleasure, sun
and the circle of shadow

Letter 7

But the buried walls and our mouths of fragments,
no us but the snow staring at us . . .

And you Mr. Ground-of-What, Mr. Text, Mr. Is-Was,
can you calculate the ratio between wire and window,

between tone and row, copula and carnival
and can you reassemble light from the future-past

in its parabolic nest
or recite an entire winter's words,

its liberties and pseudo-elegies,
the shell of a street-car in mid-turn

or scattered fires in the great hall
I would say not-I here I'd say The Book of Knots

I'd say undertows and currents and water-spouts,
streaks of phosphorous and riverine winds

Dear Z, I'd say it's time, it's nearly time, it's almost,
it's just about, it's long

past time now time now for the vex- for the vox- for the
voices of shadows,

time for the prism letters, trinkets and shrouds,
for a whirl in gauzy scarves around the wrecked piazza

Messieurs-Dames, Meine Herren und Damen, our word-balloon,
you will note, is slowly
rising over the parched city,

its catacombs, hospitals and experimental gardens,
its toll-gates, ghettos and ring-roads,

narcoleptics and therapists and stray cats
Ladies and Gentlemen, our menu for this flight,

due to temporary shortages,
will be alpha-omega soup, Bactrian hump, and nun's farts

As we enter the seventh sphere, you will discover a thin
layer of ice just beginning

to form on your limbs
Do not be alarmed, this is normal

You will experience difficulty breathing, this is normal
The breathing you experience is difficulty, this is normal

Dear Z, Should I say space
constructed of echoes, rifts, mirrors, a strange

year for touring the interior
Should I say *double dance, Horn, axis* and *wheel*

Dear A, Scuttled ships are clogging the harbors
and their cargoes lie rotting on the piers

Prepare executions and transfusions
Put on your latest gear

LETTER 8

(cirrostratus)

So A's finally, alephs and arcades,
the bone-dice thrown

beside the chained gates
And the cawing of out-there: bells, charged hearts, old films

threaded past narrative's lip
But what does the whir- the wer- what does the word

need - world need to be gone - to perform - what
does the world

before you need
to become perfect

They are swimming below the cliff-heads and the wind
Brickworld, chimneys, when-if-not-

Michael Palmer

When-if-not-when, foam
and wrack, wheeling of terns

And aloud, unearthed
as a language of nets

Actual blue and citron
Actual grey underleaf - so

many bundles to burn - take them to the woods
and burn them in heaps

A's before B's
Take the versions in your mouth

Take inside into your mouth
unearthed, all smoke, blue

and citron, actual word
for that earth and that smoke

Italian Sequence Comma With Italian Words Stop One Stop (Architextures 8 Dash 14)

Nathaniel Tarn

—To the wounded spirit of Andrea Mantegna,
ad majorem gloriam

ARC8 : 88

Stress on seven intense from plethora of clocks. Had he been there another hour would they have stressed time too? For now, weight lifts from familiar recitals: organization withers to rest. Maternally for him it can do nothing more. Weight sinks back then and blooms of glory waver on the abyss instead. His radical surprise! Force of decisiveness! It is as if they were names: in his mind, will it not be so with their perfumes? Letters of these names hard to abscond with, yet he has known of their alphabet always. It is only that you have to follow the aleph with the beth—and so forth down the years. He found it very needful to seize this hour before such buildings claimed him. You arrived in that somnambulant pink air pleasance was famous for—although it was at least seven of evening and you knew you had been granted into another world.

Grace of that new root which is so old for him, it is his anchorage: he always cuts from it! Here he is, so clearly assisting his own birth. Maternities pour down afresh from all his ceilings; showered with infants of all sexes as if in a squall of flowers. Is it not the truth these people mastered size as no others have? Seize the hour! For buildings here are larger than any made in his own era. He may run the danger of disappearing into them forever, dissected in small corners no one would ever recover. Buildings smiling down on small, cross towns around them, huddled from roof to roof, swarming with dwarf contentions: have you noted how they speak to each other in streets and plazas, these folks, as if there were time for nothing other than to be violently born? Whereas his people! As if manifest destiny existed in silence—unspoken, unspeakable, the very alpha of wealth itself! As if they had not precluded wealth by concern for no other repression!

Is it not frequently that "to write" is an act which is not to be followed by "to read", unless a "to read" were to be experienced as a "to write"? But this would alleviate from the original "to write" would it not? If such there ever was, would it not? But they do not know that there was such an original ever. Thus do they not retreat over and over? Until they reach no beginning—and, in that circumstance, come to understand there is no other life?

ARC9 : 88

Where to enter the round? Round? Comfort to think "round" but may be line instead, interminable, and, at that point, will it matter where you enter or leave? Would it not have been wonderful to feel secure with no residue whatsoever? He had tried sunlight, a father's road. Had held father as if holding sun, but a dead sun, in his night realm not his day, bundled, mummified. Poured out love by night impossible by day. Refused to respond. Come out then *en trompe l'oeil*, holding his hunting lance, girt with horns and hounds, and could be seen far down a closed-off access, in one of the private rooms, making toward the round. *A la Veronese.* Gods peeling off the ecstasy, falling on them like rain.

Huge sunflower fed by force. Over and over had he not let himself be born as sunlight, stealing through windows, pooling over white ceilings until he had them chastely changed to gold? Understanding this play of space in time. Space speaks to space as actors on stage, treading an adequate distance. Whereby enduring vistas held, that do not shift or break, rising straight always, no matter from what angle. Now you go into endless colonnades (a colonnade interminate itself, leading into another likewise, the product of these likewise). Orange and red throughout the city, sun melted into walls, each one standing in for a dream. Your passport is your innocence and grace. This city. Other cities, above, below. All visible avenues (and the invisible) leading away from this scenario. Had you not, on a map, chosen the semblance of a circuit, closed, irrefutable, and seen but fractions of the possible? Whenas all roads now led into a parliament of gold. Thinking "*gloire, gloria*, glory." Ceilings burning, your neck aching as you look up at them. Immeasurably they drink up your eyes. Singing etches a life into a likeness.

Whereas if the finite become smaller and smaller until you look into the very intervals of the world's body, is it not so that this vastness, this golden universe, will shrink into a minuscule stone, incandescent with wrath? He ushers in the other accredited worlds. Side by side, crushed into images, these stones shine forth together. From domes, like novel galaxies. Brighter than desert nights falling apart with stars.

ARC10 : 88

E quel mistero: how had they ever fallen to this life? From high domes, those you do not examine, in forgetfulness, so close you are to walls, to center stage. Emperor throned on eagle wings. Sun weighs on horses; hanged man, head broken on the balustrade, falls to distract your own. Blinding white wall brings out the mandorla of empire: plangent honors, legions at exercise, caracoling horses, shimmering uniforms, somber wine tunics, red or blue, awash with gush of silver. Cannon, sabers, lances, pikes. Always the eagle's shadow to bewitch the plains. Out of the mountains, armies waterfall, cavalry cataracts, artillery blares with the long roar of thunder trapped in crag coffins. Dancing along huge fronts, a godlike forehead moves to the smiling plains of our most memorable country. Did he not always seed imperious republics: shining, fresh-minted coins of his new currency? Pigeon-bosoms heaved. Arts praised.

Intimate fountains. Wine pours from sexes, breasts and mouths to escalating moss. As once the milky way expressed a goddess motherhood. Stairs rise and fall from fountains up to doors now leading nowhere, through halls grey with dead voices, ghosts packed into old cradles. Leaning against the balustrade over these hanging gardens, stares down into the lake ringed with ancient counties. Seizes from castle, keep, tower, villa, palace, names needed for a story told in so few days. Were you not able then, two hundred years later, to follow his round, digest his plot, intimately desire each of his characters? Who had launched himself from the glorious wings of his new empire when it had first begun to dawn over interminable sleep?

What he liked about these gardens. That they came down to the water as lip meets lip, no intervening cut or noise of street along the kiss. Small blue pavilion against the lake knits sky to water as the swallow will, housing a choice of ancestors. And the light struck her, overdone in her laces (the real had rushed to all extremes), but light had struck her from behind her shoulder, against expectancy, with such a tenderness, marble had come alive. So much a mother might have kneeled one night over an infant's bed, time leaning into sightless eyes, perfume alone afire as if with light. And he had done with conquest then, though conquest not with him—shaken he was by it until he died.

ARC11 : 88

He stands in ravishment of this country. Sleep given back to him by the epiphany of it: never need he fall again—as long as he can somersault from vision to vision. Imperia to rule his vocables wherever on the map. So early, stretched its wings over the land, this aegis. So early covered all the goddesses, bound them to bridle. Scaled thighs, standards inclined between them, advanced at siren moats. While palace painted with these *amorini*, flesh ridden divinely. Ransom: states soon breakdown, family-choked so many centuries, when other eagles swoop to reunite them. After which, a great farce: empire in fascicles. Now, the whole nation perpetually restored. One third of monuments green-gauzed, gnomes busily unseen below. To see or not to see: the cosmic lottery. Country falling to pieces, in repair, invisible (all the time); fleeing him (most of the time); refusing him (some of the time). Anxiety force fed between fish-scale thighs, for the almost unbearable weight of worship carried there.

Nth legion about to leave *PI / PR* or *PA; RA / RI; VI / VR* or *VE.* N captured troops, *la fanteria,* tails between legs, stubs up their assholes—who had been writing pre-verbal testaments. Courtesies wear the stars one by one in their velvet earlobes. Catastrophic rain: the town falls over in its sleep. Unable to assimilate more monuments that day, over to acquisition. *Cartoline?—si, di aviazione, per favore.* Shops had reached out to them, window by window, purchased them in—both in the general and the particular. Whose currency privates despised on this occasion.

He in front, forehead of the tale, light-hearted, ever newly born, young, flourishing, *camina di pari con la Natura.* Ah, morning freshness! Dawn poems written only! Renew those days (so long ago) when eagle-claw could grip his shoulder—anywhere . . . the most unlikely places . . . pitch him bodily in. Kingdom of the holy word, moving from sight to sight! *Sine qua non* his sight. Feet, as if argus-eyed, bearing him on. Burn down insulting darkness! Torch temples where enthusiasm has absolutely died! Let in the light, more light! *Francisco! Domenico!* Here would Imperia arouse herself again: labor light lights in air, on earth, in heaven. Lineage depend from it.

ARC12 : 88

To banish annoyance. So near the workplace, these pleasure-palaces, to singe a city with joy. As if roses were brought here after hours, hour after hour, wherever you were to be, no sooner opening a little than taken off, replaced. Deep blood of rose, like blood to him, arterial progress! Schematize the months. Ingratiate the gods at sky-level; your governance in symbols at the belt; choice moments of the royal life down here on earth. Munificence. Justice. Righteousness. Administration. After which, a joyful massacre of birds and animals. Some darker sport: running of idiots on mules, whores and heretics on foot, chased down by stallioned courtiers. Races in the so-called "humiliating genre," *le gare umilianti.* Upsky, of course, paradise: soul meets with soul, discourse is through the iris, love would rather pass through the eye of a needle than risk a loss of heaven. Your lords and ladies progress, drawn by unicorn, swan, eagle, lion, dragon, ape. Through their heavenly bodies, as water falls, to the plots below: are they as informed as this, ever, as fortunate?

Spring lips he could not reach though he longed to. Subsistence economy of thought alone. Informing the gentle face he saw each day, in and out of sight: he would have had her swan-drawn if he could, all the hours of her life. Facing her on his knees, full-armored and yet chained. Who came with roses crowned, on dove-winged air, breath warm with breeze, perfume on woven waters. Where he stood before his own subservient form, hands raised in blessing. Who had been brought from hell live and triumphant: by whom you think, by whom the air repeated: should you not smile on me whose epigraph is music?

Self-concern to the winds! Move out of body's burden, leaden breast heavy with worldliness; step in front of it, naked to the hilt. Armor kneels behind you, empty as air. Mandate all thoughts back to that weight, servants to scullery. Mind owns that leaden one; let him look to and after it, above and under it: you are in no case sullied. Light shines from back of *you* now, shadows *your* shoulders as you bow to her. Summer lips reached as arm crooks over neck, no matter face desired pensive to one side; her hand as if embarrassed that will soon caress, gesture learned in a school for ladies largely since. This kiss outlasts a culture as they witness it. They learn it on their lips.

ARC13 : 88

Siren noise outside, robin clatter nearby, sleep into waking and back to sleep which would go music music. Tapestry of one texture as if woven in water. As wood falls from mountain crest above green lawns, so thrush song to lake in a rush of quick trills. From bird to bird his canto goes as two will mate with veers of white wings. No architect resists this edifying air, ghost thread of mortar through imagination: the only buildings which cannot fall, or be pulled down, or added to by others. Through which song echoes—as if all operas were being played together in a dream, none warring with another. Such space for music, depth in the terrasphere, no singer flies alone but, in marvelous choirs, spreads satin voice over all your stairways.

Whereas, in cities, the infinitesimal souls of dogs look up at him from cobblestone or pavement, weaving along beside their masters, full of their own preoccupations, caring no jot for palaces in air he'd raised day after day on *terra firma.* Who remember waters in which they'd swum, canals through which their paths had been appointed when all these millenary houses had dumped their surpluses to flush land dry. But, perhaps, you will have thought, these are very large, capacious souls—huge souls compared to yours. Conserving plans of immemorial cities: avenues, crossways, streets, parks, plazas, pleasure groves, numberless cuts through lots linking one to another. See, once for all, how dogs' eyes meet at their own level, deep layers of conciliation in them from centuries of care, and tell if you do not believe eyes meeting high above them are not more full of murder and assassination.

Had he not promptly decided, on realizing the grandeur of this task, that, were he to miss one, two, or three of these cities, it would not greatly matter? Since they'd be launching other voyages and would invariably catch themselves up? While on this very expedition, had he not planned these subsequent, for fear that, once returned to their own home, they would have lost the necessary details? Did he not own vast repertoires of cards, slides, indices, guides, catalogues and maps from which to draw *periploi* for failing memory? Too, there were matters of advancing age which threatened to curtail all explorations. So, likewise, he took counsel with authority, contracting that if he weren't to see some cities in this life, he would reincarnate in the vicinity to see them in the next—and so forth till the repertoire of cities should be entirely exhausted.

ARC14 : 88

How they rise, one after the other, like clocks at small intervals, these voices sounding deed as sole measure of day! How they lay ambition to sleep in modest achievements! Raised this great helm of the extended world that nothing can depart from, circumscribed glance from single possibility: the planet has looked you in the eye and blinked: enough! you have changed time to gold and purchased vision from . . . a holly leaf! Free (inasmuch as conscious of volitions and desires) men had thought themselves. But, ignorant of causes by which led to desire, they do not even dream of their existence. Now stand these palaces erect against your woman world as generals advancing to their lands with casual caresses. Avenues part, lined with tall trees, let buildings in, vistas of generation open beyond the property. Pillars march martially into the city's thighs and you can rest now, declare day vanquished, *passegiare.*

Whereas striving for wisdom is the second paradise of the world. Master of staring eyes sees not in this domain; questions won't stretch as far as this, nor any research whatsoever. Gloriously have you departed into the silence of pure sound! Capitals crumble that were built on desire; the city is sold to broker and pawn; shares in her tumble to deserted streets; rivers surrounding her float cat and rat to their graves; ocean awaits it all with open arms—until the sea itself dies of these fabrications. And there *he* is, our Zeta, asleep in his tree, held in his forest! Her boughs encompass him, lyre music only he can soar to, hear on the midnight wave. How moon struck through her boughs that night of nights, winkled your heroes out singing for renaissance, while an exhausted mist covered the lake and no shore shimmered from the further side!

Sometimes, you will see need for courage nowhere described in any human book, pleading the divine. There will be those to have made bread, in time of famine, with no tangible flour; wine will have flowed, dark as the west where ocean had been clarified with sunken bells. You will have looked again over the landscape and with astonishment noted it had not changed one jot. His voice known as sole agent of any transformation. *Lascialo! Lascialo* (be!) None will have come to feast beheld as he had been beheld—whose step drew out no mark in sand, breath moved no air, touch raised no welt on fire, mind moved like water surrendering to water.

From Over the Hill
Sarah Menefee

it wasn't the moon that went down behind the granite mountains it was a red neon sign the desert was glowing with radium like a new casino rug this land I walked so often in dream and also in waking whose heat rose up and embraced me like a mother's

was I kissing one of them in that room or was it that other night when I left the movie to meet him my hair all tangled I'd forgotten my comb no that was in another apartment a basement room Jackie was on the bed she was fifteen the older guys called her a bride because she gave out she liked it making out on the bed he was on top Peggy and I at the table with a deck of cards

when the sun comes up early in the morning it shines across the railroad tracks through big gold and lilac clouds and the plate glass window into the eyes of the drinkers at the Circle Bar so they blink and squint and stagger out

the man looked intellectual because of those thick glasses and sort of dissipated bloatedness usually didn't gamble was so excited winning awhile calling from the poker table for drinks and tipping a dollar each time until he was broke came to the bar I was having my after-shift drink I'll drive you to Pyramid Lake and eat you out up there he said I'll do it for an hour come on it'll only take twenty minutes to get up there and you won't regret it the last time I went to Pyramid to swim I thought about his words wondering how it would have been like his words sucking at me passing the raw bulldozed area of a huge corral on a flat between two desert mountain ranges full of hundreds of captured wild mustangs

Then one of the young men whose function this was went into a cubicle to lie down with me. He was blond and rather chubby. He lay down on his side, and I saw the green phosphorescence glowing out of his anus.

you see the landscape of their bodies it lets you in built so solidly the clay of them the woman we followed along Saturday night downtown street with elaborate pompadour all puffed and ringleted Miss Kitty you know Amanda Blake a real Reno woman pastel pleated skirt high heel sandals a little wobbly yet a sure step smoking a cigarette in painted mouth in the clear air soft as borax water

I used to see you come down to the bus depot in shining shoes he said he stopped in the alley and gave me a ride down to Lake St was I wearing shining shoes black flats that made my heels bleed walking home from school I looked at his big Louis Armstrong face seeing myself so young twelve years old in patent leather shoes and understood he was saying that he was shining shoes in the stand outside the bus depot down on Lake St the Negroes the Chinese the Paiutes the x-movie women bent over fifties' hairdoes high heels g-strings the Keno Queen on the radio that first summer the murder at Henry's Corner over a fly crawling up the door of the bar one man wanted to kill so the other who didn't went and got a gun from his room at the Mizpah Hotel and shot him dead

Half a glass of red wine, embarrassing people in the bar with the weeping, and home in the rain, tears on my face again, over the hill on the bus. Far less drunk than last time. Oh god, here it comes again, it laughs and falls on my head.

she said it in Woolworth's I have a pain that a pill can't cure by the rack of paperback romances a pain that a pill can't cure it had to do with running down in front of the theater she taught me to say over and over the lights coming on goddam sonofabitching asshole goddam sonofabitching asshole it had to do with men and women I drempt it was evening the river just beyond the shadows of the buildings on each other in such a sad way

When my husband came through town, all thin and wasted with arthritis, he slept against me like a skeleton from behind. Oh, woman, woman. It makes my pain go away for a few hours. How have you stayed so young? Now that I didn't care he desired me; what a petty triumph!

the other Peggy was thirteen too lived in a flattop by the rendering works on the rise above the fairgrounds where we'd hang out she knew Rodney Day the fast guy who was sixteen in the ninth grade had a car I was in love with him in the same study hall we held hands once in the movie saw him again when I was eighteen his buddies threw perfume on him in the car sitting there abashed my family laughed not a very bright boy who'd made my heart ache at my desk writing dear lover I love you deep in my heart plese keep my word

I'm working night shift in a morgue. Feeling lonely, I open out a drawer and start to talk to the two stiffs lying on it.

wasn't that the Plaza Hotel that used to be the original opera house turned into a fleabag we stayed in one night we just hit town and he hit a number on the roulette wheel with his last dollar no that was torn down some years ago another street this is the Gospel Mission somebody told me they make em pray for hours before they feed em no neon on this block Third St hardly lights at all people hunkered against the side of the place waiting a husky young woman with lank hair growling at her little bald baby in its stroller the only thing she can safely yell at

that night of winter rain the child of my dream who was my bartender John making love to me became an old man who said I've gone to live in the Old Indian's Home soon I'll go to the Land of Many Rivers my friend at the Home can already hear the Tribes singing and I saw white rivers flowing from a hilltop

A Baltic Tragedy
Robert Kelly

1.
Oelbewoelbe, a place or beach
by scant reprisal

near infarcted, as by sky the Chinese tower,
the empty. These

are the scarcities of number
not by counting

as a tower not by seeing stands.
As.

What a surd does in the sky.
This is by the old tree

trash among shadows loved or
some things in fresh supply,

a town's name or a mother.
Redaction of a piccolo gazette.

2.
A kind of being out of focus,
example three and a half year old child in blue

on a seacoast in physiological
saline solution swims

with eyes open and sees a Wellington
sink a Red Cross boat

an enterprise of agony not adequately
impacted by 'remember'

willy-nilly corpses on the shore.
Tariff quibblers lose the fresh of life,

dawn squat or hump of bread
for nothing is indifferent when you pay the price,

counting doctors to assess disease.
Numember. Turf quest

a grown man with a perfect golf
(sarsen stone, aerial metagraph).

Woke vexed into mathematics
or wear good shoes, his boarhide bluechers

muddy Bight of Helgoland. The night.
I hear the kettle sail

over the hoof tops and skirl
into the maiden windows of a skittish town

trembling for its privacy in the lord's day a.m.
A horse by watching.

The town's name sees enough.
Bloody Old king and the news of sparrows

and what is hawked in mark't, a spill
to light your history with,

good governor, postwar return of cents
to their proper musical impost

pay a carrier for his blood, a belle
for being. For a child a war

is mostly not eating. Go no further
into not knowing, The plane

was bright but the sky was brighter,
the war is never exactly over

though it's hard to find the soldiers now.
The sea was red at first

but then they cleared the mess away.

3.
This edited me he said. It edited it
was more my sense of that column

stretching from the Baltic Gate to the commissariat
where No one served Some one in a cloud,

steam table and a silver fork
cui bono for an old judge in a periwig

as my green by ground advanceth
earth upon Neaptime. The wet.

We stayed in a cheap place on the Tenison Road
not liking to pay a lot to shut the eye.

Men waiting to die still young yet
their oily bassinettes with pacifiers

jammed into the harley's shivered muffler
hurry round the corner to the other place

the one your mother wouldn't let you say
and now you can't see though you try

saturday weather but the thurs is on you
you shake your fist around the porn.

It was the town's name that eluded me
for all my root Parmenides my dog my bark

(look in this eye) each Virgilian afterthought
afternoons the lagoon. Day weather

the dry, the station's down the block, to go.
Skeptical, I married.

Terminal resonance, fast quarried
from the silences of ordinary time

specially made for your mother, carved now
by more hand than wit, a mild clavier.

I sat among Palestinians in their loud grief
mourning a century more than a country,

even the dignity of being wrong was gone them.
They are right and they lose and they lie

like the Union dead at Chickamauga.
Where am I selling? Would a man say

anything to get into bed. Noise restaurant,
parliament of cheese.

To ask you the true remaining question:
fix what would make the rest work,

any? Blood was water first
is feeble consolation, not that I asked for

or you are ladylike to give.
A color called murray and a deer across the yard.

Collar on yet, dad, with a miser waiting
and the mine weasel writhing and the bell

banging the sky apart over the methodist steeple?
Your coat on then and a white scarf

a finial? We are the only who are beautiful
with our nosegays and our final mandolins

and the girl thinking I felt your hand acrost
my whatyamacall I like it but I'll never tell

and I'll never tell by harry, cat in a window
and all the rest of us one single child

remembering a beach full of dead Jews.
I'm stuck on his remembering

burdock on my sock I can't get fast
what the cat wrote and what the dream remembered

truth finding ridiculous questions
typically rare, filling out questionnaires

confused about their original intents
(they have none, they come in cars

and wrap themselves at night in stars
like the heathen rest of us and Jesus weeps)

what do you do with what a boy remembers
inside the body of a man grown old?

That is the burden here, boat. That is the wanton,
wife. That is the kerning, friday,

that is the dog in the dump and fresh hay on the moon.
Hat for sale, will you buy me?

I read a book that told me not to count
all the numbers had a different look

and some were red and some were hooked
and some came off the page and bit me

and all the men who wrote that book
believed in ghost opinions on a vanished world

creepy as a constable in fog, his billy poised
to assassinate dissent or kick my dog.

What's your hat like? My dead is in it.
Does it feel? It feels like remember

—and that's a nice girl whatever they say.
So please forget your cunning Portugals,

there are no islands here but numbers
and the numbers have no clue. The boat I meant

is gone beyond beliefs, like the color
of the orangeman and the heart of maplewood.

Uninhabited memory far sands of Thebes.
People my hat. Every word I say

sells you my hat. Whether you buy or not
is nothing but a market question. Turf

quick to yield beneath those heavy shoon,
a shandy and a capital and not just Jews

but men and women of every white
pickled pink by that sea. I'm angry now

can you read my age? Mad at the war
reminding, mad at the gaspump and the fox,

mad at the mind. Rescue
this ardent hypotenuse my remnant life,

accuse each artifice of being so
and if you do that hard

you'll find the room for me inside you
and with wet tip lip or lap

my coarse silences you of all characters imbed
in the sudden actual. My hat

is off to you, Columbus. My coat
soon follows and the smell of my chest

throws round you like a summer sky
when you woke up wanting christmas, who?

Robert Kelly

You'll find the room but the waves
will wander all the floor and men

once dead will not so easy come
sparrowfast through Edwin's living room

to illustrate the fondness of the world.
Hurry to reply. Yours, a farrier.

(A centaur even needs such handling,
ostler weather, priest on clitoris

declaiming, rites of Pan and who
dares to ride or not decide or sit

motionless while his hands caress
surgical amplitudes of your slim weather,

nay?) Some feel a tower
breaks its local sky as a boat

violates the contract of the sea
to be apart and spare all islands

from boredom by categorical philosophers
(Eve counts, Adam raises honey)

not far from where the Orinoco goes.
Serpentine though a newborn stream

an idea beginning to impose itself
local values in a fractal town

what he remembers and what the sea took down.
Call Oelbewoelbe the name of the small resort

where clouds over what the infant tells
transfer sunlight by wet mediation

through the analytical conversation
(smells like pork) onto his uncle's straw-yellow

eyelashes he will remember all his life
till he too lies in the surf and dies,

the cold clean eyes of philosophers
looking the other way. Escapist grammar

but buy my hat anyway here
give me your head to put it on.

What do you care about the numbers,
we are valves. Can it be such music

that the tower stands but the sky falls?
Hear thirty-two roads flow quickly east

a mute number of escaping slaves.

Page
R*achel* B*lau* DuP*lessis*

—"Exegi monumentum aere perennius"
Horace, *Odes,* III, xxx

1. Waste places from the very first.
Grubbed marginal plots,
where daisy aster, hairy petaled, was.
Saw sheaves of stirrers strewn by the loading dock.

Stepped and stepped
up the hill under the gate over the road through the field

into the reaches of some certain dead.
Spent mum
inside their rage

that every day decides it will not heal.
"This has been going on for years now."

Rage, range, some other "r" word, a re- or ru-
some word-hunger rampaging
its repression:

thus barely beginning, world, word, wood
would, as all varieties of clouds' lush chaos

BLEW.

2. She gave me loose crayonings, just
a few colored marks, and I was
frightened, first
folded my gift up.

"It looks terrible."
There is nerve involvement, codine-sweetened pain,

negative dung. Without value.
In which becomes legible

a vacuum from the plethora of materials

and in this space a birth of enigma
to which one owes one's own enigma.

3. It was snow turning to rain, was soft sleet
sheets,
runnels of grey air, was melting on the asphalt, was nothing
to last?

All the words of light,
light among ancient people, navigators,
hidden.

Irretrievable estrangements and
unanswerable despair primed
thick-weave canvases which I stretched here.
It was almost too much, it was almost
smothered.

4. For the canvases already primed with words
were to take more.
And the line-streaked white
wobbled

perennially ready
to hold another mark or counter-score.

Eggshell colorings when cracked
show turquoise signs
upon the over-boiled white.

Softly silted S's silver water
silk the misted phosphorescent ground
beyond the river's main meander.

A space for deep wake
(screamed "something wet is chasing me"
or "there are worms in my bed") then
the deep wake, passing.

5. Dawn white
Sunset green

Muddy turgid dirtlike clouds
rainbow arch, and driving madly toward it

rows of makirs
litanies of dead, and dead too young

sequences
interruptions

"making light do what I want"
"weaving webs and webs of silver"

whose very whiteness may be thought too blank
to "tell the white marks from the black."

Apprenticed to it
tripping, my nose down, one corner of an iris, a stick,

light making me do what it wants
and it wants me to weep.

The luminous sheet, the open space, is living air and bright;
or dead, a waiting white like night.

6. What do you want? Is the poem a pony?
You want it to be "noble"
and "stronger than bronze."

You talk of funerals.
I have put a half-sprig
on a coffin above what once had soon before
a face. But was no more.

The poem immortal? you guarantee?

These page-space presences the
negativity
of written words; "parsley" or "bronze," are
airy

as if they turned beyond dimension
and cast the shadows
of what nameless void, whatever voiceless space collected
behind,
and beyond.

Dangerous their generosity
coupled with that shadowy randomness.

7. I crack the spine
of the book, split its muslin glue,
chip the endpapers in a raggèd rip.
Inside, folds
and mats of list
camouflage as lines.

It's hiding its impulse even from itself.
Does it want to speak?
Does it want to weep?

Mist. It's four. Rigid without sleep.
"To know what my motives are . . ."
(unfinished)

8. Line marks names
wavy registers,
a note with folds on the edge of a used sheet
a note with staples and tape
crumpled paper, pencil smudges half illegible
"isolate flakes" hybrid, subversive, inchoate.

The writing on the open page
the underside of itself
as if the underside made words

and, when the busy ripples on the surface stilled,
one saw that other taking shape:

the abstract rush of untranslated words
the space a presence possessed by other spaces

white trace
blank trance
whisper hold.

9. Being the thing that light comes round, it comes to know light.

Black, and black and white;
yes, and no, and yes and no;
being and not:
the flicker over space—rectangle, letter line,
spatter marks, irregular alphabet, rath and late;
a scrape, a set of incisions, a score in air:
for various work
has been done in and over this place

various works or workings, works
by,
of,
different hands

hand-space tracks
trek lines

(a trace of spotted light
gleams around the tricky edge of substance . . .)

Horace, *Odes:* "I have completed a monument more permanent than bronze and loftier than the regal memorial of pyramids—a monument which no squalling rain, no gale-force winds can overthrow. . . . I shall not wholly die; a lot of me will escape the funeral parlor." (My modification of a Penguin translation of III, xxx.) "Making light" and "weaving webs" are H.D. on film; "tell the white marks" is Williams on Marianne Moore, and "isolate flakes" alters *Spring and All.*

Prom in Toledo Night
Ann Lauterbach

A new heat comes up on a grand scale.
Were we waiting for it, as for a link,

Ask about sugar? Well, the heat is
Here. It thought I would speak of it

For someone to adjust the antenna, to

The recent suburban content, how much
Sky is now blocked. I have run into

Coolly, as flatly as possible, given

Chatted with both florists. Boys have
Been born to two nice women: Raphael

Numerous persons I know. I have

On a trial basis. I don't know why but
This heat is like a quarry dug into

And Penn. Some friends have separated

Omissions, intuitions flying out of the
Cranny or slot we thought irreducible,

The side of a hill. Intangible

Some things, uninteresting things,
Colors, pigs, toys, the usual river.

Earlier, I had written, mentioning

Radio: *I saw a good one, It looked like*
It could run. That was before the heat

I noted a couplet from a song on the

Cabaret. Another poem begins: "But
We were drawn away again by portraits,

But after I had won the howling dog at the

Those who were still living, but who
Had forgotten while the violins

Pictures where we could be idle against

I don't know that that means. The poem
Continues: "Beautiful faces

Explained the conditions

'It seems someone else was in the room.'
'This is a Mercury Production.'

Turn in the light; the two walk, stop

Evolving like the slow surge of history."
That part ends there, but

And then the spectacle

Room to its original strangeness, "I
Have better things to do with my time,

Then another: "Restoring a

I mention it was prom night in Toledo?
Have you noticed how the specific is

Now that I am in the city again. Did

Ann Lauterbach

Continuities of what we want.
Of what

Always a gash or wound in the ongoing

Unravelled speaks for itself, a mask.
I'll stop concluding that desire is

We want to keep, to cure, care for. The

A girl rides from the field in hot sun.
We stopped, once, at a lake to swim

A good place to start. I'll quit, as

The old red Ford. Last night you said
My dreams would improve but

When the heat became intolerable in

And after April, when May follows,
And the whitethroat builds, and all the

You were wrong.

On a black table, some around your house,
Some around mine, and the specific looms

Peonies weighted, three in a white vase

We turn and turn through always and ever
With as between us. When you laugh my

Again. In my mind there is a carousel,

The point of entry: the gash on the hill,
What we see as we ride. From the log:

Arms feel light. Your voice has become

A small Pa. town. Ducks, chickens, geese,

Eggs. I had some bacon, too, I

Two your time. Stopped for lunch in

About that duplicated hill. As I note
Duplicated hill, look up and the first

Never eat bacon or eggs. I'm thinking

The sign says bridge may be icy. My
Mind revolves around where and when.

Big hill appears ahead. We walked East.

Trying to describe a miniature calla
Lily only makes matters worse, and

Passing Presque Isle

I grasp at particulars when I am a
Deposit of hermetic, avid cares

Proves your point about dimensions

Be, found in the radiant furl of skin
As it plummets, seen from under a

Whose known qualities could be, might

Akin. I can feel the city's nearness,
Its less than equal attitude in

Cluster of new foliage, or something

My bracelet got hitched to a girl's
Sleeve—a frenzy took place around

Skirmishes—elbows hit elbows, wrists

Is this a form of exaltation or despair?
I love conjecture, although its stipend,

Ann Lauterbach

Some running shoes on sale on the street

Linear vein pierced, is too delicate.
Interspersed among these less than valiant

Day after day of weather reports like a

My love, this is the bitterest, that
Thou/ Who art all truth and who dost

Innings I'd turn to pure lyric:

Among the temporarily stricken; old
Litany of passage. Against a glass

Love me now . . . warble of language

I've come to see through nothing, ad-
Mit to only a haphazard verisimilitude

Back-drop and its brilliant flanges

Eyed art. Of course you, as both
Occasion and witness, pull me through

Similitude of the story-teller's wide

Gloss it amuses you to touch. I had
Planned to leave earlier, but these

Like a thread of feather whose pale

Suddenly the sense of prelude becomes
A hard spray of contingencies,

Keep making their mobile shadows

The most essential. She turns to look
Into the glass, watches as the image

Adamant, refuting, like a tax on

Of a gate closing off the garden for-
Ever. The model, exposed, could not

Expand, shifting to the calamity

With the rest, and nobody would know
How it ended, as nobody had known

Last, but would be shredded

Briefly wild; a fan eeked its rotations
In an alley; her friend, a girl,

I have but to be with thee, and thy hand
She reads from the open page

Told her mildly, obliquely, to rescind

To increase or ease the new implication.
It was as if a lance, aimed into the night

Of a nearby volume, hoping for chance

Of a passing stranger who had been surprised
But had remained diffident as he plucked it out

Hit a real target, had stung the arm

He had taken a rag, knotted it,
Walked uphill in the direction

And watched as blood poured from the hole

Asked, handing back the weapon
This tale boiled up from the flat black earth

From which the thing had come. Is this yours?

To breach the destitution of our aimless band's
Hungers. The more familiar pattern

One long spring whose sole aim appeared to be

Became interesting only when we decided
To participate in it. The room

This habit of one thing leading to another

Airless so that she, in it, felt
Breathless, reckless, faithless

Painted a virulent green, seemed

As I sleep, an unnatural extremity prevails.
Entrusted to a stranger, harnessed

I have but to be with thee, and thy hand

A spill I prevent like this.
Did you use a cup for the dice?

Or yoked while floodgates are lifted

With either the actual or absolute.
In the full heroic flush, we

Am I A? Each is a quibble

How to keep an even keel: "Single tree
In brown field: two trees: flashing

Could not be more discerning, note

Empty corrals white fences cows
Arrows your fingers your small bird

On barns silver wrists your fingers

Like a beacon the smell of oats
Right lane ends; merge left you

Attacking hawk: shade that green silo

Ann Lauterbach

Different hair: your . . .
Being marked

By the river, those girls with

Solitude cheats, it is to you she speaks
While at the same time wanting a world

As thought: what to suggest, what elicit?

Of how it looks but how it is. You
Are the constituent object; this distance

Others might recognize, not because

Others will say
She was just passing the time—

An argument. Against what?

Animal allegiance—makes anything from scratch
Abating or diluting while the last thrash—

A milder form of discourse

The river is nearer. Little conversations
At the check-out counter.

Still to be seen against—I am less at ease—

I remember the room I invented you in,
How happily captive I felt in such

At last, a reductive mood

Exactitude in this, an idea of being
As being with. This is rudimentary

Confinement. There was, and is

Ann Lauterbach

Say love is an attitude toward difference
In its freest form, adhering, inimical

But festive, if the subject persists

Now, let's leave to the cartographers
While the music lasts, the privileged

To time's jurisdiction. Space, for

Most intimate, most entailing.
Abundance and loss are the terms.

Information a display, a harbor

The arch or bridge or catapult—
A dart piercing an arm—is how

Earn the right to ford those rapids.
That she wants to converse in silence

Redress, reconceive our predicament

The unutterable collapse of particulars
Yet speaks its priority and stillness.

Is how desire crumbles disbelief

Men skip over the drawbridge
Muscular and vibrant in the distilled age

Pleasure is the cost of time, as may be

Some future proverb in which complexity is
Soothed: give the infant beer for her tooth.

The women darken with expertise, hum

Blooming above the pond in memory. Out task
Is to be less defeated by these children

But the fireworks were only partly successful

Girl is out of control, she reaps her hunger
On small things, rips handfuls of blooms,

As they shrilly discard the air. The golden

Seeing what I contain, as one contains
An ancient song. *La La La* spray of notes

Rips hair, my only sight, now actually

Stick to cloth, home sweet home as awful
As a flood, a crowd, an epidemic beyond halt.

In heat, an absent, singular source. Words

Cure for the incommensurate. *La La*: who cares
In the fresh air to which we, even now,

Rapture is the antidote, as may be.

Virtual Reality
Charles Bernstein

—for Susan

Swear
there is a sombrero
of illicit
desquamation
(composition).

I forgot to
get the
potatoes but the lakehouse
(ladle)
is spent
asunder. Gorgeous
gullibility—
or,
the origin
of testiness
(testimony).

Laura
does the laundry, Larry
lifts lacunas.
Such that
details commission of
misjudgment over 30-day
intervals.

By
the sleeve is the
cuff & cuff
link (lullaby, left offensive,
houseboat).

Nor
let your unconscious
get the better of you.
Still, all ropes
lead somewhere, all falls
cut to fade.
I.e.: 4 should always be followed
by 6, 6 by 13.

Or if
individuality is a false
front, group solidarity is a
false fort.

"Any more fussing & you'll
go right to your room!"

She flutes that slurp
admiringlier.

Any more blustering & I
collapse as deciduous
replenishment.

So sway the
swivels, corpusculate the
dilatations.
For I've
learned that relations
are a small
twig in the blizzard
of projections
& expectations.
The story
not capacity but care—
not size but desire.

& despair
makes dolts of any persons, shimmering
in the quiescence of
longing, skimming

disappointment & mixing it
with
breeze.
The sting of
recognition triggers
the memory & try to
take that apart (put
that together).

Popeye
no longer sails, but Betty
Boop will always
sing sweetlier
sweetliest
than the crow who fly
against the blank
remorse of castles made
by dusk, dissolved in
day's baked light.

Three Poems
Martine Bellen

CAMISADO

Across the bridge a basilisk waits for breath and your past with the weight of what you live—a complete description moves inside a universe indefinite because of finite matters. And stars unbounded by direction. No one must note the secret, though it may be known there is text stored in the solar nervous system which we will never enter. The knowledge is possible but not its possession:

A castle deep not of this time we sought for what the dead take with them with a rigor that frightens; eyelike spot on ocelot looking nothing toward. We are drawn to the lazy pagan majesty where once a mortal error breaks the crawl-space lock all falls into the cellar. What wails lie open in this game with inner moves?

Turbulence expands universe, and black groves suck the donjon dry of ineffable drift. We enter the missing sin through water though Iris, inseparable seer, cannot dissociate wind from air on any one layer. Hold on to the rim of this linear sea.

Spheres of seen perish when washed by fire; a chorus composed of our female friends seeks the things obscene. And after his face you are no longer, but make too much of leaving the cellular by star. Being detaches itself from its inversion. At bottom it may collapse onto the beach at your skull, a circumstance of mortality where every wave breaks and rejoins. What you were ends frozen across the horizon.

Martine Bellen

THE STILL-BOUND

Lay thee down the dwarf from under earth, a moon may climb the darkest side and we will reach in memory as chasms can. Divvied up by color this fear annihilates shadows before what later will exist. We fail to dream but only what's believed.

She looks not through the clerestory window though sees something going out her eye while stain changes vision and she reacts with involuntary mental movements. Meaning extracted as light is caught between living and its look. She thinks farther than the traveling show, an imagining that soon as a new soul appears the last one is gaseous. And imagination: like genie from an inkwell it cannot be drawn. Even there, walls break the earth into corners.

She could not live someway outside herself in a room she lets for sleep and to hold her in, but she is mostly aware of the terrorism, not how she found her way lying between its walls. There is a place of bodily grief. As long as it exists mind cannot destruct though it has to be as complicated as what is left under. If she detaches emotion from the external cause one mistake contains more truth than another, the kind of analogies that exist between them. Errors played backwards eradicate the previous from the new and an object of regret ceases to be a passion when becoming an idea. It cannot recollect anything without obliterating the distinction between factual and conceptual sensations. Imagine what would happen if the thought aroused emotion and the game kept something of itself? She might feel movement in common with the inward ear, sound off body; sometimes one can only believe where music leaves. It falls down from pain and the assignment of place. At the ocean she was warned not to break what others made.

ABSOLUTELY

How far have you gone this evening or passed between remembrance other? The vacillation is ours, pure, not land outside the sin fenced in.

What makes it space, a trace-wound wound around hide so far back that she carries her body through it with the notion there is always something behind: A memory, a confused constellation, a white substance of which the heart cannot take the purity and cannot be conceived out of this world where her deepest errors steep suspended on gossip and even if she stays awake, shift in placement occurs when air's gone astray or the spirit's sent off without flesh; for there is nothing so fearsome as no image and no thing to recognize we near.

In weather she is timid since last light finds a way down to set free from above and turns away tidings. Always an absolute span as it curls out of her, withdraws, while snow accumulates, must mist over a moment of loss that is an image, not meaning and deflection of passion is depicted by drowned river or heaving sea. If she were a bridge drawn between two spans of spirit she'd be walked over.

Field of identity sustained, still part of the entire surface, a kind of thought that walks through her into a snowy field; she is all but a ghost, and he can talk freely about matters outside her. The more she fades into the woods the sharper her outline and dimmer her concupiscent flesh. The words spoken about home automatically enclose in the roof or framed by windows while she is climbing a tree and can only be sought on branches pointing to what isn't known. Into the recess she freezes needles, needs breath no longer and footfalls of small animals replace her but she accepts this as the part of nature she'll never be a part of. Acts can be played in absence and the world is that much changed.

When done in a glow there might be an estuary that lay ahead.

Safe inside magma, the blind daughter and her brother with translucent skin feel no whether or which, just wet light lost to the clouds. With a telescope she brings it into sight of escape and who the devil also compels, pointing to the line from his heart and his private parts in the brain where we buried him so he could begin in a lone direction, already canonized for admitting the most souls, flesh-shed and supine. Each one masked so she could recognize them in herselves—their motion and sensation of sound in encamped concentration.

You try to remember where you came from but with each step there is less trace to your past.

After he steps on her wrist, disturbing her intravascular volume, ocean closes up, though he can't cry in her high concentration of salt and peace. Anywhere is the same and motion the distance between everywhere he is not. Nor does the distinction between earthly and celestial bodies become obsolete with the acceptance of flight and the possibility that what he sees or where he is could be other; the alteration of something into else makes self-evident identity is not a relationship between objects. She could not be seen before he saw her, though nothing allows us to conclude he sees by eye.

and how this body relates to where it is or the bodies around it.

She is the wall of water from where she sees. Before her—a window with solunar ice, behind her is devotion. Before her are bare trees, behind her the world starts from what she imagines. She's not sure they are eyes though wishes he were present to know the snow casting shadow melts into crests.

Her land has this sin in it but not that one though the sky overarches and turns it around as she holds herself out into morning and names its possibility toward back thinking where she exists already as a stranger lurking to loom wonder in suspense.

When sketching, she takes the pose of her studies to understand their feats, falls to her knees to feel the flame around him, and in charcoal, draws the ashes to her fingers, scarred as she unlearns years. It is already simpler. She can turn all situations into pictures on paper and question the possibility with the irruption of speech. If she conceives a body as its movement then something else exists that depends on her life and greater, more complex bodies in mission. She can't think of his name without changing shape. There is much outside the facts that concentrates into questions through three incarnations and many miles of motion. Across the way a friend is wiping with a photo of Ceausescu's blood.

She can answer to where spirits and ideas have an absolute exterior existence, where space with trimmings out of reach absolve her, but even if what she sees is not correct there is sense in that we always conceive another who is greater yet never satisfied.

If you turn to follow your markings the tread has all but been erased,

After falling out of the forest he forgets all secrets, forfeits cards and earnings. He has memories of feelings but one cannot hand over a promise of the sun and its arrival with mauve strokes, the color of liver without delineation and the inside of her. An amassing of images, of magic, passes away and right or wrong fade from a bruise. One need only proximate experience; death flounders around skeletons, is attracted to light like the buzzing. When the dutch door opens you'll be able to answer most questions.

before you a trace of what night might come to

Without warning her home became dangerous, tears from other parts of the train she traveled through and observation intersected into infinity with written women; it is the nature of scattered memory; it is the privilege of re-entering renaissance and finding herself in his pockets of flesh; it is important to analyze how this particular feeling is composed and then dissociate all persons and things so it is only her own. The spectacle is doubly visible if her footprints are carried away and pulled into her pieces as she bursts from east to west. The gaze disappears and they diminish.

and is trampled upon by an imprint that was once yours.

Looking through a window one thing is sought and another seen, so what she sees when she looks at him has two heads, little to do with looking at the window and this she is aware of but it's right before her on the other side that she sees. And she knows part of it is a secret and can't even be saved, and she has to be, and she is in him breaking laughter with the danger of mixing aspects from a real realm with what exists in the other, so that some characteristics seem so plausible she passes over them while some bring her straight back into parts of herself that couldn't be recognized around the eyes nor does it affect the body, but only the feelings made possible by the knowledge of things invisible. Movement influences passion and property too so the snow falling everywhere makes him an ocean away though why the eyes bulge in space where there is little nothing to see has not been explicated, yet she believes that it has to do with the theory that she could ride light to his face and know him by reflection only. The soul has to be made desirable

it was once yours.

Three Poems
Marjorie Welish

DANBURY, CONNECTICUT

1.
While winter remains without shadow
that brings lasting credit, it is possible
that the air's panopticon inserts new

bird calls—a burst almost, in the upper
slow latency. And still
there are no forces in this going abroad;

the solid observer is here before the rebirth
of space. Yet, another voice breaks,
then successive voices every two weeks,

new excrescences of the invisible
spectacle moving a process
well in advance of seeing.

2.
Advance or gather, then,
the gravel driveway,
but one strand of a tree
as a list in slow time.
As list differs from lyric,
so, too, these growing pains:
First railroad from Danbury
to South Norwalk opens in 1851.
Here, take this
catgut and wire
treated either as suspensions
noticed to have arrived late

or as green glass
of some sporadic good.

3.
That the air's indeterminacy inserts new
bird calls—a burst almost, in the upper
mid-range,

in the upper portion of the portrayal
of vocal coagulation—.

Acting on things: "I reproached him a thousand times."

DESIGN, WITH DRAWING

1.
And slowly, Monet underwent a conversion from wrist
to shoulder and thence to the ambit
of paint dragged across surface unappeased:

plasticity without an appointment
or trace of retinal light.

Unimpressed, an editor asks, "Was Pollock even seen
standing before this canvas opining 'Monet,'
Monet, ceasing to exist, I want to paint like you?"

Apparition. Really, I swear it.

And wearying.

And slowly. And somewhere other than observable water.

2.
A mossy bank, schoolgirlish

Of lacunae passing through literal mentalities
a few pages later.

A parapet, an undercurrent

of misplaced exactitude these odysseys transcended.
Why ask the artist? Ask the art:

rock-ribbed

breakwater, to mark the hue and cry of forgetfulness
and gray areas.

Addressees,

what constitutes evidence in stylistic transmission?
Disbelief "much bigger and faster"

or problems corroborated,

in a more efficient axe.

KISS TOMORROW GOODBYE

1.
Among us are those who apply
dysfunctional tactics to convened ordinariness
of setting, as in certain booby-trapped stories.

For similar reasons,
a narrative complete with lunch menu and stereoscopic thugs . . . ,
complete with cigarette yet for all that a narrative clad in itself . . . ,
or a ventriloquist and dummy, minus the ventriloquist . . . ,
all threaten the logical unit.

Complete with cigarette
yet disturbing the infinitesimal trash, the depiction,
this ventriloquist set a bowler-hatted dummy
on one knee, served up a twin
on the other.

Thus translated,
and torn limb from limb, "naively,"
the rivers ran

and Osiris spread showering selves, showering down
existence after death.

2.
Death served up a twin
the rivers ran
limb from limb
trash the depiction
minus the depiction
as in certain booby-trapped stories
for similar reasons
narrative clad in itself
on one knee
on the other
convened ordinariness
complete with cigarette.

Variations on a Paraphrase

Keith Waldrop

Beauty foreign, my heart
empty. Love signaling
from her face.

In a grassy clearing, the woods
crying *Waste. Why*
bother?

In the shade of a beech, I
come to myself,
empty, turn back. It
is almost noon.

* * *

And while in this wise I
meditate, the tables are laid, nigh
on to noon. She holds my
head between her hands, as if
thunderstruck.

*

As for the front steps, they must always
be an odd number, so that the right
foot—with which one mounts
the first step—will be first to
reach the temple.

*

Beauty cries out, crying
with a foreign accent. Before
the head, within the body, with-out pitch.

*

Between fall and rise, without
pitch. Consider well
the enormity of
what we must brook.

*

Bold knights, who've not their
hearts in their boots, and a thousand
foot, in a grassy clearing, footloose. *Why?* Full
speed, says the king on the third
day of battle. Unaccented
syllables, rapid, my
heart empty.

*

Building, so far from shore, these
shadows of the high sea-waves.

*

The distress which these notes cause, the
central part swollen and un-
graceful, open to the sky,
without a roof. When tiles are
broken or thrown down by
wind, we may yet be
preserved intact.

*

The doors are lattice-work. Extraordinary cadenzas, ornaments
serving to connect the notes,
enliven them, em-
phasize, elucidate. Without them the best
melody might appear meaningless and
empty.

*

A good retreat. Love
faces signals, would destroy
the gardens round the town. Tell
how great a madness: machines for
war, armor, salted
meat, a heap of the whole, the whole
set on fire, blasted,
dishonored, written down, greatly
dissatisfied. Now, faced with
noon, come awe-inspiring pronouncements in
love's unmistakable mispronunciation.

*

Heavenly houses should be
arranged so that passersby
can glimpse the gods.

*

If solid ground can
not be found, nothing but loose or
marshy earth to the bottom, then
it must be dug up, set with pilings
of charred alder, olive, oak. A dim
scale indeed, ascending hole
by hole, admitted only as passing notes.

*

If they touch, they
begin to rot.

*

Inky darkness discovered in
the doorway. In
such cases, love
signals: did you
see her yesterday? did you see

how pale she looked? does
she like dogs? have you
put the kettle on? My
heart in my boots.

*

In unison on the right, on
the left in counterpoint.

*

Low, broad, clumsy-roofed: let the
width of the front be
divided into eleven
parts and a half.

*

Many processions re-
joice the heart, conduct us
safely to the earth.

*

My harangue scarcely
pitched, I'm
troubled. No music from these
times remains. *Why
bother?* In spring
all the trees become
pregnant, lap up water, return
to their natural strength.

*

One must not build temples
to the same rules to
all gods alike. While
Valentine Snow plays, we
dispense with space, with absolute
pitch, with a steady scale.

*

On the lowest tier, up the
curving slope, at the top of the hill,
right in the center, there is
a mistaken idea,
colossal, out of
place, of remarkable clarity.

*

Players behave differently. But
still the temple is
empty with an emptiness
like the sun at noon. Exactly the
pitch of my own voice. Void, I
marvel in this marvelous
waste.

*

Rise or fall.

*

Speed, says the shade. Such
syllables within the body.

*

Spring infects us on the extreme
left, an evolution
of temperament.

*

Such delight in foreign
music—a taste for
exotic timbres. Between
the entire body and its separate
members, we have nothing but
respect, so vital
the delicate vacillations.

*

This arrangement involves
dangers: continuous
glide, columns cracked by
reason of the great
width of the intervals. Too
sensitive to permit any
answers, roaming across
Mitteleuropa, having no
rules for pain . . .

*

Towards noon, I turn
to this tremendous beech and
move into its shade.

*

We counteract ocular
deception by an adjustment
of proportions, the air seeming to
eat away and diminish the shaft.

*

We have no example of this.

*

What's there to
follow? Will you
come? At the sound of the
horn, perfect
peace restored.

*

With due regard to
diminution, let a line
be drawn. The higher the eye has
to climb, observing more anxious

values of symmetry, the less
easily can it make its way
through the thicker and
thicker mass of air, long
reiterations of single notes, constructed out of old roofing tiles.

* * *

Sun nearly to
noon, I turn
aside, seek shade.

Why follow
nothing? Why
waste the woods' green cry?

Love signals, but my heart
is empty, beauty
foreign.

Geisha Mime
Phillip Foss

. . . a mute soliloquy that the phantom, white as a yet unwritten page, holds in both face and gesture at full length to his soul.

—Mallarmé

Beneath kaoline, the skin is damascus. Death
or ceramics; the image is frangible, entity.
Love as a magnetic enclosure, white water
dissipated beyond mirroring face.

Reflection is a path, labyrinth of recedings,
toward and against desire, as when one walks
backwards toward lust; or knives as doors,
odor as warning.

Her mouth is wet with stars; the curve of her
waist is inevitable failure, acquiescence.

You hold yourself in your own arms and are enamoured
to have become the pretense. Or you are her.
Or her pretense.

Opulent forests. Decay. And mannerisms.

You clothe your skin in skin. Hallucinating oblique
passions antecedent to dawn, great flavor of blood.
Or illuminated eyes, flammable dance,
at the delicacy of insight.

Your hands are retroactive calendars; she is a drawing
in charcoal on rock.

Ocean waves are not random: predestination. As gifts
enameled thighs can be returned.

When in a specific perfume, your body is displaced,
or dismembered.

Or flesh is brocade. At a birth,
the face is bound to compel neoteny.

Mirror or lithography. What she puts in her mouth.
Conceptualizing reproduction. Or moonlight and frost,
which in walking, you find is a lake.

Lace gloves and aggregate collapse.

Seven versions of the face, all face in control.
To police the singing, abandon the way. Syphilitic
grin: ecstatics define vibration.

Define dissonant appetite: she takes off her hands
with her gloves; misplaces her tongue.

To exist only as print or light. Painting of light
where she puts her tongue in her mouth: speech
or sustenance.

Lace is frost. The tremors are kinetic: dissipation
of heat and orgasm; the heart is painted on the thigh,
lips painted on the mirror:

Amputation of name.

You are permitted to define that which is beautiful.

Phillip Foss

The fluent absences. All in the eyes.

There is a great vertical wind which attempts to elongate
and separate you from earth. Porcelain. A breast. Wheat.

Her asymmetrical body: gravity, moon. One black iris bleeding
horizontally into her hairline, cartography: lies.

Pursued by a storm, memory; indices replicating
each, twisting pore, follical, track of spittle
down the bereaved occasion of your smoke, hold

your fragmenting grace, slit, lick absence

in which you wash your face clean of semblance:

a porcelain breast as bowl, filled with milk: white

as absence of color. No, confers the non-iconic,
nacreous laughter.

Colonnade of painted spruce. Laceration of space,
or the value of weapons. Impaled. Feral intimacy:
cloven and seizure. *The painted snow.*

Red intimacy: *painted mist.*

Structure defined, behavior articulated: representation
to compel emotion: hairlip with tines, impassioned hair,
horse and violet sky; *in the painting,*
the painting.

Frozen swoon. Ceramics to portray disease. The balance
of white to black: nothingness in every corner.
The current cannot flow; revelers do not swallow.

In tiny strokes the ocean occurs on the eyes. *Painted*
hallucination: stars in the hair.

In the painting, she holds a paintbrush; licking
the hairs to define the eyelashes,

or a needle impaling alphabet into flesh.

(In the mirror, the lithograph depicts a man
reading his future from the entrails of a pig.)

Glass skirt. Voyeur exile. Blue silicate or obsidian.
That which is beneath That which is inside That which fills:
kaolin That which is or is idea.
Skirt glass: sustenance
to what eye? Mercantile dice? Mendicant poker?
A state
dependant on optics: voluptuous convexity, telescoping
impassioned.
The skirt is a perfume bottle? (Olfactory optics)
Optics of synesthesia Or your hand in . . .
Or your hand in
water. Or your hand in darkness. In snow.
But within
the glass skirt is a perfect vacuum? De-articulated
skeleton?

Sleeping in a goat mask to offend death:

Red lips suspended in a glass of ice:

Black hair as camouflage:

Cleansing blood from genitals with milk:

Gold ring through the lip:

The ceiling painted with nightmares:

Concealed in a block of air:

Seeing through flammable sustenance:

(In your—her—final disappearance
what then will saturate the space
so abandoned, orphaned of flesh—
the damascus, the brocade—other
than breath—kaoline—or desire?)

Emptiness is then empty of emptiness:
Costume.

Seven Poems
Bruce Andrews

Dear World, *fuck off* advice ingredients, empty swing. Studies show that couples who try to avoid arguments tend to average higher happiness scores. Sizes carried, class analysis, men's consciousness-raising, medieval robbers, no one seems to know how many. There are freshly dug graves, but children were buried together, driven to obscurity by the unconscious need to cover up the defects of the argument. 'I'm a knee fetishist,' sit up, arching the back a little, the transformation of a worker into a mere hand. Noises? Smells fresh but doesn't linger = semen disinfectant, 20 kilos of heroin; if I had lost the race, I could start over, but by winning I get to race again. Eat letters! Excavations, soft minimals, ELITIST INTENSITY—institutions no more than the barricades of repression clapping his twists. Great foster argument; crabbing which count mere heart shiver joints. Kick out stiff rubbed slow far fell crib. Was eagerly—presses. Violent Crimes by Young Girls on the Upswing Across U.S. without the oppressive shadows of our protective images intruding. Clocks spike pupil visa—goes to Africa on Vacation, Returns with Bride He Bought from Tribal Chief. It's like giving your whole body a facial.

Mavericks do not become great leaders. The organization is more the weighing of one part against another within a whole than the building of a whole through systematic succession. She is a child playing house inside her own enthusiasms, the kind of success that can only be measured in loss, a lot of useful scrutinizing, the insidious connection develops between economic dependency and sexuality. S, S, S & s & s, an intellectual: someone living articulately beyond her or his intellectual means. We have no other, a phrase that badly needs study. Nonsense bargains. I don't want an art of visual aids, this is the problem of an index. Events now followed with bewildering rapidity. What shit about loaves and fishes? Meet-me-tonight-cowshed. Vestiges of illusionism do not overpower but assume their place in a revealed activity—"the terms I like to see," . . . Faith-less Love, "defensive communication." Well grubbed, old mole! Taken as a whole, they are like quicksilver do's and don'ts—what is the status of 'always'? Ten trillion flies cannot be wrong: Eat shit. Like a searchlight that had found its target, man's auditory equipment is similarly elaborate. ('No beliefs to propel him, only imposed but arbitrary obligations.') The touchdowns are the triumphs of will.

With a tact, with a tact that renders them almost subliminal, the surgery constituted unreasonable search and seizure: refuses us admittance—a deft grace note. Papal nuncio. I gotta get a shower curtain before I die, even though the odd marriage creeps in among the corpses. Obelisk exposition; well, two aperçus. The Marines who landed in Lebanon in 1958 brought atomic howitzers. Can one weave & masturbate at the same time? No more white gloves. The President, himself, repolished these claims. To sense what he should do if he had time is not enough, it was made to take your sleep. It was an army whose bayonets could be trusted to think. As you can imagine, the rhythmic problems were considerable. No feelings at all was exactly right. We shall see why shortly. Now we have had Eisenhower, you punch them in the pocketbook. I don't know if I can say this in a way I can understand what I'm saying. That would be a scandal, but not a theoretical problem, of brilliantly backlit cigarette smoke: refer Mr. Hunt to Mr. Liddy. Did you ever have a blackout in Johannesburg? I mean lonely where you're afraid to mix with people. Maladroit throughout may excusably be thought. Everything remains unfinished business, they have the doing of whatever he wants done—they probably discuss me in bed, without harming the many things that made retreat worthwhile. My argument is not the physicality of vertical sex in a dark room—you used to need a prescription to get medicine this strong. Obfuscation lay on the air without psychological support. But most have been mobsters. Now, even the lacunae are eloquent—plausible verbal models are quite easy to formulate. Nanny goat vibrato. It was me that I heard it, talking at length and alone they shriek louder than the rest. The class struggle is obscured? —I do think you're letting your conscientiousness take advantage of you; drooled on my penis. Becky's studying the muscles & memorizing the bones not as if as though it were swerves—a sham move may modify or soften that. In Chapter 2 we cited France and Britain's joint threats against Peru in 1844. Contra underconsumption, contra mechanism, the buzzers are broken. Does violence beget violence?—the summer usually brings a high demand for blood. We ought to have more articulate rules: fry an egg on my lips, I feel drowsy. These voices seem to be grasping at strategic straws. I get drunk just licking your face. Someone calls up asks 'you watchin' American Bandstand?' Law as the fine print of class structure—the imperative implication in English is not very strong. Compensation is the key. This generalization is too weak. You smell like semen—surfaces are so nonporous in their high heels, with perhaps more assurance than the argument deserves. There are tweezers & then there are tweezers. The emotional technology of dog shows. Liberals for whom the Cold War overshadowed all else. I am always reading about moundbuilders. We are pulling the firemen off the ladder.

Let me try to explain this rather cryptic statement. Ahh—the discursive redemption of validity claims, achieved without pathology, and strengthened, snookering, picky, picky, picky. I have run ahead, desperate will. Why not radios? Reform efforts repeatedly stumble because they tend toward systemic change. The larger the print, the more believable it is—HE IS ALL ELSE BUT. Go to free. Angrier and angrier. . . . Do I read you right? Used hooks? See (and use!). This involves considerably more than waving the flag, just how close these ties are is revealed in one remarkable statistic—on that topic, however, I have already said something. The decay of the voice, as is fitting, by way of expiation, inhabits upward. But many men are born policemen. Right now I guess I believe in individuality more than anything else, political space is curved: there is a difference between seeing marks on a page and reading words. Silkily evokes it. I hate dealing with messages that may not have been intentionally transmitted delicacies of randomness. I'm glad you got into the material, implications in wording. Yankee Doodle Dandy—I'd like a cupcake. And yet there is little repetition, no lassitude, nothing predictable, legible sounds provide comely obligation, slackened, humid embouchure.

Looked like a flip visor, a 'technical mother lode,' one loser called it. Black bombazine—bloody assizes, a profound caesura. His chordal improvisations and arpeggiated flourishes were largely in the service of clichés. I like being smart. Thank you for the great mugs. Michael's into clad. Bring back the gerontic laxative denture crowd, the connotations of all the words we use are controlled by the ruling apparatus. The talk is going to cause most of the talk. Ominously much—under cover of awards, having failed to overthrow capitalist society. You gotta learn to take the shit with the toilet paper, all these leaks are interwoven with each other. I've taken enough odd shoving grinds out limp wrists to loosen the bands of confidence. Are you fuckin' up my beans, boy? But what a head of steam the thing build up! Aquinas would not disagree with this assertion—in Walter Bagehot's charming phrase, "no man can *argue* on his knees." A lay-up is a lapse of imagination. You should dress up a little bit just comb your hair look nice. And yet we never know who they are! I played stop-time to the piecework in the ghost factories—the klieg lights recruit us. To ask the question is to answer it: it is a seductive image, but a totally inadequate one. My father dying was a picnic compared to you. Two words which are never caught with their upper cases down . . . he had not mastered the public relations of failure. It's *not* ironic. You don't have to worry about where I am, I've been thinking about you. People learned to carry candles with them twelve years ago. Not just images evoked [invoked] in the mind's back, but a tangible filling of the real space between speaker and listener. How things develop, verbs too. Revolutions have never been made by bums. It looks nets, crepey around the neck and arms and another confusing one in the panties —there's no way to say everything, the fender had to fit the car: you look like a *crayon box*. Collectively they are known as 'The Illegal Alien Problem.' Why is a broken heart the only one thing whole in the world? It's not as if what wants spread thin—help, though, is synonymous with trouble. I thought the bird life was fascinating. The self-immolative scenario cannot be ruled out entirely, though it probably deserves a low-probability assessment for the medium term—I am not satisfied to feel that civil liberty is just a matter of prosecutorial discretion. The way a research question is posed dictates the data that are needed: you're literature, I'm a language. No doubt he did *as he wished.* Here Amin falls into ahistoricity and formalism again. In her later years she declines depressingly into glossolalia. Lenin still seems to be winning. Suggestive less of mastery than failure—the failure of attempts to gain an end by softer means. Whether bushwhackers were paleo-socialists or thieving bums, my reasons for asserting this can be put as follows: in prose a single word represents an entire complicated argument. Some tweezers don't rip very well. Everybody gets greasy & they laugh a lot. There might not be no afterwhile, I guess integration used to be in somewhere too. Elevator etiquette—people migrate or vegetate, there is a discomfort with sexual maturity: fix burners. The facts reek of reasonable doubt, we have a new system where everybody shares the violence. Patristic literature or parasitic literature, I am not interested in a slice of life. 'Defeat' is admittedly rather hard to objectify. Her recent rhetoric of lust succeeds admirably as such. In so far as this offers anything except evasive insinuation, it invites a quick answer: I'm one of those knowledgeable innocents, I am a private person—structure; are we robots? To the whip, the seeds; flower their language. I'll stick with my little hoops, an ocular promiscuity has prevailed. Who was it that called scabs, 'little blankets'? Androgynous catatonia is the answer to repulsive macho, earnest, respectable, unexciting. There is no furniture. What prompted?: all purpose. Only fools wait.

Half-willed absence. Neckband; cosmetology, it's o.k. To understand too much is to destroy: the containers are distorters inevitably. Women have not been enthusiastic over war. Every word forms occasions for a sentence—'beauty and misery are so unutterably manifold that there is no time for triviality'—stoves extinguish the imagination. I haven't had a dump in two days; I'm worried I'm dumped up. The automobile is an accessory of the tire; they never want you to over-muffin it. "You're sixteen. You're beautiful. And you're mine." Sentences veil paragraphs can be unending events going back, it's just that you can't go back. Sure does. Even so, the orgies should have been still more dramatically curtailed. Gruesome's in there with stencils one better. Not I. I want myself back to move the situation off dead center. If it lights, it passes, instilling in us a feeling of ennui, often bordering on pleasure. This rarely corresponds to reality, you can't do as much in a dress. It suits me fine if that's all down the drain. Today it was as hot as disease. How many paragraphs can sit inside a sentence? How many sentences can fit inside a word? This war will never end.

War: trading real estate for men. We are all put on this earth to suffer, what has become of Piper Laurie? The Nelsons portray themselves; Ozzie and Harriet used to *read* in the bedroom. Drums? Singing? The dates concede this fact. Religion replacing politics as the exciting recreation of the young white middle class; Woodstock *5 years ago* will be redone—at the Houston Astrodome. I was lying on the floor, bleeding like a stuck hog—they turn water blue in bath bowls— . . . I'm a little unsure of myself whenever I crawl out of my briefcase. What I'm selling is worth as much as the person who buys; he has to learn to run with the other horses. "You see, we could have prevented a lot of confusion about this thing called jazz if Fletcher Henderson had listened to me in the 1920s. I told him, 'Let's just call it Black music. Then it'll be clear where we are and where they are" (Duke Ellington). Just lucky I guess—only the West was fully carnivorous; he'll charm the gold right out of your back teeth. The corporation will continue, nonsensical, but with inflections. I got as far as the altar.

Eggplants and Lotus Root
Forrest Gander

TEA SCRIPTURE

1.

or her hair. Its rain. Her face juts out from. Winter rooms of electricity, her hair lifts. The rug coarse as hog stubble. Musk her hair. Held down by the neck. Or in. At once recognizable by intimate: near-burning smell. White mole to the right of her cocyx, those hairs. Inside of her ears is sweating. A sense of duration spilt across the pillow. Vague and specific like. An analogy, undislodgeable. Pubic hair under tongue. *Words spoken into*

2.

Dead of winter barechested in the Green Forest bar. Each wears a cap, roughly half "backwards." Frog-eyed son of a bitch. Claimed his hound was Death. On snakes. Want to put it in their pocket and walk around with it. Floor's tongue and groove. Tiny hexes of dirt from their Redwings. At the window, among neon letters, with no arms, stands the reverend. Admonition's gargoyle. Glass fogs out his face. Hours pass. Then. Who bursts in holding one shoe. One foot in a paper bag.

*Because men love them, eulogies are an ideal introduction to the world of reading.

3.

When the schoolbus, lights
flashing, confronts the howling ambulance-
which pauses?

Forrest Gander

"There is a ruttish
perfume, proposition
inexpressible
in a human language,"
begins Death's phosphorous
voice, a little
in drag.

Marbled evening sky over.

Rutilant.

MONITORY

1.

full suddenly. "Still through the hawthorne blows the cold wind." What I wanted to say was her hair. At the dressing stand or lies she made. Mouths in a glass. With her hair let down. Among the cattails redwings. That I could feel how sharper than the cold wind was. Undone like an illumination. The mornings it happened. Echo. Simultaneously. Disturb the black mud of the ferruginous mud of the. Poem. Such as torture, a simple fact. Having nothing to do with. *Departure, its logorhythms of description*

2.

The upper gate rail's sticky green surface—momentarily gripped—was nearly invisible under a dense layer of dead and dying insects caught to the paint, like a pale arm taken over by black moles. This he vaulted this. Approaching the mansion, couldn't stop imagining how she'd look pregnant, his brain an acre of hissing grass. A cold summer's 2 a.m. The ocean's slant eye closing and closing in sand. Someone forgot to turn off the lawn sprinkler. The wind shifted, wet him. Froth on her nipples, from deep sleep sits up sits up and stares, the monophthong of the jimmied back door captured by, lost to receding dream. The man he was the man who the man who. Invoking room set apart by red ribbon.

*He'd come from the bar in a blue Corolla.

3.

It is often possible
to take up a point of view—
crude palimpsest of memory and sensation—
other than one's own
as a dog might piss on a horse's leg.

Caught by her longish
hair she flew around the room
attached to the huge pulley belt.

And is passed away
into the adjoining fringe
and selvage of this fragment.
But the clarity
of the word "is"
is a deception.
How many times

have you descended?
Which the largest bale
you will metabolize.

A MACULA OF LIGHT

1.

never so much as. An oblique angle. Primitive oath, blood horizon. Her light cholera and one hundred more questions. The dreamt achievement of scorpions at audience. In the furrow weeds. Then double combs her hair. Pallbearer's vintage. When the bird begins alone the light. Its steady fillip into drain. Similarly but later, directed against telephone pole, its pizzle's hard pulse. Absence propped in her chair to preach. Critical orchestra. Low man among stinging arachnids grips the spade. *Dawn's on him*

2.

Didn't he have a loincloth over his gentiles. And Goody's Headache Powder. Objects in mirror are closer than they appear. Disconnected last thoughts. Between the white center lanes a large red stain. Ascension Parish. In the shaggy tree lodges one hubcap. The radio song finished. Without the driver. I attend Gloryland Baptist Church bumpersticker. Visible. On the bumper. Impaled on the bridge rail. Remember, someone had joked, rubber side down. In humid air the wheels each freely spinning. Who's going to tell?

*The soft spot in the floor wakes him.

3.

A dog manages to catch its own tail. At first the traveler laughs, but then shouts and weeps. No news will ever be obtained regarding that about to be lost.

Rain for forty days. Surrounded by mountains. When it brims, the water has raised him to the peak.

The responses to death are sometimes funny. A man opens his wrist without drawing blood; a woman opens a book with nothing inside.

CLOSE TO WATER

1.

some form retains. Hair at nipple. I of. Sperm. She wipes her cleavage. How would you sit full of news on my lap, facing. Guillotines raised over dark eyes. Crossed a bare common. We, surrounded by neglect. Or drunk, the bridgelights, watery, bridgelights sputtering in the river's mouth. Curious syntaxes as intimate. Menstrual flow, the moon from Guanajuato, the pock-faced dead clutching their genitals, gaping. *To mean anything*

2.

"But don't they leak," he asked the Harley dealer. "They don't leak they leave their mark." Chirping so loudly. He woke. Continued when he mentioned this. The phone rang reminding him of the call he had forgotten to make. Which now could not be made for the line was busy. Etc. Flowing from eyes nose mouth tears. Night birds' dialog: one note bent up like an eyelash and the other double combing her ferruginous hair, tsk tsk tsk tsk. Sudden desire to see a woman's pubic triangle where there was no such desire a moment before.

*Imagine being regular for the rest of your life.

3.

Strange
that we come
to worship

silence as an aesthetic
activity, a gift,
that we draw it

to the heart of our spiritual zone
let silence ripen
there with its absences
of gesture in the ungulate night,
silence's anniversary, of our penetration.

MOON IN THE AFTERNOON

1.

harshed her. Lied she was thick skinned as a gator. One of which was. Too longish for the painter's. Nor- and also sibilantly curved- a brush bristle. Imbedded suchwise in the wall under a smoothed surface. Like anaconda beneath thinly crusted water. Otherwise a merely enacted principle. She left several hairs. Their curved flanks quivering, their necks like beaches, an unbearable pungence speaking. *But equally nonindicative of any direction shy of loss*

2.

People who did things with their lives. To his eyes they brought tears. Cardinal in bamboo. His arms thrown out then sneezes. Morning, more sneezes, their sticky taste. Answers to ding dong. Seeing the horrible rubber mask touches his heart. Reads aloud every visible sign from hearse window. The whole trip. As though illuminations. How the tea grew bitter. Hank Williams you wrote my life. Lump in his pants at her funeral. To armless preacher is the coffee served. The gate itself a hell. Barking for Bank Patrons Only. In the summer of Elvis sightings. No shoulder. A head.

*The rims of the open graves began to steam.

3.

Out from the ordeal
came silence.
Substituted for intention,
thunderstruck by a tongue.
Otherworldly relief

abolishes sthenic sobbing,
rhythmic heaves, wind-whipped
funeral banners. All the less

strange since it is death
who constructs silence
who climbs into silence
by her longish hair.

CODA

and the birds: canthi loosed at a distance. Aquamarine backdrop, scratched out several. All symbols buried in the sand. Nor a cardinal's color nor point, so only smooth and hush come clear. Unfocused and as if winked upon. Where the wind, dehiscing sand, does not omit. In a synoptic way, surrounded: already the eye whose perceptible tearing: "how the rain swung from the rims of." Even if it is possible to remain noncommittal about an endpoint. Winter, thumbprint of black birds smudged across windshield, in a premature language. An ocean

Three Poems
George Evans

HORSE ON A FENCE

We might have died by now
could be among the dead
where the numbers are greater

but for courage   course
or luck,

meeting like roads
only to divide like roads,
or regenerate,

wild,
performing the act
out loud, in the open

forgetting what
made us want to kill
made us kill
ever

believing ourselves invisible

though passion makes us
visible
even
strangely out of place
the way the present always is,
our hold on it four hooves of a horse
stopped mid-flight in a leap

standing now on a fence
between two worlds

George Evans

WHAT I MEANT WAS THIS

The moon crushed everything
ruined the whole deal

but one wants people who speak with both a desire to be heard

and fear they will be

making it worth all

the light which surrounds us

in its many forms   and histories

POPPIES TWISTED TO PEAKS BY EVENING LIGHT

A mourning dove coos, placid and sawing
the great wall of trees squeaking

suddenly up

the hawk hovered over
unsure of a head

snapping thistles
and yarrow
in the field
below

on the slope mission
blue butterflies bounce among lupin, paint chips,

there is no control,
there is only control.

Flits in lupin,
dies in lupin.

From Herself Com Passionate
Theodore Enslin

That she who is my love is all of it
resists my naming her.

My girl's a weave of many things   I
do not know the names of all the threads
or lap or warp which make for colors
several in delight yet supple.
It is cloth that will not fade
the dye was fated not to bleach
or soak away. Her heat has burned it in
and if I look to see more there than
what she shows me   I will find
a pleasure in each shadow
taking form for what is not
informed suggestion   is so woven.

HOW SHE SURVIVES ME

Not close not usual
not anything I know
of heightened sense
her sleeping such
that color shows her
parted lips return
to quiet
stillest air
of night   and this is
morning   one ray
touching alien

to stray beyond her.
I must rise and
go away.

The center wavers
so I think   it does not
love's a burden   how it
wavers   no I step aside
and see no loved one
many objects   love's a pest
it lights and stings   a
temporary insect   yet my
girl   the proper one
remains   a flame at times
and I'm the moth
so close I'm singed.
She'll laugh   well
let her   some of it
will soothe the very wound
she made. The center's whole.

ON SPELLING LOVE

I hesitate to tell
this girl or any other that I love
love's spell   for if I do
she does return to me
a void   then love's a double
and a dupe   a love not meant
the same thing   and a word
divides us   as the simple lust
in cleaving   thrust received
does not   I will not say I do
yet do   and if she does
the spent both strayed and spelled.

She will not know me.
Many times she'll think
she does   nor I know her.
The flares of anger
stray around our bed   each sigh
may carry us a cutting edge.
We will not know until
the word has bled us
faint. Still there is source   all
source renews the chance
is always equal   so
for now let's take it.

Maid's eye   as flower
yet the flower will not open.
She who holds it asks me
wait a bit   the curve of thorn
she asks for   wait and
skirt the petal   flower
yet the flower will not open
if it does no maid remains.

Which one shall say
I love   am loved?
And if she will
how will I know her
if she looks at me?
Of all the moments
periods   this loving
is the hardest part
to us. It does appear
as fact at times   but
timing is its element.
It is not often

we are able to
immerse ourselves and find it.

Whenever blossoms blossoms fade
wherever heat the heat turns cold
as love is embers dampened out
unless another season's fuel
brought to bear is ash.
But to insist is force in winter.
She will not want that
nor I a fumbler in the freezing.

Of many questions never
answered I return
to give the questions up and
she may take them
if she will or laugh
that I am bothered
by them. Love if anything
is practical.
Her wildest ecstasy is
common sense.

To herself she will not
admit what she
admits to me if I
see in her delight
a mirror of my own
I must turn away from it.
I gave her nothing
but my pleasure yet
it might have been
a mingling that her heat and
waters flowed in mine.

Whatever we have shared
has been a single choice.
I do not know the sense
she brings to what we
both have seen   and if
in desperate attempt
to stay together   either
says we think alike
I know it is a fiction.
We do not   and
something not our own
has made the bind
a commonness   but
one we do not share.

She will   and yet she won't
to talk would be the best
of it   no   and yet she
has. I've heard her
falling in and following
the water sounding
what's up is down is
will and won't. I
catch her legs and hold
them   the distance here
is not in walking
will I? yet I won't.

AS AN ARGUMENT

Whatever voice we used
what   ever longing in
despite of what was voiced
it was in tone   an accent
how could we receive

what voice was used we
spaced it what we
longing used in spite.
She never asked
I never answered.

How cloudless her eyes
have been I've seen deep
through them far enough
to know that what I've seen
is not a film the distance
colored only by its
distance yet she laughs.
Her eyes are laughter.
What she hides is clear enough
yet something mocking me.
Say on she says I'll listen
yet you will not hear my answer.

AN ETERNAL EXODUS

Each time this girl and I
come into a new place
a land or time of life
it is a different
yet the same place.
Everything is memory
yet it is new to try
to move in comfort
and to open locks
which have made of us
familiars to ourselves.
We had wished it
other simpler yet
we are still ourselves.

Her seasons
and her colors
change
          they
are the mark
of her cover
as the varying hare.
It   is similar
and will she cower
knowing the bitter
cast
      to seasons
all my own?

So often I have thought to turn away from her
and yet I won't
to find another   yet there would be same
a face   a voice   its timbre
yet the same
I won't.
What is familiar is not sameness   nor
a place to settle   merely that
I love her   merely that I chose
and still do choose to fight it out
our faults are various.
Difference will survive us
that we fit   so often joined.
We'd not do well to
try again
          (however
what she wills.

That fine wiring
tense with jewels
strung along its

noble metals   gold and
silver   that we burn
to touch   our longing
reaches one another
one   the day for all
its shining   is outside.
Our bed is here.

How many pressures
brought to bear   we feel
the short delights
together   nor will we know them
longer   what they are
they were   a gentle
stirring   sound of what's
beside us   time to turn
from this one thing
to many others   look across
her eyes or mine   forget
to touch what other
senses did and will
the lasting pleasures   so and
as we were.

Five Nails
Charles Stein

1 : AIR

It is quiet on the beaches.

There is no one around. And the sounds
of the breeze and the waves
are as no sound now. No one to hear them.

But soon a person comes to enjoy the silence.
And then the sounds begin.

Someone is sitting there
absorbed in the sound
of the surf as that sound rolls
wild across the dunes.

And soon the wind begins to blow from over the water.

First it disturbs the gulls that stand on the wharfs.
Then the wharfs themselves begin to become
disturbed from the strength the wind is developing.
Little by little

the wind makes a larger
sound and increases the menace. The garments of the person
seated on the strand
flutter in the gathering wind.

Now all is a tumult of sand and sound, water and air
aswirl in an enormous turbulence. The person
remains
as long as that is possible. But soon this person too
flies up on the wind.

It blows his hair away.
It blows the skin from his body.
Soon the bones and flesh are strewn among
particles of sand and mist the wind sends. Soon his bones
are blown to powder
and bones and sand
swirl in the wind.

Only the sound
remains.

2 : FIRE

Dweller in cabins on the outskirts, lush. Luscious
jungle growths enclose.

And on the outskirts of the outskirts, little fires
start up.

The marshals are not concerned. They continue smoking
at their posts.

And now the little houses start to burn. The paper walls
go up on sensate flashes. Quietly
the persons depart and only I myself
am seated
unconcerned.

I am seated on my mat and the sounds of far off fires
begin to reach me. I am not alarmed.

I can hear the susuration, the sizzle, the wings
of birds, the crackling of exotic bark.

I am at ease, at leisure.
There is time as large as the wings of birds
beating above the encampment.
The fires now ring the encampment.
The sounds and cries and rushing
of groups of mammals reach my ears.
I am unconcerned. I listen

as the roar of conflagration closes round me.

The flames reach far beyond the tallest trees now.

The flames
commute
with the sky. Their momentary turrets pierce the cumuli.
The heat of it rises in huge ballooning canopies.

Waves of it fan across the porches where I linger. Soon the
walls will be aflame. Now the walls
are all aflame.

The searing heat consumes my cubicle. It cannot be endured.
My clothes begin to blaze and the flames
needle me everywhere. I am unconcerned.
Enormous sensations penetrate and consume me.
My belly my hair my skin take flame.
My singed flesh blackens
and bubbles up like crust.

Flames from the end of the Aion flash about
till flames consume themselves in a single nature.

Then :

Two red signs
shine in the void.

3 : WATER

All of us, sitting in a park, in rows and rows
and rows of rows and rows. Filling it everywhere.

As far as one can see
rows of beings sit on quiet couches
smiling, aware, awake; cognizant of all the other beings
sitting in rows, resting on couches.

The air is clear, the breeze
vivifying, wafting pleasant vernal smells,

pungent temple smells, or no smells,
just as each requires, sitting as each pleases.

To each as to each is pleasing. The sky
is quiet, shining.
Each is still.
Blissful feelings pass in constant waves across the fold,
rising simultaneously everywhere,
passing from each to the next and quietly subsiding.

. . .

Across the vast expanse
a perfect cloud appears—
to each of us it seems to form itself
a distant point above the far horizon—
to each an interesting speck, a salutary blemish, increasing
the perfection of the sky

growing slightly, slowly, showing a perfect shape,
ovoid, ivory white
with delicate puffs and ruffles,
buff, or flush with vermilion, edged in gold.

To each the colors to the pleasure of each.
To each increasing in volume and variety
as each commits attention to its forming.
A gorgeous object poised in the center of the sky,
compelling the sky, controlling the vista for all
and each. The luminous shining dome of perfect turquoise
fringes the clouds. And columns of skylight fan about it.

. . .

And now in the edge of the cloud a speck or blotch of grey
cloud first appears. It appears as if a doubt
in the eye of one of us, a mote in one of the eyes,
sent to test a doubt.

And soon another of us marks the blemish—
some being off somewhere,

far across the park in another row
assumes the doubt
and knows the speck.

And another blot appears in the luminous cloud face.
And spotted across the field of rows and rows
doubting blots appear across the clouds—
clouds and specks and blots—

to each according to the doubts of each.

The air is clear.
The beings sit in rows.

. . .

Now rain falls from the cloud.
Rain falls from the clouds.
The grass is moist.
We sit in rows.
Mist moves in from the sky.
The park is drenched from the downpour.
Little rivulets rush from the park pavilion
meandering rapidly between the sitting rows.

The rain seems more than rain.
Waterfalls crash from pavilions.
Across the shining sky the sea appears.
Enormous, white-crested billows approach from afar.
We sit in rows.
The water rushes at us
loosening the trees
dissolving the knots in the mortar of pavilions.
The roofs come crashing down.
The people sit in their garments, soaked in the over-flush.
The trees of the park, uprooted, roll about,
the bark dissolves,
our clothes dissolve.

Now naked rows of persons sit in the flood.
The water lifts up one of us out of the row we have.

And now another—lifted, tossed, deposited
into a maw of waters.

Soon across the fold
waves of water break the seated rows.
Persons tossed in the billows—
the mind of each intent upon the water.
The thoughts of each arush in growing waters.
Soon the limbs of one of us, softened in the deluge,
fall into the deluge.
Soon the thoughts of one of us floods the world.
A deluge of rushing memory and intellect
commingling with water-sotted digits, limbs and torsos.

The thought of water rushing
fills the scene of water rushing—
vermilion billows roll across the minds—
billowing intellects (flecked with gold and black)
flash across the flood—

water into water passing—
flux into flux resolved—
chaos swallowed up in its nature—
doubt swallowed up in doubt—

Three thoughts:
three white signata
sign the Void.

4 : SPACE

There really is no
space. The blue
room
resumes the mind.

All of them are gone now.
All of the other creatures—people or whatever.

All of you are gone now

All of me are gone now

into the open space
the mind itself
resumes—

The things of sense relax in their true condition.

The houses relax—the walls
remaining walls
give a little—

The furniture responds to the weight of people or things—
the joints relax—
the brittle glue grows moist again

The things of mind relax—all one
blue gust of oxygen,one bottomless
sky. The platforms floating down it—

And on each platform, each of us, sitting absorbedly—

The body of each of us

Blue—absorbed in its nature . . .

. . .

Blue the Dark

and Blue the Work . . .

5 : EARTH

The earth is still.

You are sitting there

on your little wooden bench
knitting your shoes.

Or using a delicate hammering instrument
to curve the copper object cupped in your hands.

Or talking to friends in the summer afternoon
sitting on long benches
around a wooden table.

A house with a porch and a lawn
upon a street
with other well-kept houses—lawns and porches.

You hear a sound on the air, dark and rumbly.
Distant thunder, one of the friends proposes.

You sniff the air for the odor of thunder
but there is no odor.

You watch the upper branches of the maples.
A little breeze. No sense of impending motion.

You sit on the ground.

Or stand.

Or adopt a definitely hunched posture, leaning over the
table.

A few old stones lie about the feet of a few old trees.

Some rumbling once again, far to the north
a bit like a herd of mammals from afar.

The sound is a sound approaching—
subtly ominous.
Each wave of approaching rumbling
rumbles closer still.

The intervals of time between the sounds

Charles Stein

grow shorter now

and louder sounds overwhelm the softer ones
and larger sounds
supersede the small.

You all are sitting now or standing, no one hunched now.

No one talking or attending the little tasks
upon which each had been, but a few moment earlier,
occupied so intently.

You notice the many little sounds within the larger sounds;
crackling sounds and whistling ones; the noise
of a huge thing, striking the ground with a thud;
the metal parts of intricate machinery
toppling to the floor with a cascade of crackling sounds.

Things are shaking now.
The objects and the table rattle and buzz.
The hammer falls to the ground.
The leaves of the maples are all ablur.
The stones roll over other stones
and set off on a course—then leave that course.

You sit alone. Holding your bench.
The others sit alone.
Or stand.
Holding the beams of the cottage porches for ballast.

Things are moving in the air now—
shingles from the slanted rooftops fall from the rooftops
and start upon random courses through the trees.

The shaking of things increases.
The clothes upon your body vibrate oddly.
The seat upon the ground begins to exert
terrible pressure against you. You stand.
Or sit on the ground.

The ground is moving now.

The sounds of falling things ring all about.
An enormous tumult encloses on all sides.
All the buildings are falling down
rising in the air and crashing to the earth.
The earth itself rises up
thrusting boulders into the air.
You can see people everywhere
attempting to assume control of their motion
popping off the earth, falling, scampering,
being thrown across their porches onto the lawns.

The things in flight begin to vibrate uncontrollably.
The outer surfaces are first to fall away.
Then the inward machines disintegrate and scatter.

Shirts are torn from bodies, bodies from themselves.

The sky is a welter of human parts and thing parts
streaming in a vast display.

You yourself are among them.
The thoughts you have
begin to come asunder.

You see your thoughts rattling in the foreground
rapidly becoming other thoughts.
Your memories shake and vibrate—they fly out of you
as you yourself are strewn
across the vast expanse.

You see the thoughts of all things come apart
from each—each person thought and thing
an item in a centerless turbulence without gravitation.

. . . .

All things grow smaller now.

Everything that can be shaken loose
has been shaken loose.

Charles Stein

The parts are as small as they can become.

An infinite dust rains across the void.

The motionless void consumes the dust.

Four black signs remain

at the front of the world.

Mise en Scène

Peter Gizzi

Not knowing the name for something proves nothing.
—James Schuyler

The shortest distance between
two points is around the world,
and commerce is a word we can
appropriate to use *here*, but more
than this it is our achievement
of evening silence. A billowing
scarf draped upon the door latch
in fragrant air. Vulnerable is
another word to attach to this
opening, a vivisection I fill
with eyelash teeth. Although
there was no piano to state the theme
there is music in our night space.
Breath making skin upon ribs taut.
That the formal alphabet of silence
(with or without a future) reveals
a language of the spine and sphinx
of wrists and ankles. Hair blue
black in china braids embellishes
this setting. In the book of my
archaeology your rib cage means
everything, because for years
absence has been my collarbone,
and I a sorry border guard of this
sad state. An invisible X marks
the spot where you touch me,
right here, between wanting
and understanding between revelation
and the secret. This intersection
at the extremes of our walk.

Covers

Rae Armantrout

The man
slapped her bottom
like a man did
in a video,

then he waited
as if for shadow
to completely cover the sun.

Moments later
archeologists found him.

The idea that they were reenacting something which had been staged in the first place bothered her. If she wanted to go on, she'd need to ignore this limp chronology. She assumed he was conscious of the same constraint. But she almost always did want to proceed. Procedure! If only either one of them believed in the spontaneity of the original actors and could identify with one. Be one. For this to work, she reasoned, one of us would have to be gone.

"Well, look who missed
the fleeting moment,"

Green Giant gloats
over dazed children.

If to transpose
is to know,

we can cover our losses.

But only
If talking,

Formerly food,

Now meant
Not now

So recovery
Ran rings.

If to traverse
is to envelop,

I am held
and sung to sleep.

The Attraction of the Ground

Rosmarie Waldrop

In the beginning there were torrential rains, and the world dissolved in puddles, even though we were well into the nuclear age and speedier methods. Constant precipitation drenched the dry point of the present till it leaked a wash of color all the way up to the roots of our hair. I wanted to see mysteries at the bottom of the puddles, but they turned out to be reflections that made our heads swim. The way a statue's eyes bring our stock of blindness to the surface. Every thought swelled to the softness of flesh after a long bath, the lack of definition essential for happiness, just as not knowing yourself guarantees a life of long lukewarm days stretching beyond the shadow of pure reason on the sidewalk. All this was common practice. Downpour of sun. Flood of young leafiness. A slight unease caused by sheer fill of body. Running over and over like the light spilled westward across the continent, a river we couldn't cross without our moment, barely born, drowning in its own translucent metaphor.

The silence, which matted my hair like a room with the windows shut too long, filled with your breath. As if you didn't need the weight of words in your lungs to keep your body from dispersing like so many molecules over an empty field. Being a woman and without history, I wanted to explore how the grain of the world runs, hoping for backward and forward, the way sentences breathe even this side of explanation. But you claimed that words absorb all perspective and blot out the view just as certain parts of the body obscure others on the curve of desire. Or again, as the message gets lost in the long run, while we still see the messenger panting, unflagging, through the centuries. I had thought it went the other way round and was surprised as he came out of my mouth in his toga, without even a raincoat. I had to lean far out the window to follow his now unencumbered course, speeding your theory toward a horizon flat and true as a spirit level.

My legs were so interlaced with yours I began to think I could never use them on my own again. Not even if I shaved them. As if emotion had always to be a handicap. But maybe the knots were a picture of my faint unrest at having everything and not more, like wind caught in the trees with no open space to get lost, a tension toward song hanging in the air like an unfinished bird-cry, or the smell of the word verbena, or apples that would not succumb to the attraction of the ground. In a neutral grammar love may be a refrain screamed through the loudspeakers, a calibration of parallels or bone structure strong enough to support verisimilitude. A FOR SALE sign in red urged us to participate in our society, while a whole flock of gulls stood in the mud by the river, ready to extend the sky with their wings. Another picture. Is it called love or nerves, you said, when everything is on the verge of happening? But I was unable to distinguish between waves and corpuscles because I had rings under my eyes, and appearances are fragile. Though we already live partly underground it must be possible to find a light that is exacting and yet allows us to be ourselves even while taking our measure.

Although you are thin you always seemed to be in front of my eyes, putting back in the body the roads my thoughts might have taken. As if forward and backward meant no more than right and left, and the earth could just as easily reverse its spin. So that we made each other the present of a stage where time would not pass, and only space would age, encompassing all 200000 dramatic situations, but over the rest of the proceedings, the increase of entropy and unemployment. Meanwhile we juggled details of our feelings into an exaggeration which took the place of explanation, and consequences remained in the kind of repose that, like a dancer's, already holds the leap toward inside turning out.

Your arms were embracing like a climate that does not require being native. They held me responsive, but I still wondered about the other lives I might have lived, the unused cast of characters stored within me, outcasts of actuality no stranger than my previous selves. As if a word should be counted a lie for all it misses. I could imagine my body arching up toward other men in a high-strung vertigo that scored a virtual accompaniment to our real dance, deep phantom chords echoing from nowhere though with the force of long acceleration, of flying home from a lost wedding. Stakes and mistakes. Big with sky, with bracing cold, with the drone of aircraft, the measures of distance hang in the air before falling in thick drops. The child will be pale and thin. Though it had infiltrated my bones, the thought was without marrow. More a feeling that might accompany a thought, a ply of consonants, an outward motion of the eye.

I began to long for respite from attention, the freedom of interruption. The clouds of feeling inside my head, though full of soft light, needed a breeze or the pull of gravity. More rain. As if I suddenly couldn't speak without first licking my lips, spelling my name, enumerating the days of the week. Would separation act as an astringent? Ink our characters more sharply? I tried to push the idea aside, afraid of losing the dimensions of nakedness, but it kept turning up underfoot, tripping me. Clearly, the journey would mean growing older, flat tiredness, desire out of tune. Much practice is needed for two-dimensional representation whether in drawing or rooms, and it emaciates our undertakings in the way that lack of sleep narrows thinking to a point without echoes, the neck of the hour glass. You may be able to travel fast forward without looking back, but I paint my lashes to slow the child in my face and climb the winding stairs back to a logic whose gaps are filled by mermaids.

Many questions were left in the clearing we built our shared life in. Later sheer size left no room for imagining myself standing outside it, on the edge of an empty day. I knew I didn't want to part from this whole which could be said to carry its foundation as much as resting on it, just as a family tree grows downward, its branches confounding gravitation and gravidity. I wanted to continue lying alongside you, two parallel, comparable lengths of feeling, and let the stresses of the structure push our sleep to momentum and fullness. Still, a fallow evening stretches into unknown elsewheres, seductive with possibility, doors open onto a chaos of culs-de-sac, of could-be, of galloping off on the horse in the picture. And where to? A crowning mirage or a question like What is love? And where? Does it enter with a squeeze, or without, bringing, like interpretation, its own space from some other dimension? Or is it like a dream corridor forever extending its concept toward extreme emptiness, like that of atoms?

One to Bet: A Jerusalem Pamphlet

Peter Cole

"to lift up valid signs"
—David Jones

I.

TILTING A LITTLE to the right and into an echo of the childhood shift that marks, somatic counselors tell me, the source of my displacement, I came after work one noon across a heap of grayish junk wood on Rashba Street, down the block from my apartment. A rusty-nailed structure of some sort had been dismantled, a makeshift fence or workers' shack, and fragments were scattered about on the sidewalk. In particular, three short, inch-thick boards held together in the shape of the Hebrew letter *bet* caught my attention. Beside them lay a figure which looked like the numeral 1.

I brought the two drift-pieces up to my rooftop porch and set them out to weather among the flowerpots and herbs there. Gradually a poem began to precipitate around the two foot-and-a-half-high finds: awkward stick-like figures that seemed to be uplifted and stumbling at once—figures whose shapes in space evoked irreconcilable presents and gave rise to emotional alloys whose names they were struggling to sound.

A wince: a wince in which: a winch.

ABET

Wanting to say 'first of all' the book of the law begins with *bet*, the sign for two. Traditionally the rabbis understood two worlds—this mirrored, ghosted corridor-world, and the less echoing one to come.

Redemption, the loop of currency through which we repossess what's been sold out from under us, begins with a descent into the most elementary combinations of materials. The heady beginning recast: "Between the ears and the eyes Towardgod created the alphabet of heaven and the alphabet of earth. And the earth was a gaping. And he was in it."

Like the Genesis sword blocking the entrance to Eden, redemption reads every which way: a propeller.

BOATS

Only two hundred or so yards long, narrow Alfassi Street winds inconspicuously through the sleepy Jerusalem neighborhood of Rehavia. Conducive to ambling, the street, like the sound of its name, was something of a refuge for me from all things linear—shaded on both sides with lush geranium gardens, an occasional pepper tree, several soaring palms, a small dirt playground, two grocery stores, and leaf-hidden limestone homes, the best of which exemplify the Jerusalem Bauhaus, sitting smartly but without ostentation in the domesticated Judaen landscape, much like the grammar of many a German immigrant in the contemporary Hebrew vernacular.

Three quarters of the way down the street, walking west to east away from the olive-studded Valley of the Cross and toward the center of town, the Alfassi Cave, a Hasmonean family burial site also known as Jason's Tomb, withdraws into the coolness. Hewn out of a gentle rock slope, and capped with the standard pyramidal structure, the cage is surrounded by a small grassy park almost no one ever enters. The front gate is always locked, the back gate is difficult to find. Of note inside are several drawings of ships, there in the mountains, overlooking a desert, some twenty-five hundred feet above sea level and forty miles from the coast.

Peter Cole

AURICULAR

The ear is orchid to the *aleph*; *aleph* is its scent.

AARON'S ROD

Beer Sheba Street was Chagall-like with its patchwork of roofs, steps, and laundry full sail in the fall billow of Nahlaot, an outcrop of a neighborhood where the city dips westward into the Valley of the Cross and northerly down to the market and toward the central bus station. I had a room that opened onto a small triangular courtyard. Beyond the kitchenette's greenhouse windows, and framed by the neighboring roofs, an equally triangular patch of deep blue sky opened out; jutting up into it were three young pomegranate shoots, a rose bush, and two almond trees. The latter flowered just as the most painfully tenuous layer of green fuzz had begun to grow back across the fields and vacant lots and nearby desert—blossoms like panties, I kept thinking, or a knot in the blueness untying itself.

One Sunday, after a weekend away, I returned to find the entire little park gone. The trees and bushes had been sawed down to painful-looking nubs; broken glass and tin cans were conspicuous in the soil. "What happened?" I asked the old lady next door. Her eyes were set deep into her face, and her raspy voice seemed always to require two gesturing arms in order to make itself clear. "My sons took it out," she said, in a curious use of the singular. "But there were almonds and pomegranates." "Mah," she said, "it's just greenery. It attracts children."

ARABESQUE

Irreferant. The burden of the easily overlooked *aleph*, unsounded and ummarked: the bass.

BURNING BRIDGES

Bets not hedged. The far side of the reader.

BOUSTROPHEDON

These pages, written from left to right and conceived from right to left. English duration in this model runs to the right, along a line, into the future of the Hebrew origin: into the arms of the open letter *bet.*

The ground-slug and smear of existence.

ADVANCE

In the *fin de siècle* suck of unknowing, our panic politics and horror vacuii culture are stripped in the negative art of the conceptual, which sets itself up between us in our borrowing and our increasingly pathetic idea of an original.

Peter Cole

BLACK AND BLUE

Legend has it that the Ineffable Name, the Tetragrammaton, was engraved at the center of the Temple on a stone whose power checked the Blue waters of Heaven above and the Black waters of Abyss below—in a scheme whereby the name which is not not a name protects us in the slippery exponent of its significance.

According to Tacitus, "most authors agree" that the Jews dedicated the golden bust of an ass in the Holy of Holies at Jerusalem. When the conquering Gnaeus Pompey entered the forbidden precinct, however, "the place was empty and the secret shrine contained nothing."

AURAS AGAIN

Summoned by a medium who works exclusively through answering machines, Walter Benjamin is asked to update his notion of aura. He praises the camerawork of two young Israeli artists, "the particularly clever and brilliant" Diaspora returnees Clegg and Guttman, then takes his morphine-leave once again.

Skidding toward the lip of Millennium, in our hocklife.

AS THOUGH THE EXISTENCE

The unrest of Hierosalem is incurable. Its poesis of apartness—of **dedication** or **holiness**, from the verb *le-kadesh*, to set apart—breaks into the radical forever of the distance that Emmanuel Levinas has in mind when he writes:

> Objectification is produced in the very work of language, where the subject is detached from the things possessed as though it hovered over its own existence, as though it were detached from it, as though the existence it exists had not yet reached it. This distance is more radical than every distance in the world.

Peter Cole

ABARBANEL

Abarbanel Street (named for the financial adviser to Ferdinand and Isabella of Spain) is sister to Alfassi, equidistant from the carob-canopied central Rehavian artery of Ramban. Gershom Scholem, the German kabbala scholar of revealment and concealment, lived there, on slithery Abarbanel.

> "That's the last time you'll see me"
> Scholem at eighty-three said and kissed her
> on the mouth in baggy pants circled
> her fishnet blouse eyes lowered the table
> promised her would come when it should
> when she got there, The Land, midnight
> banging his books dust clouds above Abarbanel . . .

Mauve leadwort, metal mailbox nameplates, a marble bench, late-night clicking fruitbats, the street confused with *aleph*s and *bet*s.

ANTIDOTE

Leviticus is really a Guide to Temple Choreographers. Unlike the padded double lore with which *Genesis* begins, *Leviticus* opens with a summoning from the Name. But its technicality serves as antidote to our spiritualizing tendencies, as alloy to the useless precious mettle. Students traditionally begin with it, in the sink-or-swim method of religious instruction: the Book of the Rites of Salvation, or, as clerical suffocator, spirit repellent.

BOILED POTATOES

Snuff, boiled potatoes, cardamom coffee, the mucussy greekseed condiment *hilbah*, whiskey, sweet mint tea, three in the winter midnight chorus and counter-chorus, soloists facing. The shop-keeper-beadle in tacky plaid sports jacket and jarring fedora bangs a table then bangs it twice—a low rumble beginning *ael mi-sta-tair:*

Hidden god, in the pavilion of concealment,
the mind withdrawn from all conceiving.
Cause of causes, crowned with the crown
of supremacy, a crown they'll offer you, O Lord.

Psalms and medieval canticles stretched out over quarters of an hour; letters ascended, letters slid down. Choral shouts, a fist-fight, an eight-year-old's voice cracking along his narrow solo and the chorus resuming as though with a blanket to cushion his fall and toss him up gently back to the scale. Kaddish, the street, a platinum sky, purple basil, a walk through empty downtown home.

BRIARS

A nation of priests, those adept at drawing near and being drawn, the ready ones. Not a collective of slaughterhouse functionaries, or spiritual engineers.

Brecht, whose ministrations were directed to the mule-god, distinguishes the seriousness of the priest from that of, say, the silversmith, and declares the former incompatible with art, or—at any rate—with the art of the theater. But he also qualifies the category of priestly seriousness by including in it the image of the doctor stooping over his patient. The serious discussion of those engaged in a text "behind locked doors," however, he welcomes.

Priests, then, in the evolution of the tribes which number stand-up comics among them also. So it is that one comes upon curiously vaudeville qualities in the most serious of 5th or 8th century rabbinical texts.

ABRACADABRAKAZOO

Aaron, the antsy and Orphically inclined Levite, older brother to Moses, remained unsatisfied with the givenness of light on the one hand and objects illumined by it on the other. So he conceived of the oracular devices, the Urim and the Thummim, which, encased by the twelve gems on the high priest's breastplate, bent the originary light across him in a lexical-cum-aesthetic rite the Greek and Latin translators understood as **revelation and truth**, or **true instruction.** The oracle could be consulted only for the king, the high court, or someone serving a need of the community. The priest would read the light as it angled through the gems in order to determine its relation to the Urim or the Thummim, the Yes or the No. The bejeweled priestly vestment came to be known as the "breastpiece of decision," and the fuss-pot priest was established not as bureaucrat, but spiritual sommelier.

According to Jewish legend, the Levite could call upon the oracle neither silently nor in a loud voice, but only with a Hannah-like muttering "on her heart."

ACCOUNTS

"Sing us of the songs of Zion . . ." (Psalms 137:7)

Birah, or **capital**, whose economy—in the rabbinic imagination—reflected a delicate if impractical understanding of currency's dual nature as signifier at once of both substance and emptiness:

The comptroller's office was outside Jerusalem.
and anyone wishing to settle his accounts went
there. Why? So as not to do one's calculating
in Jerusalem and be sad there, as it said [of her]:
"Fair in situation, the joy of all the earth."

—Midrash Rabbah, Exodus

Jerusalem, *Yerushalayim* in Hebrew, exists grammatically in the dual form, reserved for words that refer to pairs. The root of the word is disputed, but seems to involve a compound that includes the notion of foundation or inheritance on the one hand (*yeru, yerush*) and peace or fullness (*shalom, shalem*) on the other. According to scholars of a more historical bent, the city draws its name from its being dedicated to the Western Semite god Shalim, or Shulmanu, the god of what brings peace, that is, payment (*shilem*, or paid)—Jerusalem being the city wherein one's interest is always compounded; where one's debt, even as guest, is assumed; where one pays at least twice, in the unfair economies of song.

BODY REMEMBER

Ruach, **spirit**: akin to *revach*, **interval**, **gap**, or **profit. Soul** (*neshama*, which also means **breath**) engages where the gap between inner and outer is momentarily canceled, where outer and inner abut, before one's expression changes, before something else gets said and intervals reopen—accounts to be risked, payment to be made.

ATTITUDE

Put your mouth where your money is.

BETWIXT

A slyding quheill us lent to seik remeid . . .

—William Dunbar

II.

Our attraction to buildings in the process of being gutted.

As they lead us back toward the sources of speech, the aphasics, even the stutterers, raise the hair on our language. Person to person, first speech emerged through the snake—the hedge-glider, who slips his skin and leaves us his souvenir husk: a hoop.

In the babel-prism of our sign-center.

Speech is a given, "a spoon-knife, death on one side, life on the other." (Leviticus Rabbah). (S)He who would seek the *aleph* of Adonai and through it The Infinite (*Ain Sof*), is admonished to seek righteousness and humility, and to remember the snake—he with the dust in his mouth. "Let him put his mouth in the dust, perhaps there may be hope" (Lamentations 3:29).

ABOUT NOTHING

Omphalos—the snake eating its tail. A sphincter. Zero. Circumcision. A fence about nothing at all.

ADZE

Teach your mouth threshold.

BOTTOM'S UP

There were several "heads"—in Hebrew, literally **houses of service**, or **use**—off the courtyard that first year. All the way across the cistern, mine in the corner was a dark, mossy alcove that established the act in the order of things. Barefoot or sandalled middle of the night trips were especially Levantine as they involved the blind negotiation of what with dark turned into a minefield of fat, mucilaginous slugs.

My neighbor's, on the other hand, was a plastered closet directly beside his kitchenette, also a plastered closet. Both formed a tight

right angle to the door to his room. A pensioner, Herzl worked, he told me, part-time at the Ministry of Education. One day when I was walking into East Jerusalem, twenty minutes from my house, the sky opened in a mountain rainstorm. Drenched, I turned around and began walking home. Suddenly I heard my name being called. Not my name exactly, but one that now belonged to me. "Biton! Biton!" It was Herzl, who from the first had trouble with Peter, hearing Buhtter, and then, after I'd corrected him, settled on Biton, a common Moroccan last name.

Sure enough I was standing outside the impressive Ministry of Education, which was housed in what once had been the Italian hospital and was constructed in perfect Florentine style with a large tower and sensitive sloping roof of sienna tile. Herzl, the parking lot attendant, ushered me into his booth. "*Bo, Bo, kahness.*" (**"Come, come, come in."**) He took out his electric fork and began preparing a cup of tea. I was making conversation. My Hebrew was new, but good. Herzl would always comment on my reading as he puttered around the courtyard in his tattered pajamas, setting cucumbers out in the sun in a big pickling jar, or doing the laundry. "You're going to be famous," he'd caution me, wagging his surprisingly fat finger. "But do you have a Girl?" His own Hebrew was halting, after nearly forty years in the country.

Suddenly the news in Yiddish came on. He held up the finger and concentrated on the voice coming out of the black box on the shelf in the booth. "That," he said to me sharply, "is Yiddish. That you *don't* understand!"

Another time we were sitting in his dirty one room, crowded with nick-nacks and his tailor's equipment and orders. He was serving up the usual tea and cookies with brandy on the side. We were watching a big black and white TV. I asked him if he'd ever been married. He looked up at me, startled, his idiot-blue eyes glittering uncontrollably, his white hair slicked down around the side of his head. He had several gold fillings. "Of course," he said, proudly at first, his voice oddly rising toward the end of the one Hebrew word—*beh-taach*. "I had a wife, children, a telephone. . . . I had EVERYTHING. HITLER took them! . . . What do *you* know?"

ABYSS

> Immediately below was the Valley of the Kidron, here seen in its greatest depth as it joins the Valley of Hinnom, and thus giving full effect to the great peculiarity of Jerusalem seen only on its eastern side—its situation as of a city rising out of a deep abyss.
>
> —Dean Stanley

Gehinnom, adjacent to Kidron, is the valley whose name yields Gehenna—the vale of child-sacrifice, and one of the names for Hell. The first Jews defined themselves as a people of The Name, not the miasm. They were opposed to dismemberment though they incorporated its specter into their rites and eventually came, as a people, to a faith of splitting hairs in the name of the One.

"Said the Holy One, Blessed Be He, to David, 'If you seek life, look for fear . . .' "—Leviticus Rabbah

So the laughter which lends Isaac his name is a nervous one—Isaac, whom the rabbis associate with the attribute of fear.

Peter Cole

ASKEW

When a poem works, it's as though a conduit opens within it toward which the entire world begins slipping.

ALMA ASSOCIATES

Alma de peruda, **the world of separation**, wherein consciousness of our mirrored-window nature receives the association of the English Alma into it.

The loneness of soul.

ANGELIC DISSENT

Some angels objected to the creation of people because people were destined to be liars. They were overruled. Rabbi Solevetchik talks about the fundamental split in our being, a kind of virgule, irreparable by a Christ in time: a split, akin to that generated by language, that is "irreconcilable" and leaves us in "a state of ontological tension and perplexity."

AT A CERTAIN POINT

At a certain point he felt the spirit emerge and begin. Shortly thereafter it looked into the night of the Valley of the Cross and began the walk out along the tightrope of its calculation and into morning.

AMELIORIST

In our purities beyond repair.

BABBA BLACK SHEEP

Bourse-like pages that gauge the relationship between poetic debt and available tender.

Hoping to redeem One by letting it stray farthest from home.

Not coinage exactly, but the near-money of feeling.

BARELY, BARFLY

Abstract: not taken out of context, but as in the etymology of its Hebrew equivalent—stripped, revealed, made bare; i.e., something to be ashamed of.

Not withdrawal from experience, or abstraction from written accounts. But access to principal.

AMNIOTICS

The bus to Netanya and then the old, domed British shore hut at Beit Yannai that Meyer Levin used to write in and that his writer-son Gabriel maintains, Olson's "I have had to learn the simplest things last . . . It is undone business/ I speak of, this morning,/ with the sea/ stretching out/ from my feet" tacked to a closet door. A familiar childhood fraughtness in getting there, and likewise familiar comfort in being carried across the landscape in the national coach, the various landmark turns and yaws my body recognizes in the dark, my eyes shut, into the orange groves, past the prison and through the Ayalon junction, the salt-smell picking up, my thinking split into several directions, sparking back and forth without extension along any one line. In part a drifting back over what's happened, but also the rip out of Jerusalem—even temporarily—to the actual sea.

Peter Cole

ATOMIC THEORY

The call from the muezzin during the heat wave, as though the electrons holding the air together in their motion were a muffled alarm that had been ringing through our joints from the beginning of time.

"Words," said Coleridge, are like "hooked atoms."

B-MOVIE

Putting water up to boil one overcast March morning I heard the high-pitched ripping sound of the swifts returned for a season's assault on thinking—which they open with their flight and call, exposing hitherto guarded pasts and locking one out of the present with thwacking discovery at the hub of cliché.

ARGUMENTS

How much of mideastern instability and carnage derives from clashing ethoi of interpretation, of arguments over how to read?

On The Housetops of Balata

> The three-day curfew's blanked out a lot but they're up here. Sky's legal, reached by a staircase. Up here, at least a floor higher than the troops.
>
> In this fable by Aesop, men manage to become birds. They salute each other across little parcels of air. "Space be about you, Raja." "Double space be about you, Marwan."
>
> —Dennis Silk

BLASPHEMY

The most beautiful psalm, legend has it, was offered up by the sons of Korach-the-Equalizer from a ledge where they landed as they fell into Hell and began remembering the water brooks and meat of Life on Earth.

BELATED

In the smoggy nimbus of our innocence . . .

The poem not as mnemonic receptacle, but as Levitical enactment. Leviticus as the Book of Approach, or Ramp.

BELLY BUTTON

Sacrificial fat presented with smoke and blade. Like what we offer up with a quip, or belly-laugh, or something so clearly seen the mind repudiates it—having been tricked out of its husk by the glaring quality of the appearance. Thus, as is regularly the case, we accommodate what we most intricately resist, and everything counts.

BITTERS

As in "liquors impregnated with wormwood, rind, etc., used to promote appetite and digestion. . . ."

Or, sarcastic: from the Greek *sarkasmos*, from the Greek *serkizo*—to tear flesh; back-to-back with the Hebrew word for prayer—*lehitpallel*, which is derived from the root *p-l-l*, indicating a cutting.

ALIEN FIRE

Nadab and Abihu were incinerated for having offered alien fire in a mysterious deviation from the cultic rite.

What Scripture means to say is that they were licked to death by the cold flames of excessively right intention.

ACCIDENTS HAPPEN

The car careened into view, lifting onto two wheels and flipping over before hurling itself with a crash of glass and thud into the oppositely powerful trunk of the olive tree on the corner. I froze, and three women dressed for Friday nightclubs crawled screaming and bloody out the shattered windows and windshield. I started toward the wreck, running—it seemed to me—more backward than forward, as several cars pulled over, 2 a.m., King George Street, downtown Jerusalem.

A fourth passenger was trapped in the back seat, and five of us, shot-through and suddenly depressed with adrenalin, began rocking the car to turn it over. One of the five took charge and went in after the trapped person, a young blond man wearing a white shirt; ribbons of blood were running out from the top of his head, down along his forehead and face and chest. The other four of us wanted to wait for the ambulance, which had already been called. I was, as now, watching myself, feeling that I'd written myself into a scene but was unable to write myself out.

AIR

Walking down the hall before class at the high school his mouth suddenly begins stretching his face for air in a particularly hideous yawn. Is he bored? Tired? Hungry? No, he is afraid.

AUTHORITY

The third time I found pieces of my mail blowing around in an adjacent alley on my way to the *shuk* I wrote the postmaster general a letter. Within a short time I received the following handwritten reply:

> Honorable Sir, Your address is quite familiar to us. With the amount of mail you receive don't you think it reasonable that you should purchase a larger mailbox?

BODYGUARD

Confident that he has earned the right to his phalanx of opinion.

Peter Cole

BABEL

"Through *bet* I confounded *[beelbalti]* the language of the world."
—*Midrash Alpha Beita de Rabbi Akiva*

Babel *(bavel)* spelled backwards is *levav*, or **heart**.

> You have ravished my heart, my sister, my bride;
> You have ravished my heart with one of your eyes.
> —Song of Songs 4:9

APPARATUS

Dualism is like the game in which two steel rods, like legs, are gradually parted in order to guide a small steel ball up along them. Inevitably one loses control of the ball, either when the rods have been spread apart too suddenly, at which point the ball drops into a little notch marked with a number, or by opening the rods too gradually, in which case the ball goes nowhere or rolls back down and lands with a click at the base of the apparatus, where the rods are attached to a hinge. One tries again.

And thinking is infinite, and the angel is a ladder leaned against it.

III.

Not the sweet medieval lyric of When; the dry, piss and jasmine scent of There.

Dusk with its pink streaks and startling Giotto light settling onto Mt. Zion; nationalist kitsch drifting up from the community center choir in the valley below to the left, Palestinian drum corps *shebab* in paramilitary youth group rehearsal marching up and down the same few permissible streets in percussive crescendo one neighborhood below to the right.

Zion, from the Hebrew root *tsiya*, **parched land**.
Other possible etymologies relate the word to *tsayon*, **stronghold**, or the Hurian *tseya*, **running water**.

The aspiration to dryness on the one hand, a satyr-like shade on the other.

ABU TOR

Dennis, asking the visiting writer from New York what his plans were, how long he'd be staying—"three weeks"—what he'd seen so far. "And how long will you be staying?" "Oh, two and half weeks or so." And if he's been enjoying himself, and "How much longer will you be here?" "I'm *not* sure. Maybe a month." And how did he like his stay at the arts colony in Virginia to which Dennis has been invited for the spring, far away from Abu Tor and the "sinking aircraft carrier the country has become." "Fine, they leave you alone and bring lunch to your room on a silver tray." "Is it," Dennis asks, getting at last to the point of his conversation, "far from New Orleans?"

Peter Cole

AFTERNOON

Yesterday afternoon I came into the room after school and noticed that the gray wool blanket was chalky, from the wall plaster no doubt, I thought, and went over to brush it off only to discover it was sunlight caught in the blanket's weave and couldn't be brushed away.

ALONGSIDE

. . . may *always* be the false *aleph* in the basement beneath the poet's Earth in Borges's imagination . . . which posits alongside it the memory of Beatriz.

BALCONY

Sunset over the Valley of the Cross, all Jasper Johns and quietness—opium eaten.

BRIDE

Whatever

But who'll be the man,
he'll come or he won't.
And if he comes—fine.
And if not—but he will.

Said a man to his wife,
we'll get ourselves a cow.
If it gives milk—good.
If not, but it will.

Let him come, let him come already,
this man-who. The next one.
From here on in
he'll be with the bride.

—Avot Yeshurun

הכניסה
אסורה
NO
ENTRY

Peter Cole

AMOUR

Ahava, or **love**, in which *aleph* and *bet* are combined with *hé*, the fifth letter, through which, according to yet another midrash, the world was created. *Hé* is also the letter that signals the unpronounceable, wedged between and after the *aleph* and *bet*, like the trick pitch and surface of a fun-house runway between two ghosted rooms. So that the word itself, *ahava*, is like the medieval wheel of fortune that spins one into the vertigo of the full circle in motion. In medieval picture books the figures on the wheel cling as desperately when they near the top as when they begin their descent. Hence the notion of a "shit eating grin."

> Bot for to se the sudayn weltering
> Off that Ilk quhele,that sloppare was to hold,
> It semyt vnto my wit a strange thing,
> So mony I sawe that than clymben wold,
> And failit foting, and tio ground were rold;
> And othir eke, that sat aboue on hye,
> Were ouerthrawe In twinklyng of an eye . . .
>
> And sum were eke that fallyng had sore,
> There for to clymbe, thaire corage was no more.
>
> *A King's Quair*
> James I, King of Scotland

ACKNOWLEDGMENTS

Into town for dinner at Ruhama's with Dennis—the usual *malawwah* and meat. He told the story of the Israeli writer who, being honored at a dinner on his 65th birthday, rose to deliver the following address:

> Friends, I thank you for this dinner. Its occasion prompts me to tell the following story. Once there was a man, in Greece, who was condemned to die. When the day of his execution arrived he was led from his cell, chained, and taken along a path by a very fat Greek Orthodox priest. The priest explained that they were going to walk to the gallows, which were on a far hill, barely visible in the distance. It was a terribly hot day, and the path was arduous. They began sweating profusely and breathing heavily and the prisoner started to complain. Finally he stopped in his tracks and refused to go any further, claiming

> that it was unjust to force a man condemned to die to labor so in order to have his sentence carried out. The priest, every bit as exhausted, looked the prisoner in the eye and said: "You think you have it bad. I have to make it back."

And with that he sat down.

ALL THE REST

The kike-like chorus of one-liners and smirks, modulating through quibbles, on to commentary.

BANK

Just as being tickled as a child would send me into fits of laughter and then suddenly brush me up against terror and finally rage, which in turn could as easily give over to cruelty, so when news of my younger brother's death by car-crash reached me in Jerusalem, I wandered out onto a friend's porch overlooking the dusty, sweltering July city and burst out with a huge pitbull laugh which

I tried to swallow back down at once, even though I was utterly alone.

Nine years later, I've worked his name, like a mint, into my ATM code at the bank.

ACCORDINGLY

Within myself I've discovered
an opening—

imagine for a moment the cave
of Pan at Banyas—

and was astonished
at the shiftings of meaning there—

that what's wanting we call an opening

and that opening we call the past

that the past has the supple body
of a young woman

and she told me
what no one's ever told me
(what I always wanted to be told)

and as much as she told me
so the girl grew in me

deepening and deepening and deepening

the past

and, accordingly,
the openness

and, as it were,
all became wanting.

—Aharon Shabtai

Peter Cole

BIRD FOOD

Schimmel by after a morning at the Institute. We take the back route to the *shuk*, along the western slope of the city, past the high-rises and condominiums—good for at least one teenage suicide a year—and then into the older religious and semi-religious neighborhoods, crowded with two story houses and 'be fruitful and multiply' families. At lunchtime one can see long ant-like trails of yeshiva students, dressed in white shirts and black trousers, making their way toward a given house, designated 'the dining hall.'

Then through the poorer Sephardic neighborhood, an occasional arch, and up Shiloh Street into the market. We wander into the various canopied alleys inspecting the fish stands, stop for specific tomatoes, then again for cucumbers. At Canetti's all the way at the back behind the main stalls for dried, oil-cured black olives and the cracked green Syrian kind, then large, still warm *pitot* fogging up the plastic bag they're wrapped in. Wine, and finally the day's catch of tiny mullet, which Pythagoras warns against, and which the fish monger says you can eat whole, "like french fries."

We start back, gathering wood from building lots we pass on the way. It's the first really spring-like day of the year, and the lizards are out sunning themselves on the rooftop cement. Harold quickly has everything arranged on the makeshift table, including a plateful of sparkling gutted reddish fish, each with a yellow stripe so densely hued it appears to have been painted along it.

The fire is burning down to coals in a small tin tray, and we move on to the wine and tomatoes and small unwaxed cucumbers. Everything bears evidence of Schimmel's touch, which makes me think of a grove of pepper trees filled with finches. In fact, everything about Harold is birdlike—his crowish, rivered hands, gatherer's eyes, leathery skin, and, most strikingly, his print on notes, letters, and in the margins of his books. It's a shore bird's script, like tracks in the sand closest to the water.

ANXIETY

Is one's hunger for complicated pleasure aroused by the pain already incurred? Or does the vision of one's putative enjoyment determine the kind of pain one will be required to go through?

In the calculus of meaning, how will the price of one's pleasure be set?

What is extraordinary pleasure but mutual credit extended along a line of perception? Who extends such credit? And who could deny the usuric nature of such an economy, wherein those who have the pluck to borrow are given the chance for greatest recompense, while the fundamentalists of an aesthetic barter system are left to squabble over crumbs?

Against what is this line of credit drawn? Against a debatable notion of naming—a dignity.

> "[The artist] must work within the limits of his love."
>
> —David Jones

AXES

"Rabbi Yehoshua (the coalheaver) was undefeated in his confrontation with the Athenian philosophers:

> "Salt that stinks," they asked him, "what was it soaked in?"
> "In the afterbirth of a mule."
>
> "Does a mule have an afterbirth?"
> "Does salt stink?"
>
> "A chick that dies in its egg. How does the spirit get out?"
> "The way it got in it gets out."

. . . This isn't the voluntary style of someone who borrows an axe and goes down to the woods [Thoreau], but that of a man compelled to exhaust the material at hand.

Rabbi Akiba, who was a shepherd until the age of forty, would get by on a single bundle of wood: half he sold, and half he used. The neighbors, complaining about the smoke, suggested that he sell the second half also and buy himself oil for his lamp. He preferred the wood: 'I meet several needs with it,' he said. 'First of all I learn from it; second, it keeps me warm; and third, I can sleep on it.' This ethical exigency also finds expression in a story about the same Rabbi Akiba, who was found weeping on the Sabbath. His students said to him: 'Our teacher, we were taught—*And call the Sabbath a delight'* (Isaiah 58:13). He said to them: 'This is my delight.'"

—Aharon Shabtai, "Where They Come From"

AUGURY

Twitches at the absolute with the concentration of a horse working its withers and tail, to keep the blood-sucking flies at bay.

BOTH

At the root of the word for **gentle** *(adin)* and **pleasure** (ednah) are the respite notions both of Eden and Robert Duncan's "snake-like beauty in the living changes of syntax."

Describing Adam and Eve, the J writer uses the word *arumim*, or **naked:** "The two of them were naked . . . yet they felt no shame." Then the writer employs the homonym *arom* to characterize the snake as "the **shrewdest** or **most subtle** of all the wild beasts—" establishing the Edenic origin of the flinch between innocence and wit along the shifting length of the serpent.

Hence the Hebrew *begidah*, **betrayal**, akin to *beged*, **clothes**—relating to exposure?

A kind of kiss. A bite. An altered tack. A wise crack, through which one's love slips out and in as it pleases.

BEYOND IT

A kiss to the wall,
to the *alephbet*
that hung there.

And Mr. Pah asks me:
Still on the
alephbet? Still

not beyond it? . . .

—Harold Schimmel

Peter Cole

BURGLAR

D., whose voice I'd fallen in love with that fall when she came to the door looking for my neighbor, was asleep beside me. Her skin was calm. It was August, early in the morning. The light was already streaming in through the kitchenette windows which faced onto the courtyard, and I lifted my head a little to gauge the time by the color of the sky. I noticed a blur some ten feet off. As it came into focus I realized that it was a man in a dark, striped polo shirt by the kitchen sink. He was concentrating on something in the sink but I couldn't see what it was. A distinctly un-American instinct coiled me and I sprang up and shouted *"Tseiiiii!"* **(GET OUT!!!)**—at which point he fled, pedalling air like a cartoon character. I jumped out of bed and hopped into my pants, grabbed a shirt, and gave chase. He chose one alley and I—it was soon clear—chose another.

For several months thereafter I had the recurring dream that someone was breaking into the room while I slept. I would hear him trying to pry the door open, and I'd anticipate the moment it would give, so that I'd be ready. Just as he broke through, I'd wake up sweating.

One afternoon the next spring, I was working at the table with my back to the window when I felt suddenly that someone was watching me. I turned around and there was a man looking in the window. He said that he'd heard the room was for rent and wanted to know if it was true. "No," I said, annoyed, "it isn't and it won't be. Stop bothering me, please." And I went returned to my work. A minute or so passed, and then the questioner's face came back to me, familiar from that August morning.

That was six years ago. Just now I got up from the desk and went over to the kitchen table where a book I'd recently purchased but not yet read was lying. I opened it at random. My eye fell immediately on the following words from Canetti's *Auto-da-Fé:* "Then Kien felt something unexpected and soft, thought 'A burglar' and closed his eyes as quickly as he could.

Although he was now lying on top of the burglar, he did not dare to move. . . ."

Peter Cole

BOXES

Fleshy, farmer-like, Gershuni is showing us his Tel Aviv bunker studio whose walls are huge with spirals and blackened turquoise night skies swarming with cypress and arrows and Hebrew and stars. He dreams of the day when every Israeli will have one of his hand-smeared paintings over the household TV. "Shalom soldier!" "Beautiful soldier," they cry. Moustache and helmet and Marilyn Monroe mouths.

We talk for several hours, and he shows us everything, including the new kiln and his porcelain dishware, painted with swastikas and liturgical scrawl. He and May, my Chinese friend, get into a long conversation about how best to exhibit them. Now we're

deciding where to have lunch. I explain that May had her first gefilte fish the night before. "I loved it," she says. Gershuni is handling a set of plates and trying to get them back into storage. He doesn't seem to be interested and smacks his lips, missing their cigar. Still looking down at the plates, he says, as though turning a corner, "Be careful May. You start with gefilte fish and who knows where you'll end up."

It's time to go. He's given us three powerful miniatures to take back to the States. They seem to be waving what Shabtai has called "the flag of ugliness." Two are shoebox paintings with cracked lacquer, smeared Hebrew, and acrylic; blacked and red maculate praise from the psalm that says "Pray for the peace of Jerusalem; May they prosper that love thee." Gershuni has the next verse as one of his themes for these flattened scrap-heap boxes—"For the sake of my brethren and companions, I will now say: 'Peace be within thee,'" which mixes sex, history, and religion—like Tennessee Williams said you shouldn't if you want to succeed in America.

Then there is the rejected lithograph from the Bialik series—the blackest twisting trees and pan-erotic holocaust inscription: "And we'll remember them all."

The poems quoted in this piece are as follows: In "Abarbanel"—*from "1880" by Harold Schimmel; in "Arguments"—from "Stingy Kids" by Dennis Silk; in* "Bride"—*"Whatever" by Avot Yeshurun; in* "Accordingly"—*from* Love *by Aharon Shabtai; in* "Beyond It"—*from* The Beginning of Wisdom *by Harold Schimmel. "Stingy Kids" is from Silk's new collection,* Catwalk and Overpass (*Viking 1990*). *Translations of the Schimmel, Shabtai, and Yeshurun are my own, from the Hebrew. The photographs were taken by May Liang and the author.*

American Writing Today: A Diagnosis of the Disease

William T. *Vollmann*

> Approximately 90% of neoplasms originate within 2 cm of the anterior midline of the mouth.
>
> —Dr. Rodney Million and Dr. Nicholas J. Cassisi, *Management of Head and Neck Cancer: A Multidisciplinary Approach* (Philadelphia: Lippincott, 1984), p. 251.

AS THIS QUOTATION SHOWS, the mouth is a veritable fount of pestilence, vomiting forth its unclean words to infect all who are not armored with ignorance and earwax. Worse still is when the virus is sealed into a cartridge, positioned with a click of the pen-button, and squeezed through the ball-point onto a sheet of permanence, where spores of words wait gleefully for library centuries until they can attack new victims. Of course there are also saintly books which heal us with word-light; yet these are now sparse. Indeed, the American scene suffers from a plague of writers careless and even putrid. With the assistance of many learned doctors of oral and anal health, I now propose to set forth our responsibility, and some rules for reform.

This first requires that I set right all the woes of the world.

THE FAILURE OF AMERICAN SOCIETY

It is a commonplace that our United States are in decline. On the part of our government we have at best a shortsighted reactive strategy to specific events, lacking in any vision which might influence basic causes. As for the governed, our apathy and misinformation grow hourly. The terrifying increase in random violence and racism of all colors bespeaks a nation polarized halfway to impotence. From homelessness to schools where nothing is taught, from impending environmental disaster to continued environmental assault, our failures illuminate us as Selves incapable of comprehending others.

Our policy toward Nicaragua demonstrates that we cannot put ourselves in a Nicaraguan's shoes. Our laughable War On Drugs does not address the question of why people use drugs, or what people might do instead. Our suppression of abortion is not even hypocritical; it is simply, astoundingly, blind. And we truly have the "leadership" we deserve, for when we see the Other, what do *we* do?—Suppose that you do not rent whores, and a whore approaches you in the night-lit street, brave and desperate. Suppose that a member of some cult sets out to convert you. Suppose that someone begs you for money.—No, suppose simply that someone sits down beside you in your subway car and begins to talk to you. In how many cases will you answer?

THE FAILURE OF HUMANITY

To fail this test is only human. But survival and happiness depend on knowledge. And knowledge can only be obtained through openness, which requires vulnerability, curiosity, suffering.

The vicious Christian ignoramuses who are determined to end abortions in our country are cousins to the Muslims who preach murder, the Maoists who restore order in China beneath their tank-treads, the terrorists who shoot tourists in Peru or Sri Lanka. These will have their day, because they use force. But ultimately they will be defeated by force, and it will be a force they do not know. Why? Precisely because they will not know the Other. As long as they do not know it, how can they guard against it?

We must take care not to be like them. How can we best do this? By knowing them. By understanding without approving or hating. By empathizing.

How best to do this?

William T. Vollmann

THE GLORIOUS ICE-CREAM BAR

Through art.*

A RHAPSODY OF DESSERTS

Art takes us inside other minds, like a space capsule swooping down across Jupiter while the passengers can see strangeness and newness through the portholes, meanwhile enjoying all the comforts of Standard Temperature and Pressure.

Of all the arts, although photography *presents* best, painting and music *convey* best, and sculpture *looms* best, I believe that literature *articulates* best.

THE PRESCRIPTION (WHICH MUST INEVITABLY SOUND DULL, LIKE A DOCTOR'S COMMAND TO TAKE MORE EXERCISE)

We need writing with a sense of purpose.

GENERIC DRUGS REJECTED

What about beautifully useless books, like the French *Maldoror*?—They too have their place. But there is too much writing nowadays that is useless WITHOUT being beautiful.—On the other side are those scarcely mentionable works which strive to be useful and fail in proportion to be beautiful: "socialist realism." In our own country we rarely fall into that mistake, but it does happen, as in the spots where *The Grapes of Wrath* is mildewed.

In this period of our literature we are producing mainly insular works, as if all our writers were on an airplane in economy seats, beverage trays shading their laps, faces averted from one another, masturbating furiously. Consider, for instance, the *New Yorker* fiction of the past few years, with those eternally affluent charac-

---

*Here one might argue that it would be more efficient simply to be GOD, or failing that, to join the CIA. However, the first is not within our power. As for the second, it has now been established that our spooks are wrong as often as our meteorologists.

ters suffering understated melancholies of overabundance. Here the Self is projected and replicated into a monotonous army which marches through story after story like deadly locusts. Consider, too, the structuralist smog that has hovered so long over our universities, permitting only games of stifling breathlessness. (The so-called New Historicism promises no better.)

So how ought writers fulfill their role, and *accomplish* something?

THE RULES

1. We should never write without feeling.

2. Unless we are much more interesting than we imagine we are, we should strive to feel not only about Self, but also about Other. *Not* the vacuum so often between Self and Other. *Not* the unworthiness of Other. *Not* the Other as a negation or eclipse of Self. Not even about the Other exclusive of Self, because that is but a trickster-egoist's way of worshipping Self secretly. We must treat Self and Other as equal partners. (Of course I am suggesting nothing new. I do not mean to suggest anything new. Health is more important than novelty.)

3. We should portray important human problems.

4. We should seek for solutions to those problems. Whether or not we find them, the seeking will deepen the portrait.

5. We should know our subject, treating it with the respect with which Self must treat Other. We should know it in all senses, until our eyes are bleary from seeing it, our ears ring from listening to it, our muscles ache from embracing it, our gonads are raw from making love to it. (If this sounds pompous, it is perhaps because I wear thick spectacles.)

6. We should believe that truth exists.

7. *We should aim to benefit others in addition to ourselves.*

Fragments from Aeschylus' *Prometheos Auomenos* *Translated by* John *Taggart*

According to H. Weir Smyth, fragments 104–106 are from the parodus of the Chorus Titans who have been released from Tartarus by the clemency of Zeus. Prometheus describes his tortures in fragment 107 and his benefits to humanity in fragment 108. Fragments 109–111 deal with Heracles receiving directions through the land of the furthest north from Prometheus and the perils to be encountered as he makes his way home after slaying Geryon in the furthest west. Fragments 113–114 refer to Heracles' shooting of the eagle that fed on the "vitals" of Prometheus.

104

We have come . . .
watchers of these your struggles, Prometheus,
fettered and chained, chained to your suffering.

105

Red all the way, crashing like cymbals,
the divine Erythras flows beside Okeanos
into the all-providing sea of the Ethiopians
where the panoptic sun returns
to revivify himself and his horses,
letting the soft warm water pour over them.

106

Here is the place where Europe meets Asia,
the place of their shared boundary: broad Phasis.

108

Stallions and he-asses and bulls:
slave-substitutes, burden-relievers.

109

Take this the straight road; no delay,
you'll feel the beak-bite of the North Wind—
swooping in cold rage—, and you thought
you couldn't be caught in the grip of winter.

110

Thereafter you'll come to a land of tranquility,
a land of cordial and hospitable people
where neither plough nor even hoe
works the fertile soil, but—self-seeding—
brings evergreen bounty for its innocent people.

111

Proper Scythians eat cheese made from mare's milk.

No's Knife in Yes's Throat
Paul West

1

One way of accounting for Dark Annie Chapman's last hours would be to say that Gull, Netley and Sickert found her at 5:30 in the morning, after many tedious searches throughout the East End, and occupied themselves with her for half an hour. Never had Sickert seen so many dark alleyways or, in the gaslight, so many blanched ruined faces attached to bodies that would not straighten or even move forward. Not even during his own nocturnal rambles had he seen such wastage of the human frame; London slept while these waifs and demons capered about in the half-light, raving or gestured, wrestling one another or trying to advance on hands and knees, vomiting or coughing with feral vigor. He had not known there was that much liquor available, though he did not know that the parade of the lost began soon after eleven o'clock, which was when the dossing houses re-let their unoccupied beds: turn-over time it was called, having however nothing to do with apples. For some reason, the exodus from the dosshouses took place about the same time as the police stations released the drunks, giving them a chance to earn their living, if they were women and not too far gone (what was the point of taking them to court the next day and imposing upon them a fine they could not pay?). So, the bedless and the fourpenceless trudged through the streets at the same time with no chance of getting drunk unless they clicked, and those who were sobering up had to join them. Actually, those in jail received better care than those in a fourpenny bed as, out of some not altogether regimented altruism, the constables and the jailer looked in on their charges whereas the M'Carthys and the Donovans who ran the Crossinghams had a business interest only, intent on warehousing the poor; those who went to jail, however briefly, had entered into an almost religious system whose formulas and rituals remained intact and even evinced a mysterious tenderness for the down and out. As Sickert knew, the clients came from other areas of London and were rarely drunk, whereas the flotsam in the streets was mainly female, few of whom would ever be primly accosted by the venerable William Ewart Gladstone, and taken home with him to be propagandized over scones and tea, or cakes and hot chocolate—whether he was then Prime Minister or not. The error of their way was what Gladstone propounded to his select few whores, with minimal effect, though he did convert several to a different, more exquisite diet designed, perhaps, at least in his own mind, to sap the voracity of the flesh or stiffen the moral fiber of fallen women. What shook Sickert was the untamed flow of the wretched, seen not, as was usual with him, from ground level, but from something in motion, so that those slouching or loitering in the streets seemed to be marking time or even walking backwards, caught in one of death's mighty rallentandos.

Through the streets they toured, prisoners of *The Crusader*, and even more so when Netley swung down and went off on foot to look. It was then that Sickert heard the sounds of Gull's mastication as he downed sandwiches and milk, buns and coffee, even a few grapes—My God, Sickert thought, *hoped*, all he has to do is eat one of the wrong grapes and this whole expedition goes for naught. I wish, I wish. But Gull, who never spoke, in the dim light retained an expression of ponderous acuity, made no mistake and seemed to have endless funds of patience and an enormous bladder, never once having to leave the cab. He must, Sickert thought, be sitting in such a way that the liquids do not percolate to his bladder but remain trapped above the belt like mountain lakes. If this thing were worth doing at all, it might be better to start at dawn, or an hour before it; Sickert found himself amazed to be thinking so prosaic a thought when their purpose was so foul. Or, and once again his hopeful side flashed through, the chosen woman—the one with black eye and bruised nose, as yet wholly invisible—were just going to be yelled at and then discharged from the audience, so to speak. Alas, back came an urgent Netley, who spat a few words at them as he remounted: *"Go'a,"* said with a glottal stop, intending that he had seen Dark Annie wincing along somewhere and would quickly get them to her. At first she refused, glaring at them in fatigue, impatient with everybody and eager to go nowhere, a being wholly unstarched, yearning for bed and food. Nobody had made any offer for her services, she had no money, no drink, no food, and hardly even her legs; her entire body still ached from the drunken brawl with Liza Cooper, and she was thinking of going back to the casualty ward, just to get herself into a chair. It was that or going to lie down in one of the overgrown yards between the blocks of terrace houses. Once again Sickert had to officiate, this time beginning with more of an argument: "You look weary, my dear, and none too well," hating himself for doing it. "We are all weary tonight, it has been a long journey for us. May we drop you at your convenience?" He was careful to keep the idiom of the patronizing toff out of his address; treat her as a lady, don't say "dearie" or "darling," even when she answered, as she did, saying "Keptin," her version of "Captain."

"Nah," Annie Chapman said, "I'll walk it, Keptin."

"Honestly, madam, it will be no trouble."

"You not *arfter* anyfink are you?"

"Only some beauty sleep, madam. Please." He smiled his most ornate smile, knowing that she did not know how this dialogue had gone, only a week ago, with Polly Nichols. He felt sour and despicable, doing it again, but the vision of a dismembered child seized his brain. He offered a hand, a big warm hand, and that did it. In she came, to Gull's gross apology for the lack of wine, a little sitting there among them on the heaped-up muslin, then a grape, her first food this day, even as Gull babbled on about how grapes, currants and raisins sustained him; he was a children's doctor, he said, affiliated with Dr. Barnardo's Home for Working and Destitute Lads, as if he knew about her crippled son. She made no sound other than a sigh, three-quarters unconscious before she even bit the grape, and Gull was at her throat in seconds, mild-mannered but swift as a gorilla, and it all began, the clothes went upward, the knife spun and floated, Gull reached into her and twizzled, then removed some organ and slid it into his pocket all wet. After that, Gull told Sickert to help him to remove Dark Annie's rings, which took some forcing, and Sickert looked at her hands only, imagining himself far away, not doing this at all, but his eyes craved the sight, the butchered belly in the tiny charnel house, the shambles in the gloaming—for art, for love, for *what*?

"Dark Annie Chapman," Gull whispered as he took a rest, "sometimes known as Siffey. Friend of Mistress Kelly and Mistress Stride. If only there were time to do another. But look, it will soon be light."

Sickert knew he had not seen it happen, or his head would have exploded. All he could hear, apart from the creaking of the cab and the sound of the horse's hooves, were the last little interjections of both Polly and Dark Annie as they succumbed without quite realizing how grievous it was going to be: Polly Nichols's frail, waning, almost comfy murmur of "Gor blimey, gents" and Dark Annie Chapman's pure, scalded sigh—"I'm goin'." Somewhere on Hanbury Street, he and Netley lowered her gently to the ground, off her coming an odd aroma of suet and glycerine. She had last been seen going from Dorset Street across Crispin Street to Brushfield Street and she was now only as far away from the doss-house as she would have been at the far end of Brushfield Street. She had gone nowhere at all all night, in fact retracing her steps in the same vicinity as if ground walked over again and again were somehow less taxing. Netley, however, had seen her leaning against a wall as the brewer's clock chimed the half-hour of 5:30; a dark man in a deerstalker hat was walking away from her, calling back to her "yes" even as she answered "No, no" without waiting for him to finish. In fact, *The Crusader* had dropped her off where Netley had seen her, as if to be tidy, but in a state of shocking disarray: her hands raised with her palms upward, her legs drawn up with her feet on the ground and her knees aimed outward, on her back, some of her intestines set on her right shoulder. Netley had made this final arrangement while Sickert, heaving, had positioned her rings at her feet along with some pennies and two brand-new farthings that Gull had supplied, muttering something about brass's being the sacred metal of masons. Round her throat Netley had wound a scarf before they lifted her out and down, for Gull had attacked the spine with such ferocity that her head was almost free. This was the very scarf she had been wearing when she had clambered in to join them, her heart faintly uplifted by their show of chivalry.

Again Sickert had blood on him when he entered his studio, shaking and aghast; again he washed it away as best he could, marveling at how fast it changed hue, wondering if she had been found yet and if he had dropped anything at the site. Surely Netley was wrong to visit the same spot twice, as something dropped on the second occasion would matter whereas something dropped elsewhere, *everywhere else,* would not matter at all. Why the return to the point of origin? Was something luring him on? Afterwards, Gull had sat still with an almost juvenile smile, his hand on whatever it was he had slid into his pocket, as if it were going to be some prodigious exhibit to startle the examiners at Guy's, whose requirements he had long since met and had indeed, in his own right, stiffened for subsequent generations of candidates. A souvenir, then? Sickert shrank from thinking further: he was not going to get away with this, he knew. Best confess. Give himself up now.

But to whom? There was no way of shedding the burden, not if he believed in the malefic power of Gull, no keener demonstration of which he could imagine than what had just gone on in *The Crusader.* Once again *he* had not been the victim; indeed, about Gull today there had been something Saturday-afternoonish and bumbling, almost as if he had been on his way back from a rather soothing cricket match in which not much had happened save a whole series of decorous stalemates. For all the ferocity of his attack, the man had been oddly mellow. Sickert told himself he would not go again, but he knew he would have to. Why, Netley himself might do him an injury; his role was far from limited to cruising the streets on foot, and the pubs, the entries, the yards. He too, like Gull, had delusions of being demonic, and they were not delusions altogether, as Sickert was going to find out.

They had dumped Dark Annie less than half a mile from Buck's Row, behind a lodging house that sheltered seventeen souls, five in the attic. On the ground floor was a cat's-meat shop, and on the first floor Mrs. Davis's packing-case business. There was a yard in the rear and, alongside, a passageway that led to the stairs; tarts took their pick-ups to both the yard and the passageway (which had an unlocked door at either end). Dark Annie had gone back to the squalor she came from. Her feet pointed at a small woodshed, her trunk was parallel to the fence, and her head was half a foot short of the bottom step. John Davis, who found her at about six o'clock, had been unable to sleep between three and five, but had then dropped off for half an hour, as was almost usual with him. He had moved in with his mother only a couple of weeks ago and he could not adjust to the racket of the carts outside. He heard the church clock tolling six as he inspected the yard door, which tarts often left open after using the premises, opened it and saw Dark Annie's remains at the bottom of the steps, abandoned-looking on tufts of grass and flagstones. For a moment he tried to go back to sleep, blurred there with his pants belt in his hand, and then he saw several men from the local case-maker's shop, called to them and said to come and look at what was in the yard. They came over, but hung back short of the steps exclaiming and whispering as a crowd began to form and screams began to fill the nearby streets. Finally someone ran to find a constable, and a workman, after taking some brandy from his flask, found a tarpaulin to arrange over the body. They had seen her face already, though, bloody like her upreaching hands, and the long black coat shoved up over the bloodstained stockings. Her left arm was on her left breast, set there by Netley on Gull's instruction, giving her a sedate, composed appearance Gull had not intended; but what unsettled them all most was her having been cut wide open, eviscerated, and then, as it were, put on display. Inspector Chandler had to tussle his way through the milling mob when he arrived to take charge; he then cleared the passageway of onlookers and awaited the divisional surgeon in the yard, which he had had emptied. He had the tarpaulin removed and some sacking put in its place, sensing that a sack was somehow more human, whereas a tarpaulin was for a machine or a fixture. Dr. George Bagster certified Dark Annie as dead and had her removed to the mortuary in the same wheeled shell that Polly Nichols had occupied only a week ago. Searching began, its yield a comb and its paper sheath, together with a piece of muslin from Gull's supply, cut away during his tantrum with the knife. These they added to the rings and coins. Then they found part of an envelope bearing the seal of the Sussex regiment on one side and, on the other, the letter M; the postmark said "London, 28 Aug., 1888." In a twist of paper there were two pills from the casual ward, for pain, and Dark Annie had slipped them into the little fold of the envelope's corner for safe keeping. Without coming into play they had stood intact between her and Gull's knife. Had Sickert seen all this, he would have retched again, knowing as he did, and the raucous mob did not, that Dark Annie had been the second in a special series. It was actually happening, and, in its ramshackle and psychotic way, it was going to happen again, as if Gull controlled the whole world, beyond the power of any queen or prime minister to stop him. He was doing it for the masons, who had finessed his way to the highest medical position in the land; he was paying his debts with a sword and a series of sleepless nights. No one was looking for a pudgy doctor of enormous repute, not yet; the offender was a Jew or a Slav, swarthy with a narrow mustache, shabby-genteel evening clothes, and a rattling, jingling black bag. Various women had been accosted by this man, who had quite openly discussed the first murder and a second and had then made an appointment with them for a drink or something more intimate, at the Queen's Head in Flower and Dean Street, say, or at the Ringers. Suave, well-spoken Lotharios began to come to mind as women began to have fits in the streets. "What's in your bag, sir?" some would say, and remember the answer for as long as they lived: "Something that ladies don't like." Several had seen Dark Annie and her killer haggling in the street, then going through a gate or a doorway together, his arm about her shoulder, where her innards were soon to repose, and this same murderer was supposed to have scrawled on the yard wall "Five; fifteen more and then I give myself up." To some other woman he was supposed to have said "You are beginning to smell a rat. Foxes hunt geese, but they don't always find 'em." In fact, the man some of them had seen and been addressed by had been the indefatigable and ubiquitous Netley, short and full of rattle, eyeing the clientele in the pubs and the talent in the street, looking for Kelly mainly, but with an eye to Polly Nichols, Dark Annie Chapman and Long Liz Stride, also gently asking questions: "Who's that fine strapping wench by the bar, then?" Moved by the variable grandeur of the whores, he had sometimes made Gull and Sickert wait while he took his pleasure with one or two of them in these very streets, to ease his nerves, he told himself. His chore was both tedious and exacting, out in the air and always, after it all, he had to canter home and clean up the mess, stripping *The Crusader* of spent and scarlet muslin, mopping and sluicing, and then restoring everything to a fine unmitigated polish. Short, muscular and vibrant, he haunted the by-ways of the East End as if he were the killer himself, and increasingly gave himself a chill by giving others the chills, pretending to be what he was not but grimacing mightily in hell's penumbra and so gaining rewards not compassed in money. If only, he wished, the other two would join him as he strolled the neighborhood, each knowing who he was and who the other two were, which gave them total power over the entire population, knowing as they did which types of knives Gull was *not* using, how Dark Annie's tongue was going to protrude from her swollen face by dawn, and how she would be dressed and trimmed.

The perfect bloodthirsty hypocrite, he actually paused to help street women who had fits (though they sometimes bit his hand) and to tousle the hair of the filthy Cockney children; he gave to beggars, he shepherded the blind and the maimed, and he bought people drinks as, in a way for him subtle, he imbibed information;

in another century he would have been the perfect totalitarian policeman, German or Russian, sent prowling in a raincoat. Curiously enough, in all his wanderings, he saw nobody in bloodstained clothes, heard nobody saying "No" behind a fence or a wall (after which there came the sound of a body falling: he never heard this either), and never came face to face with a single one of the victims, although he often enough ogled them, watched them drinking or vomiting, wiping their face or walking away with someone picked up at the bar. He could, he thought, have paid for and possessed either Polly Nichols or Dark Annie Chapman, and the sight of him on high with his whip and his barracks-room smile, with his enormous member not far beneath it, might have incited them even more than Sickert's debonair diphthongs to enter *The Crusader.* No need, he decided: after all, they might have said *Enough of you for one night, Johnnie-Boy*; they would have thought we wanted them in the coach only for pleasure, not serious business, and not got in. So, no. If, like Gull, he suffered from the *idée fixe,* the idea was usually not very good, whereas Gull, for all his depravity, had a lofty mind.

For the next few days the tenants of 29 Hanbury Street did a roaring trade, letting sightseers and sensation-seekers look from their windows at the scene of the crime (or at least the scene of the body's deposition). Some more zealous than most pointed out dubious blood stains, none larger than a sixpence, some as small as a housefly. One woman had seen Dark Annie serving at a pub in Spitalfields market only half an hour before her throat was cut. The talk was that the killer had taken the pelvic organs with one sweep of his knife, that there was a growing market for such organs as were missing, and that the amount of innards culled was what would go comfortably into a breakfast cup. John Richardson, who when he was in the market came and checked the padlock on his mother's cellar flaps, she a widow living at 29 Hanbury Street, had sat down and cut a piece of leather from his boot to ease his foot; had he done this an hour later, sitting on the top step, his boots would just about have been on Dark Annie's head. It was not there, he said, at a quarter to five in the morning. A leather apron had been found, which sent the police after John Pizer, a bootmaker who not only wore a deerstalker hat, had several old hats in his possession (ladies') and five long sharp knives as well. The going price for a uterus was twenty pounds. In the end, Pizer sued the newspapers that had libeled him; his alibis were sound, but not his short-lived fame.

2

Up to now, Marie Kelly thought she had a fairly full idea of human emotions: she had felt most of them, some of them too often, one or two like a piece of iridescent heart-stopping feldspar that made her cry with joy just because God, in His superb and awful matinees had ended up creating it: such her notion of love, of marriage, even of agonizing bereavement. Had life not been wonderful, would the grief have been so vast? When she saw, again, her husband being blown apart in the mine, in the zone of fire and dead-end dust, she knew that something good had trembled for the last time. It was given to women, she thought with stagey self-assurance, to become expert grievers, to let their eyes pour with hot acid and then go out to the site and, piece by piece, reassemble the beloved with squeeze and spit, doing upon the restored hulk a tender battuta that said it would take Evan Davis the collier back in whatever shape, just so long as he never went burrowing again into the bowels of the earth: his leg where his arm should be, his head swiveled through one hundred and eighty degrees so that he faced backward at table and had to be fed according. That. She had trained on such things, almost as if knowing the murders of Polly Nichols and now Dark Annie Chapman were to come, wrapping her heart in nettles and thistles and thorns. Polly she had almost come to accept: those who walk the streets die in the streets, and not at moments of their own choosing. But with Dark Annie gone, so brutally rearranged in full view of everyone, Marie began to wonder, not about the letters—these figured in her nightmares as eligible implausibilities already lost in the wash of makeshift righteousness—but about chance and hell, luck and the demonic, deciding that a woman had no chance, not unless she went about with a friend or two, preferably with a pointed umbrella. The trouble was that even the most experienced tart could not tell a murderer from a client; every time she cozied up, her neck was on the line, her hopes were lined up like blind mice for lascivious slicing, after which everybody was so wise: yes, well, I'd do Minories and Middlesex Streets, and Old Montague and

Brushfield, but I wouldn't venture near Bucks Row and Brady Street, Hanbury and Lamb. Every girl had to draw out in her mind the map of her solicitings. That was bad enough: being drawn to money, you were being sucked along to death as well, but who walked for the sake of walking? Worse, there would soon be nobody to talk to, not even about murders; she had been close enough to Polly, in an abstract, civil fashion, without ever getting curse-word close, as she had been to Dark Annie, but they all got sloshed together and somehow, without explicitly talking about it, pooled their hand-to-mouth joys, whether or not only one out of the three of them, or the four, had a bed for the night or money for fried fish and some warmed-up spuds. Together, they had managed to get by, thriving on a good cry as a joint act, a series of indiscriminate hugs almost sisterly in their tender blindness, sometimes drinking from the same last glass of beer before going their separate ways into the night, hoping to click before their feet went numb, and the one who was on her period never told the client, unable in the dark or the flickering gaslight to tell blood from other forms of wet. Many a night they had stood seeping the blood that made them mothers, almost as if they straddled London with a tender dew, one foot planked firm and arrogant, full of swank, in The Poultry near the Mansion House, the other in Commercial Street not far from the Jews Free Schools. A big split.

It was awful to have so little, but also to need so little, as if they had been born with desires shrunken, so that a new hat was like an ovation from within, as with Polly Nichols, and a bit of an envelope bearing the seal of the Sussex regiment and the scrawled initial of somebody who had cared enough to write, crude and cuneiform, *yew are sumthing speshal*, M., was a sample from the field of the cloth of gold, a cunt's Agincourt. On things so little, so transitory, they doted as archbishops did on their robes and emblems, the essence of these women's lives being portability: they bore with them all they had and they sometimes gave to one another the discarded hat, the spare pill from the casual ward. Marie knew all this, being the most analytical of the group, but she had now reached a point, to be talked over intimately only with Long Liz Stride, at which she had to walk abroad and devil take the hindmost, or get off to Dieppe, to begin with, then bury herself deep in Paris for a year. Just to avert bad luck, never mind the murderer who was after her too, for accosting the Queen, the P.M., even Eddy, as if they were indeed whores of the grandest caliber, high-priced, whose worldly goods not even a regiment of hussars could move, not even the finest steamships that plied the ocean. But to go to Dieppe, certainly with Long Liz, would be to turn her back on Alice Margaret, for whom she had in her blundering imperious common way done so much, as she thought. The only way was to go and ask Sickert what she should do. Neither Polly nor Dark Annie would have a funeral, that she knew; the goodbyes had been said before they began. Every night was a goodbye, every M'Carthy and Donovan a mercantile pox to bargain with, every drink a skid on the way to more drunkenness, every client a reminder of those poor, sad, ineffectual best beaux: William Nichols, now living in the Old Kent Road, his wife a wreath made of air and stolen clothing; Joe Chapman, the Windsor coachman who had sent Dark Annie ten shillings a week until death cut it off, as anger had made William Nichols cut off his five. Dirty-nailed, dreamy, short-legged, aimless but provident men, they had hovered in their ladies' orbits and then given up hope of weaning them from thrump and booze, except for the drowned, *if* drowned, John Thomas Stride, and all those children lost like new-shelled peas, and then Evan Davis collier, gassed if not dismembered first. And never mind the Siffeys or Sieveys, the Morganstones, the Flemings, the bed-warmers, those who held their women's hands in dreamtime, who came and went and made scenes and slammed them in the chops for the merest transgressions. The truth, Marie Kelly told her ailing brain, was that women were mainly alone and best off alone and, in the wind-up when facing the Almighty with not even ten shillings to grease His palm, best off alone then too. Oh God send us mercy, she thought: I do declare they are coming after us with all our rubbidge. Oddly enough, even as the loudmouth philanthropists began to rave about the easy profits from prostitution and landlording and the reformers began to inveigh against lawless, poisonous sexual intercourse, things quieted down again, from the eighth of September to the ninth, then from the ninth to the tenth, and thence to the twentieth, 21st, 22nd, 23rd, and it was as if some war had come to an end and everyone began to say: They took the sacrifice, the offering of blood was made, the dread landlords of the night have decided to let us off again if only we will talk clean and watch us Ps and Qs. The women of Whitechapel still looked behind them, venturing into the shadows to sell the only thing they had that humans wanted while those most authentically indignant formed what they called a Vigilance

Committee, something no doubt destined to remain awake forever, scanning both dawn and dusk for men with razors, apes with bayonets: *our police force is inadequate to discover the author or authors ... we the undersigned ... intend offering a substantial reward to anyone, citizens or otherwise ... One Samuel Montague, M.P., offered five hundred pounds for the murderer. Marie Kelly and Long Liz Stride began to quiet down, but not with the miserable sang-froid they had achieved after Polly's death. Now their minds were scarred. They were together, the only two; they more than many others had been close to something that tore them in half and reassembled them gimpy and slack. Their throats were sore.*

"We'll never be the same, us two," said Long Liz, hugging Marie's hand at the Ringers; they knew nowhere else to go. All places reminded them of the dead.

"Stick together, love," Marie said thickly. "If anything would drive you to drink, this would. If we had a hundred pounds between us, we'd be better off in France."

"Stripe me," Long Liz sighed, mouth full of pork pie, "the only way to get the money would be to claim the reward."

"Then we'd better wake up our ideas," Marie said, her mind on Polly's new hat, Dark Annie's black eye, both of which had blown away into the universe away from her, no longer subjects for tenderness, but final, definitive, stark, what the world was really like with its clothes off.

"Do you think," Long Liz was asking, "there's really somebody out there just waiting for the likes of us?"

"There's always somebody out there waiting," Marie told her. "Waiting's not getting, though, is it? If he goes according to average," she paused, "he gets one every ten days. Work the odds out for yourself, darlin'. He can't be having us all, can he now, whoever the blighter is."

"But he *is* waiting," Long Liz persisted, "waiting his chance, his turn. Somebody's bound to catch it."

"Well, never fear," Marie said at her most stoically jocular. "Never dare, never win. What if us women was to walk the streets with carving knives in us pettycoats? I mean, not to get him, but to shove them into just about any men around, to whip up a sort of equivalent scare. I do declare I wish we'd started it, and now the men'd be running from us like partridges, instead of the other way round. Sod them. Damn them. Look at us. Who are we? Do you honestly think women like us are worth waiting around for? We're not worth killing, Liz. We're not even, half the time, worth a fourpenny pokey. In God's mouth, it's a sin that we're not, that it is. He should have made us better. If I were not the sex I am, and I had a pair of ripe good ballocks, would I go after the likes of me? No, I'd be after the likes of Mrs. Keppel and Lillie Langtry, just like Prince Bertie. They say he sleeps wit his dicky-bird in his hand, just in case. Now you stop thinking about Polly and Annie. Their time had come, I spose. Think about all the survivors there are, think about how little we're worth killing, flower. Then you'll feel better. I'm going to cry my eyes till the day I die, but I'm not going to bury myself just yet. It's a cruel world, God love it, and you haven't to weaken, no matter what they threaten you with. No matter what," she broke into an odd brogue compact of Cockney and inebriated Irish, talking like some stock personage off the stage, "they tretten you wid. Buck up, Liz, there's animals in the sea worse than men, and we can't even swim, can we now?" Then she remembered the so-called Great Thames disaster and the five hundred drowned, among them the carpenter John Thomas Stride and two of his nine children. True or not, the sad story had irresistible poignancy now. "Sorry, lass," Marie whispered, patting Long Liz on the shoulder. "Me tongue ran away with me. I'll tame it yet."

Then she told Liz that she would go and ask Sickert what he thought about the murders; if there was an easy and cheap way to Dieppe, he would be able to find it. If she had had the faintest idea what his role had been so far in Gull's atrocious outings, she might have gone to the police; but she would have gone only half-way, stunned there by the notion that they were waiting for her, not to harm her but to put her away. She lived in a muddled world in which some facts were absolute, requiring no trimmings or modifications, and some were malleable, subject to weather, whim and desire. In the end she found herself unable to add things together: the likely and the impossible; the acceptable and the unspeakable; the humdrum, the humble and the spectacular, the lofty. So she thought she was both in danger and out of danger; desirable and no oil painting; a leader and a born pawn. Since Polly's death, she had developed a new sense, that the ground was opening up in front of her and one look down, of precipitous breath-held untrustingness, and she would whistle away out of sight, not for something done, but *because*. Perhaps this was why, now she had realized the mythic element in all courage, she tried to live recklessly, inviting the bristling bear in the darkness to hug her to death even as she howled the one word Whitechapel never heeded: Murder. In attracting the killer to her, she somehow weakened him, wanned him, and why not? If only enough of them could do it before he struck again, though he might never, they could perhaps turn the tables. Her mind's eye filled with an infernal vision of a human being spurting purple ink like an octopus, as he crouched there in rough shag cape and velour hat of charcoal black, cowering and whinnying as three or four burly trollops carved him up and passed out the pieces to the waiting horde. *That's what you call showing them.* All that happened next, though, was that Polly and Annie came humbly toiling through the darkness telling them to drop it, to get on with their work, it wasn't women's way, it wasn't worth getting topped for. For all she knew, they had all trafficked with this man already, and he was a purely spoken gent with lots of books at home and a lovely confidential way of talking, like a doctor or one of the gentler commissionaires at the big hotels, never moving the girls on but, as it were, sipping them as they hovered, his mouth where his eyes were, his braid dazzling in the sun, his hands big collops of worn-shiny gladness. Any man, Marie held, might want to do a girl in, any old time; it was in the nature of the male, half of their charm reposing as it did on throwing their weight about and being irritable. Get past that in any man, she held further, and you were dealing with soft wet bread. They had to have their greens and then they would give you the earth, even if only to have you photographed with handfuls of muck in front of you or the planet like a grapefruit above your bosom, rising in golden subordinate tittiness. She was almost ready to claim that some good was bound to come out of the killings; that was the way nature balanced things up, harsher than Satan for the Pollys and the Annies, born in eternal ruction and gone down to sewage.

"You dreaming agyne," Long Liz said. "You've got that treacly look you have."

"Well, booger it," Marie said, "I'm dreamin' horrors. Would you like some of them? A little tasty sample? No you would not. I was thinking of how girls get older but go on thinking of themselves as girls and before you can say Jack Robinson London's full of old youngsters squabbling over the next coffin, the next unmarked grave. They'll be having no decent burial, those two. The doctors'll be having a fine old time with the remains." She could not accept evisceration any more than she could explosion: some fates just did not square with a world in which the saying *Bob's your uncle* stood for a norm of impromptu optimism (the god out of the machinery coming to get you when you least expected it) and the other saying *How's your father?* was another norm, of civil procedure over the bread and butter, the boiled leeks, the fried eggs on fried bread. What you said when you wuz good.

Sickert in Hampstead was a man in the county of reprieve, living on borrowed time perhaps, in some bourgeois copy of what the lower orders knew by heart as "detained during Her Majesty's pleasure," meaning the hangman could come any time and have his way with you even in the middle of breakfast with a sausage in your mouth embedded in a mouthful of mash; the drop would force it out of you into the all-encompassing black hood. When Ellen finally decided to move her things, she would end the lease, or whatever respectable thing remained to be done, hardly important to him who owned little unconnected with painting. Some of the books were hers, but most of them his; he would have to come and collect them up, once it had been settled that the two of them would not be getting back together. In an odd way, because such a move was always for the having, or had been when they last met, he did not want it or even consider it seriously; had she refused to contemplate it, though, he would have been insisting on it daily. Perverse Sickert, he said, you're living a different life now: you have crossed over into the terrain of the forbidden, the grievous, the damned, and all these well-bred privileges are as so many snowdrops to you. Having seen what you have seen, and become an accomplice simply from not having run away and be damned to the child held hostage, you have condemned yourself to mark time with bloody footsteps. No longer a man among men, you are the monster among the teacups. You have *fallen*, do you know that? How far, and where to, are matters not for you to judge, and you should quake that one of these days you might indeed be judged, then turned out into the Kalahari of the heart, waterless and blinded, doomed to wander while pleading for an unattainable forgiveness. Should the news ever come out, that you have Gulled and Netleyed yourself to fiendish perdition, your work will have the unmistakable aroma of madness, and collectors will amass it for its gossip quality: *These were the very hands,* for by then no one will care who used the knife on whom, it will all have merged into one dismal bloodletting in a city that should instead have turned its back on profit.

At that moment, among the shriveled flowers and the faint ticking of kettles and pans as the air in the deserted house cooled and tightened up, squeezing the metal, he knew that he would have somehow to incorporate his sense of history or doom into his work, not overtly painting it, not converting atrocity into a daub, but insinuating something: his reluctance, the true facts, the background to the hideous deeds already dominating the minds of Londoners. Was there a way of saying that he, culpable, was guiltless? Or that, helplessly enmeshed, he had fought to save his intrinsic decency? Special pleading, he wanly noted. Those who had served had served. Besides, it was not over. This was merely a lull as his unthinkable allies refreshed themselves, took even deeper breath for the final act or acts. Why did not the very furniture leap from his touch? Why did not the rugs on the floors shuffle away from his feet, his loathsome step? There was no one here to point at him, but there would soon be millions, unless, of course, thanks to Gull's insane ingenuities, the truth never came out and he, Sickert, was obliged to live out his days wondering if it would not have been better to be pilloried for his part, to have it out in the open, letting the cognoscenti and the rabble watch him tear his own eyes out in Trafalgar Square, donating the profits from the sales of his lugubrious and scandalous works to the Providence Row Women's Refuge. How, he wondered, could even an only half-decent man consider lifting up the corner of the grotesque denouement that allowed him to get away with it? Who or what allowed him to even think of it? Of course he wanted it both ways, being suborned to watch and yet having the rest of his life fresh as a daisy, and unimpeded as an Alpine freshet, to regret everything in. So far, so good. He winced. So far, utterly unspeakable; how could there be a sequel? How could Gull go on with it, with his last few thousand gasps defaming the very notion of evil itself? The flayed carcasses of Polly Nichols and Dark Annie Chapman roamed through his head and did not go away, but they hovered there in the half-light of *The Crusader*'s interior: a smile like a facial courtesy; a whispering sound from the butcher's block as pressed pork lapsed into slices; almost a gurgle, oh definitely, as he and Netley heaved the bodies, one, two, into the grave dayspring of a day so apocalyptic that Londoners would forget to eat, even to cry. They would dog him wherever he went until, one day, he would lie down and end it all, with a razor in the bath, Roman style, or from a high belfry, say that of St. Jude's, Whitechapel, murmuring I was not good enough to have lived, I gave all my self-perpetuations to the devil, I helped to turn London into a sinner's drain.

He had seen the phenomenon before, of course; indeed he had discoursed upon it at one or two assemblies of painters, calling up the ghost of Leonardo, who said that splotches moved if you looked at them long enough. Sometimes, the more he thought about it, the whole Renaissance seemed on the move, coming right out at them like a train out of a tunnel, all steam and Whistler. He forgave himself the pun and looked again at Ellen's favorite chair, already abstract as a collapsed ceiling in its dustcloth, and yet it moved as he peered at its back, still in part the indignant swain angry with her for being too diffident, for respecting his feelings *too* much. Yet that was her nature: cool, a little nurse-like, tolerant as a sky. All she could not abide was his not needing her enough, or his needing a sewer to match her unicorn quality. Again the back of the chair budged, wavered sideways, and he was sure his day had come, that whatever darkness held sway in the universe had come to get him and he would not have to go off into the night with Gull again. In almost capricious relief he stood slowly up, recognizing in the movement the same thing as he had watched in self-righteous crowds who, as if to laud themselves for thinking well of something, got to their feet not to pay tribute to the speaker, but, in part stretching their knees, to stand in awe of themselves, as if such a degree of self-approval would fester, compelled to sit. Could this be Ellen, here to sign and seal? To end things with a discreet clandestine visit to the scene of her guiltless downfall? If only the chair would not waver thus, implying that he was a wavering man; this was his bed, made, and he should come and roll in it. At this point, as Sickert floundered between hallucination and almost caustic nostalgia, he wanted to paint the scene: the chiaroscuro with the furniture on the move, as in that story of de Maupassant; but his sense of smell made him float from that, drenching him with patchouli, woolly patchouli as he liked to call it, no pleasant perfume of summer flowers but a searching musk, was that it? Cheap, perhaps, and overpowering him as it rose from the bowels of an unused empty chair as if someone had sat naked in it for years and each time that person or any other at there the aroma rose from the cushion, compressed into pungency. Stench of whose ghost then? He stared, shivering with fright, wishing for something brown and yellow to arise from the chair and waft him away into the Hampstead twilight, but this time a commanding effigy came upward from the chair, slyly almost, unfolding and uncoiling: an overweight anaconda, he thought, personifying lord alone knew what viciousness in himself. He backed away, trying to exhale only, but his heart was bouncing, ready to escape and leave him confronting the lurid form, oddly plump for a snake and more evocative of something from the music hall: a padded acrobat, a horse's body with two men inside. Instead, however, even as without looking he tiptoed to the French windows, half-wondering if he needed to use his knife as he heard the voice he might have been hoping to hear, if voice there had to be, but one that was Irish done in caramel, not quite whispering in the dank stuffiness of that room, nor quite murmuring either, but gently booming what it had so evidently rehearsed:

"Now then, Walt, it's only me."

3

He was sure it was a voice, perhaps human even, but his deviant mind had taken him away to a prison, Pentonville, where he and Gull and Netley had to take the long drop after being apprehended and condemned, the only unusual facet of the entire proceeding being that Gull, as one created knight of the realm, was entitled to be hanged on a rope of silk. Was that correct? Sickert could not quite figure out why such irrelevant thoughts came to mind. No, not irrelevant after all: the shape writhing in that armchair, the voice curling out toward him, were those of a witness no doubt, ready to swear. He did not want to think. "Only me" was the characteristic phrase of the person self-belittled life-long, or belittled by others. Dying, they said it's only me going. Starving or choking, it was only ever me. This was a woman's voice, though, not altogether familiar, but not Ellen's, and then he knew, but the voice was saying something else:

"Gave you quite a turn, didn't I, Walt? Out of sight, out of mind." Marie Kelly, to be sure, rising not from the dead but from something like chronic absence, penitential hiding. His mind worked again and he now saw the link between the two: the twirling form of Gull, neck snapped, was also the form of Marie Kelly rising from the armchair like something out of the Indian rope trick, a spiral without gravity.

Was he going to need the knife? Did she have a pistol? He suddenly saw that, for bizarre reasons of her own, she might want to start wiping out the murderers, he being the easy one. But she knew nothing of Gull, though more than enough, he guessed, about Netley. He was still wondering what to say to her, both levity and lechery being out of the question, when his mouth and throat combined to say "Marie Kelly. It's been a long time."

Obviously she was not coming right to the point. "I've come to have a look at how His Nibs lives as a married man. Our Walter and his Missus. Not bad for a painter, is it now? Where is she, then, Mrs. Hoity-Toity when she's at home? I bet she's walked out on you, old Walt, because you didn't keep your trouser buttons tight."

He had never needed to answer Kelly when she talked in this vein, her voice adjusted for the maximum of near-falsetto onslaught, a whine with an accusation running all the way through it like a vein. He could smell her, too: rushes and muddy sea roses, he thought, and he quite distantly wondered how she had made her way across London, certainly not to chatter idly, but to pin him down, to make him say something culpable and definite. Whatever she had come for, he told himself to let her begin; that was what Gull would do, wasn't it? She might end by attacking him, in which event he might end up doing Gull's work for him (get *The Crusader* out there fast, Netley to help him heave the body). He was hardly in the mood for an erotic bout with her, not that, in his previous ones, he had never intended to do it; she had led him on with earthy finesse to the point at which his organs took over and put him where she wanted him. This time, though, in the gloom of the empty house with none of the clocks ticking, it was an appointment of another kind, outrageously unstated.

"You've come a long way, Marie."

"Well, old cock, at least I haven't had me froat cut on the way, no thanks to you, I spose. A girl never knows when she isn't going to be going home to home and beauty after a hard day's walking, does she? Alice Margaret, now, where is she at these days?"

He thought he knew, but they could have moved her; she might be anywhere. Nobody was going to tell him until they needed her off their hands. "Oh, Windsor, I suppose," he said in a shrunken, oddly denatured voice, ashamed of what it said before it spoke.

"And you'll take care, in the end."

"As God is my witness."

"You read the papers?"

"Do I read the papers?"

"Polly Nichols and Dark Annie Chapman. *You* know."

"Of course I've heard. It *is* Whitechapel, after all."

"They're on to us, Walt."

"Who is us?"

"All of us—Polly and Annie, you and me, Prince Eddy. They're going to wipe us out, and then there'll be no scandal left. Last of all to go will be Alice Margaret. They've got her mother already, haven't they? I was wondering what you thought about going to Dieppe, and never coming back. If only we could get the child back, we could set off. And Annie too. How can we get Annie back to send abroad?"

Her vision of Dieppe appealed to him. It was oddly thrilling to be in this big, vacant house with the mature and sensual, rather massively built, Marie Kelly exchanging treasonous whispers like two owls, as if she knew all that he knew and had done, all that he had seen. Somehow, Annie seemed too far away to care about, and Alice Margaret unreal; the only valid things were the two deaths and the unfinished career of the madman on four wheels, the royal Gull, ravenous to do Salisbury's mild bidding in the most savage terms. Never would he tell her, beyond a few vague warnings. She asked for the fare to France and he offered to give it to her, though not tonight; he would scratch around, sell some paintings, and do it that way. She seemed to believe him, asking how soon, and he demurred, saying four or five days, knowing that if he really cared he would have said let's go and get it now, I'll pack a bag and we'll be out of London before dawn. Whatever has to be done has to be done in a blithering hurry, Kelly, my girl. Why then, like some petrified man unearthed from the bowels of a cave, did he not move? Could it be that he really looked forward to what Gull was doing to do with her and he wanted to look on? Dismissing that, he thought about the hovel she lived in, that made even his run-down studio rooms seem a palace, and wished he lived in a world more just, more obliging, more maternal. There she stood, almost opposite him, but still only a silhouette, as he to her, each waiting for the other to cease fencing and deliver the straight truth.

"Have you heard?" she said mysteriously.

"Heard," he said unresponding.

"Do you *know?*"

"Nobody tells me anything," he said in a petulant lunge. "They just shove me around. Don't you remember, I'm just a poor bloody painter rubbing his *sous* together."

"Ay, but you know people, Walt. What's going on, for the sake of Jesus? If they're trying to get my attention, they've succeeded. I'm boozing now whenever I can get the price of it."

"You might as well, Marie," he said, speaking from far away where none of this mattered. "I do myself. I've done all I can do. I shouldn't have done any of it. Look at the trouble I've caused—Annie and Alice Margaret." Then he said it, like someone having a purge. "You've been doing some letter-writing, I hear."

"How did you hear that?"

"A dicky-bird told me."

"Fat lot of good that'll do you when they catch up with you, Waltie boy. Mark my words, they'll leave nobody alone. We'll all get it in the neck sooner or later."

"Talk, just talk," he said, shuffling the rug into soft ribs. "I think you'll be all right, honest," he lied. "If there's anything I can do, I'll do it. Dieppe wouldn't be so bad."

"Well, flower," she said with caustic ebullience, "money doesn't grow on trees, or up arseholes, does it now? Are you going to pay me in bananas or what?"

"I'll see," he said, wondering what his true motives were: if, having gone this far, he wanted to be rid of it all, even to the extent of being rid of her, of Alice Margaret, and then making a proper gentleman's attempt to patch up his sundered marriage, still quite new. The side of him not conscience-stricken wanted to go back to Cleveland Street and start painting, just flush this mess away and say its hosannas later. Where was it written that a man was responsible for all he did? When a man had been a sentient onlooker, and no more, how much did he owe to whom? Reminding himself that Marie Kelly could not read his mind, he caressed the dagger in his sock (his first movement in several minutes) and looked and looked for the penumbra of horror that should be surrounding her: the imminence of slaughter, the ghastly halo of Gull's grape-induced coma, the destroyed smile on her face when he stepped down from *The Crusader*, raised his deerstalker hat and invited her aboard as if he genuinely meant to save her feet and, indeed in these parlous times, her neck. Such a fate I usher you to, he thought, almost reveling in the role he would not have to play; he could revel in it, could he not, when he would never have to play it? He would certainly never go so far as to identify her; they were like brother and sister under the aegis of fornication, were they not? Was that what she had come here to find out? Could he be Mister Facing Bothways, who both knew her and could go willfully blind? Neither made a move toward the other, not even for one of those perfunctory hugs they usually gave each other; it was as if each would infect the other. If they stayed apart, nobody could trace them back to where they had come from. Indeed, she might have been followed. Where was it written that Sickert would always go out with Netley and Gull on their nocturnal sorties? What would be easier than to polish them both off somewhere between Hampstead Heath and Whitechapel? Sickert knew now that the full armature of so-called human motives was crammed to the hilt with little flecks of the random, most of all for those who flew by night, did midnight flits, and achieved the unexpected by simple dint of not thinking too hard about what they were doing. He was a traitor to someone, that was certain, but he wasn't quite sure to whom since he had to figure out how much he owed; making a small gesture did not obligate you all the way. Handing a coin to a pauper did not make you a citizen of the country of misery, did it? Some artists, he reasoned right there while Marie Kelly did her pillar of salt before him in that house reeking of furniture polish and whitewash, were not morally committed to the farms of phenomena from which they gained their impressions. He who saw in the spat-up phlegm of the music-hall songbird the germ of a new color was not morally obligated to her hungs. He was going to spend the remainder of the year pondering, provided Gull did not axe him first. "You know, Marie," he at last said, "if I can gather my wits together, I think I know where the tea is, and we can boil the kettle. I've a right to be here, daft as it sounds." Her laughter put his teeth on edge so he went hunting for wine, brandy, Scotch, a bottle of any kind, and they finally sat opposite each other on dust-sheeted arm chairs, drinking gin, not reminiscing about the old days, a fair number of which they had shared, in what he pompously called more auspicious times. She had little to say, seeming content with a moment in which she could eye him and remain alive, in which no one was on her trail, no one was sidling through Whitechapel with a photograph, asking for her. Here it was if she were in a vault, a tomb, in a house already marked for frozen debility, neither favoring her nor harming her, whereas he, he was monarch of all he surveyed; she liked that expression although it wasn't an Irish one, she having acquired it from Annie Crook in less grievous days. She knew that they were two people whose passions had a rancid side, whose prettiest delectations of the spirit had a flavor of rot. Each saw this in the other, but they had hardly confronted it orchestrally, made the most of it. Now, she thought, they would never have chance since she thought he was as doomed as she, though the horror of what had happened to Polly and Dark Annie appeared to have passed him by as some typhoons do mandarins.

"Feeling better?" he said wanly.

No answer told him; she was beyond it, almost beyond feeling, and, beyond that, beyond caring. She was ready for affable anesthesia, so he hugged her, inhaling that South Seas scent of her, and she hugged him back in the full conviction that they were victims together, two viles adding up to a convenient nicenesss. Properly meshed, they could have worked wonders together, she thought, of flesh and canvas, of exotic fame and classless grandeur. It was too late now, she knew, although her nostalgic soul craved for Dieppe, though a Dieppe overlaid with Limerick lambs and the brash rhetoric of Irish pubs. Once you got to Dieppe, you could have everything, couldn't you? All nations eventually fetched up there, for fun or something graver, like the Prime Minister, Lord Salisbury, who, she'd heard, had a chalet there. Dieppe was a paradise to which you invited yourself. Both she and Sickert made the overtures to something sexual, but neither cared to go ahead, preferring to purr together in this dismal suburban box far from shops and trains, and he suddenly thought: If she stays here, she might be safe. Imagine *The Crusader* clattering up here. Gull would never dare; he functions only in Whitechapel. But Gull was off his head, now and then anyway, and the indefatigable Netley, the spy, snoop and voyeur, would sooner or later get the right idea, and another corpse would appear, this time in an area with tone and tweed. How, Sickert wondered, did you use a house without using it? How did you walk the rind of the planet without actually treading on it? It was like asking how you lived a life without ever doing things infamous and then, on top of that, doing things even worse, as it were released by their predecessors. One wrong step was all it took, and down the gradient you went screaming, lapsed from being what your headmaster called A Boy of Ability who Does Not

Concentrate or Work Hard to a slobbering demon, a mother-defiler and a wife-strangler. Sickert had begun to believe in the criminal aspect of his nature, waiting for it to come at him in the dead central core of sulfuric darkness and get him doing things he knew nothing about, squandering his gifts on gorgeous perniciousness.

Marie Kelly was shouting, not so much from gin as from a fit of new-born irritability, and he could not fathom to whom she was calling, at least not until from the shadows there came another form, even bigger and taller than Marie, making his racing blood cool for a moment. "Long Liz," Marie said. "View met? Walt Sickert, darling, he's me only mate." Long Liz had been the surreptitious witness of all that had been said, and now she had slunk out of the darkness behind the big captain's desk to come and have gin with them, like someone quietly built out there somewhere and then brought out for testing, to see if she could walk, talk and sigh.

"No, I don't think we've met," he said, slow-motion.

"Then now we have," Long Liz said. "This lovely place is going to waste. Wives, I reckon, is great wasters of nice howjedo's, at least in my book. Folks doesn't know when they is best off. Me, I lost two children in the Great Thames disaster, two of my nine, and John Thomas too." In the dim light, Marie was shaking her head, tapping her head with her forefinger to announce that Long Liz was off again, off her rocker. It was quite like old times. "This house is like a boat, isn't it?"

"Have you two been here before?" Sickert asked sternly.

"This is our first, duck," Marie said jovially, flinging both hands outward as if to encompass the setting or make the fact flower beyond its normal range. "No, never."

"Home sweet home," Sickert said tipsily.

"She did a bunk on him," Marie whispered.

"They often do," Stride said like a denuded chorus.

"And then," Marie chimed in. It was like pub talk.

"You see, we know," Stride informed him.

"And then," Marie said, "he realized how well off he had been with a couple of chippies in the worst part of London, thrumping like a Turk in Cleveland Street and no quetchtions arsked, no quarter given, none arsked. I bet you was harder, and pointier, my darling, there than you was ever here, for all the cushions and the fire irons. I do declare I can see better now me lamps is lit." How her Irish Cockney slipped and fell.

"Oh, I don't know," Sickert responded tipsily, "even bad marriages have their moments, and good times with tarts have bad ones too. The straight and narrow isn't all crown of thorns, ladies, and the primrose path can be a stinking bore."

"Heark at him," Marie said. "Mister knowitall."

"If you ask me, and you won't," Long Liz said, "men is lucky to have us waiting around for them. Where'd they be without us to give their nastiness full play? I've seen them come and go, and I've only learned one thing: even when they like it they don't like it, they don't like liking it, they would always rather go on to do something else than do it again. An apple a day, just to keep them from getting a headache. Many a woman I know can think of nothing else for days, even when they're doing it, but not your men: men like to dump it and clear off. It's like this froat-cutting caper that's presently going on: same thing. They can only cut it once. They can only do you in once, and they only want to do you once too."

If she only knew, Sickert thought, how Gull goes at it not once, but twice, then again, slicing after poisoning, then cutting them open to be sure of something, almost like an archeologist of the flesh. He's the exception, I suppose. He never seems to tire of it, though he tires of waiting to get on with it. Yet he was never a surgeon, more a physician, so perhaps he'd always wanted to cut bodies up and apart and all they'd ever let him do was peer and prescribe. That must explain his passion for what's beneath, as if he was the head of some Secret Service wanting to know what's really going on in, oh, Italy. Let's cut it open and see. These women are guessing, cheering themselves up by thinking they understand his motives. Why, he is like some ancient loyal retainer, Lear's Kent, I imagine, saying whatever he says at the end—my master calls me, I must not say no—wanting to go out in a blaze of fidelity: nothing too crude or too awful to do for his master. He wants to be the ash on his garden, the offal on his midden.

Now the two women were almost weeping, perhaps because he was ignoring them, and then they cheered up, achieving a simultaneous hectic, giddy laugh, but Sickert held on to his thought, vaguely resentful that he had to spend his time chattering with whores in the precinct of his desolation, the house he could not abide to face alone.

Then why had he come here in the first place? For something to do? No, he had merely gone walking, the light likely to last until past ten and enticing him out, along, into the flurry and shuffle of people out taking the air in spite of the new disemboweler in the streets, almost as if daring him to pollute so beautiful a later afternoon and early evening with his ghoulish bloodlust. Had it been winter, Sickert thought, he could have taken Marie and Long Liz to a music hall to cheer them up with a song by little Dot Hetherington, all tinsel and toot. That was what they needed: a tune, a trot, a chorus. It was too late now for any music hall, though they were having one of their own, impromptu, in here, their clothes undone, their faces almost invisible, their throats raw from the gin. Little expecting anything, he asked Marie Kelly for a tune, and she responded at once, almost like a choirboy trapped high up in King's College Chapel, Cambridge, achieving on this evening a series of notes so pure he felt a tear begin; she hymned the place she had come from, a boy soprano wanting a new life out of the blue, and no more hand-me-down lovers:

> Only a violet
> I plucked
> From my Mother's Grave
> When a boy, when a bo-oy.

How poignant, he thought, in this house of broken love, to a man against his will and decency obliged to look on at the toil of murderers. She is serenading one of the destroyers, passive as he might be, singing for both dead women, neither of whom sang much perhaps, and giving them a callow goodbye. He tried to sing along but desisted, having neither the voice (as an actor might have) nor the occasion. What he wanted was not a song but bellowed grief and outrage. He tried one, but succeeded only in halting the singer in mid-"Mother," so that she sang "From my Mo—," acceptable in the circumstances yet disruptive of the mood, whose maintenance required not a syllable wrong, no splits, and no caesuras. It was as if she, or he, had drawn a white line across the night sky so as to delineate something, east from west, say, or high from low, only to end up bisecting a miracle, which meant that all of a sudden only the line showed.

"That's enough," he shouted across the yard separating him from Marie Kelly, "but thanks for the tune. Come and cuddle instead, I have a fierce desire to be held and made a fuss of." They wasted no time, enfolding him like marauding eider downs, tweaking his loins to no effect but managing to arrange themselves in such a way that, willy nilly, even as he talked he tongued and laved them without taking much interest in his accomplishment or their pleasure, and quite unaware that both women were naked on the rug with him, almost as if posing for him to paint them, for which of course he would have been obliged to retreat to a safe and dry distance. On the three of them sported, soggy with drink, but managing a sedate lasciviousness: exactly what his mood required as he licked anonymous mounds of samite flesh, vaguely his for the hour, as the tenor of their lives prescribed, but this was free or for the price of the gin, and he wondered if, deep down, this was all he ever needed, either a roll on the rug or a woman-sized udder, never, he said, never to be slashed wide open, oh never that. Surely, if ever there could be a reason for doing what Gull did, it was the apparent defenselessness of flesh, its openness to wounding. Another view would be more human, he supposed; after all, left to its own devices, the flesh and its skin made a superb job of staying together, rarely coming apart. Balloon and air, they were lovers, especially in such buxom wenches as Marie Kelly, bigger than he remembered her, whereas Stride, though sturdy, was narrower and suggested muscle to spare. When his hand felt Stride, he recoiled a little, knowing she could blast him with one poke of her arm, whereas he fell swooning into Kelly's pillows, half inclined to suffocate and have Stride tug him out like a violet from his mother's grave. They were having such a boozy, undemanding, fleshly evening that they never felt hungry, never wanted to be anywhere different, or with anyone else. Slowly their talk became fouler, their motions more overt; the women's wriggles were more deliberate, more spasmodic, while his own motions were dreamlike and soft, not what they needed. Next thing, feeling *de trop*, he found the women pleasuring each other with sighs of unsimulated gusto, none of which stirred him, but he smiled at their pleasure and wondered what Ellen would say or do if she were to walk through the door. He felt like a scribe at the mating of satiny mastodons; he tested the heaves and wobbles of those flanks and collops, marveling at the sleek rigor of female anatomy, wishing (briefly) to change sex so that he might partake of this, better far than tramping around London's meanest streets for sordid inspiration. The sounds he could never paint, and this disturbed him as their mutual relish had an exquisite, tidal timing, but he knew in what hues he would brush their pallor, their heavings, their moods quick-changing from languor to frenzy. It was a disrobing of the milkmaids on a floor of cream, in a cleft of carnal air trapped between the reek of furniture polish and the whitewash on the ceiling above, pungent and dank. He could tell flesh and skin were fluid, coppery or brassy to the taste, and naturally conductive to meditations on, drawings of, the fox's brush, the rhinoceros's pleats, the flamingo's rose-fleecy breadbasket. All of it was one, even though the two immediate samples for his consumption happened to be two fallen women; they had not fallen in his estimation but had soared voluptuously in the dismal light, teaching him about the sallow colors of ecstasy, sallow because there was never enough light anywhere, not in Victoria's England, by jiminy. In Dieppe, yes, as in the Midi, the Riviera. He knew he would have to paint Marie and Long Liz sometime, without actually having seen them at it, but having slaked their frenzy with his soul.

For most of his short life he had been able to press from day to day without having to interrogate himself too keenly about his ultimate motives: these he took as read, as once upon a time so thoroughly inspected that further scrutiny would be superfluous. Sickert knew where he was going: to the pinnacle of the art world, by thirty-five, say, and as he sometimes told people about himself he would do almost anything to get ahead. Yet to speak thus was to traffic in such banalities as fame, whereas the meatier, the nastier, question had to do with the one thing he wanted his art to achieve, and he was beginning to recognize that it amounted to full visual deployment of the lives that had no hope, in whatever segment of society; so his ambit included despair and boredom, the squalid and the sordid, the down-at-heel and the tarnished, the trite and the verdigrised. He had become almost a pastmaster of the done-for, hoping always to find it and finding it so often that he sometimes wondered if his zeal had brought it into being in an otherwise or hitherto palatable situation. Does imagination, he wondered, actually transmogrify? Magic he loved, but he felt duty bound (or esthetics-bound) to supply its counterpoint in ravishing profusion. One day, he told himself, he would drown in all his browns: all those sauces, soups and glues his mind had lingered on, as if in some coprophile's tizzy. Some had called his view of life mournful, dreary, lackluster, but he had always felt that it was more honest to take the flags and pennants and superb ribboned awnings of life as a bonus sent to taunt, as if music were a fluke from the cough or painting some by-product of conjunctivitis or literature the offshoot of the fingernail scratching at a scab. If then he thought thus, why should the doings of Gull distress him so much? Surely, in the crass and lethal rituals of the zealous royal physician there were some Sickertian elements. The man, like Sickert, wanted to reach undreamed-of extremes, like a Satan pushing beyond apprehensible and categorical fidget to feats of raw bad temper, as if he had been called on to perform in some impromptu demonstration of unthinkable behavior. Only a deity, Sickert thought, could endure the massive contradictions of the double nature he envisioned, both enchanted and revulsed by the clashes in his creation. All else was copycat, he thought, though in his moderate way he had careened off the human map, far behind Gull of course, but trying all the same to strike the very nadir until it would have no more of him. Had he, he wondered, sported with Polly Nichols and Dark Annie Chapman, the late lamented, as he had tonight with Long Liz and Marie Kelly, would he now be feeling the authentic throb of terminal shame, or would he, never mind how secretly, be reveling in having tasted a sensuality so close to oblivion: the frisson in the imminent cadaver? Was that what he wanted above all?

Now, as if they had shifted their doings to another register, they stood and began to hum and warble, then to sing "Only violet," singing not to one another but to themselves, relievedly and perhaps shamefacedly announcing that they were still alive, still kicking. Where had Marie's song come from, he wondered. Why did she sing no other? Her untutored voice had done its share of screaming and berating, but when she sang this lyric she achieved an odd, aloof decorum that Long Liz could not match, nor shambling Sickert with his unreliable baritone. They were serenading the house without meaning to, no doubt thanking it and taming the echoes. Now they sang one after the other, the same phrase, "Only a violet," again and again, he with raucous gusto, Marie Kelly with temperate reverence, Long Liz Stride with nasal incisiveness. It had become their theme song, something to haunt them during events to come, but only Sickert knew this, wondering as always if the next encounter in *The Crusader* was going to be a mere scolding or something much more dreadful—and with whom? He could not believe that he was looking at potential victims, functioning as some kind of witchdoctor, willing the future to go this or that way. Clearly, he was as close to Kelly, in his disheveled way, as he had ever been to Ellen Cobham: on a level that found them together opening their legs in front of each other, airing their genitals, and generally having a candid scratch or two, after which they came abruptly and wordlessly together. Could a man do all this with a woman destined for execution within the next few weeks? How could he endure it, romping with her thus, and with Long Liz less expertly, only as a prelude to seeing them both in tatters? As a category, the appropriate no longer grew on its old stem, bore its habitual flowers, but lunged out at him, a conger eel with conical teeth for petals. It was not as if the executioners were going to wholly other people, about whom he would read in the penny dreadfuls; he was one of the select party, his role minor to be sure, but he would nonetheless be a witness, an accomplice, and then what would he think about himself? Who would forgive him? Would self-forgiveness, if ever he got that far, work? Or did the mind seal itself off like an envelope so that one could get on with the chores of daily living? His head would not explode, but he would never be able to whistle "Only a violet" again. Marie's song would have dropped into the vat of the dismembered along with her remains, and that song would be forever accursed, yet only for him. He felt catastrophically alone just now, a cheater, a fake, some kind of Judas goat; after tonight, either woman would respond to him that little bit more warmly, anticipating a good time of whatever kind. They would come to him as a wave, a gesture, already guessing what he had in mind, and before they saw otherwise they would have become part of Gull's abominable empire of the flesh, already dead and gone in the first few seconds of grape-poisoning, hardly distinguishable from their living selves, but irrevocably switched from one dimension to another by a fleck of poison, and then transformed by force majeure with the knife. How he was able to think about such matters, even in hypothesis, he had no idea, deciding he must have somehow schooled his mind: after the first horror, the second was fractionally milder, wasn't it, so by the time he reached his hundredth (his old hundredth, he thought, like the hymn), he would be hungry for even more violent stimulants. Nothing by then would stir him, he would have become murder's leading sophisticate, destined to paint violent crimes with the same sang-froid as he painted boats, flowers and bottles of wine. Perhaps society needed someone such, whose bloody hands did not appall him, to domesticate life's unspeakable side. It sounded grave and taxing, this new career, but he was not sure he would live to pursue it; he was likelier to have his neck officially broken for having been an accessory. No, Gull said the police would give them no trouble: amid the carnal uproar of London, a few more murders hardly figured. It all depended, he knew, on what Gull did next; the furor was already dying down, if there had been one at all, and even the most imaginative of street-walkers had gone back to the game, looking behind them less than before, less than last week, as if the avengers had drunk their fill and life could go on being as comfortably wretched as weeks ago.

"Time to go, girls," he said, intending nothing immediate. It was all he could think of to say, but, attuned to orders or instructions, Kelly and Stride at once began to dress, having been dismissed. Their mercantile selves took over from their impulsive ones.

"I," Marie said, "feel just like one of them Myries in New Zealand."

"Why?" Stride asked. "What's Myries when they're at home? What's Myrie about us, dear?"

"Oh, I don't know," Marie said with lazy confidence, "I just heard about them, see, and I said my life's like theirs. They just bugger about all over the place, coming and going when they want to. Don't you feel like that?"

"You're much more tied down, to business," Sickert said, meaning to go on and say more but suddenly drained of ideas and emotion as he recognized that it was these two Gull would be after. Imagine, if Gull had only known that they could be found together in the same place, he would have been there at the gallop, grapes in his hand. He wanted none of the other women in London, accepted no substitutes. Sickert was treading on coals too hot to bear. Indignation thinned his voice and took the resonance out of it. Could he perhaps, in a hurry, sell this house not his and so finance an escape to France? What Marie, Stride and he needed was a boat, a yacht, a schooner, so that no *Crusader* could creep up on them out of the night. He felt Gull's knife score his own skin and rip through his entrails: Walter Sickert, victim number three, painter and frequenter of whores. No wonder, then; he was asking for it. All his days he had complained to himself that life rarely expressed itself in a conspicuous melody but was almost always a mess of incomplete and forgettable themes no one could ever decipher; it was not a symphony, he used to say, it was a river of odds and ends, a miscellany of canceled afterthoughts, a maelstrom of botched quotations, the whole thing unworthy of a God who surely, if any entity could, had a clear and organized mind.

Why was God not like Brahms? It was no use posing such questions, but this shabby discontent had always dogged him. Life seemed to him to have filled up like a litter bin; it had certainly not been shaped from above by a genius pounding out sublime chords during the hours of darkness.

"Look at 'im," Stride said in her broadest, stagiest Cockney, "'e's lawst in fawt, just you watch 'im fink."

Sickert stared at them from some New Zealand of the mind, almost unable to recall who they were and what they were doing in the house of his marriage.

"Darling Liz," Marie replied, "don't you let him bother you. He's a thinker all right, and he's not all fun, are you, my flower? But he's better than some of the johnnies I get between my legs. At least he'll laugh with you." His laugh, Sickert thought balefully, is going to be on the other side of his face soon; the work of oblivion goes apace, grinding his conscience down into chalky atoms, soon to blow away while the dedicated painter reduces all hues to a drainage green, like an angry child who rubs all the colors together until nothing remains recognizable. He was thinking of Dark Annie disemboweled, of the sheer visual turmoil that came to birth before his eyes in *The Crusader*. If all the forms of life were melting down, surely what they melted into should be something just as holy as the forms: the molten wax of waxworks, crammed with possibility and hope and shape, magnificently latent; but he did not have that feeling at all, he was adrift in a world of destruction and decomposition, an artist in a shambles, and he could not understand how someone such as he, a connoisseur of life's mutterings and sulks, its puddles and distempers, should be feeling so little awe before the image of the human flayed. His indignation depended, he saw, on the holiness of the human effigy, as on that of rabbit, elm or thrush. Shape, he saw, was the thing God-given, and not flesh, not offal, not blood. He loved the dry.

Having made a perfunctory attempt to tidy up, the three of them walked outside, still tipsy, and chatted loudly until he decided to walk back into town with them, reversing his usual walk home. Now it would be Hampstead to Primrose Hill to Islington to Canning Town, and so on. He walked between them, an arm round each, cutting back the usual stride of his long legs, and pondering the irony that, because he was escorting them, they were safer than they would have been, except that he was who he was. What on earth would he do if a cab rattled up behind them and someone, doing his role, leaned out and offered grapes? Was Gull making Netley drive him around London without telling Sickert? It was doubtful; the team was small enough when it was three. Long Liz and Marie had no idea what he had been doing, as unable to smell the blood on him (if any) as to pick up the horrific images in his head. People were amazingly apart, he thought. Nothing was more private than a brain. "How you getting on, Walt?" He wasn't sure which one of them had asked, but he answered facing forward: "Nothing extra, love," and kept going, his head aching, his eyes full of nettles, and what seemed the beginning of a summer cold in his throat, clogged with iron filings. He kept trying to clear his voice, but it remained fogged and costive. He had always felt safe in the streets of London, and now, the third in Gull's trio, he felt even safer, although that was surely an illusion: just because he was among the doers rather than the done-to gave him a degree of safety only from Gull and Netley, and that itself was far from being a sure thing—one of these nights they might strip *him* on the piled-up muslin instead and dump him in some East End yard, whether he had a knife on him or not. A shotgun would have been more useful. Should he show Marie and Long Liz his knife, slide it imposingly from out of his sock, and so enliven their walk with a touch of bravado? No, why on earth? It must have been the drink thinking; all he had to do was navigate, a toff roaming home with two tarts across the face of the vast hecatomb of fear and levity that London was. What he was doing was not far from what he had always liked to do, even in winter, so as to attend the music halls, but tonight he was not going off with Bessie Bellwood to her rooms in Gower Street, there to dive into tripe and onions and rough-tongued talk. He was going back to Cleveland Street, either with Marie and Long Liz or not, with nothing in mind more than a good sleep, although these nights he never slept well: *The Crusader* pounded through his dreams and Gull's firmly upholstered face loomed from windows, balconies, kennels and oil paintings, his mouth so stuffed with grapes that they protruded, making a proboscis. What Walter Sickert needed was something to keep his imagination sweet, although Long Liz Stride's wide, pliable mouth, the horizontal epitome of tolerance, turned to him now and then, elongated by a smile, made him cheer up when he looked left, as did the big scented polar bear of a woman called Marie Kelly on his right. They advanced as an unsplittable phalanx, spinning unattached pedestrians this way and that, never quite colliding with anyone but presenting even from afar as a weapon bearing down, all three of them in step more or less and *aimed* at a distant point. So it seemed to passers-by, who gave them knowing grins and patronizing nods. That was what too much money got you: double pox, but for double the pleasure. They saw a tall, gangling fair-mustached rake with a sardonic mouth, flanked by one middle-aged tart and one young one, unlikely to be his sisters or even his maidservants, all three the worse for wear with skittish laughs and occasional bursts of uncoordinated humming. They did a slovenly march, inhaling each other, and sometimes, for show, deliberately veered to the side and walked straight at a building or a wall, halting in giggles at the last moment, then veering off the other way into the street. "Woops," Long Liz Stride would cry on these occasions to Marie Kelly's pungently whispered "Jesus," Sickert kept his peace, happy to have histrionic women on either side of him almost as if he were on the stage again and they three were doing an impromptu music-hall number, hardly a caricature of his Affable Arthur (long in abeyance), but the walk of rhythmic good nature, the well-timed strut of Cockney resilience. They had a willing audience, a long perpetually unfolding carpet of stone flag on which to perform, and a superb velvet evening for a backcloth.

Now and then Sickert felt an intense euphoria, marching forward like this, as if the three of them were on the prow of a vessel aiming westward to discover America. He, Stride and Kelly were the new Londoners, clicking their heels to a new cadence, perhaps even a foretaste of the twentieth century. Breasting the wave, he thought, chucking the past behind us, and all murderers, all mutilators, all careless guardians. As they went, gasping, they exchanged sloppy kisses, much to the amusement of those watching, and Sickert felt quite at home between Stride's emphatic, heavy features (those of a head nurse *manqué* except for her debonair, flexible mouth) and Kelly's voluptuous bloat, set off by her small almost rosebud mouth and her delicately sculptured petite ears. If death was waiting round the corner for them, then they would pound toward it with elated arrogance, daring it to come to them, treating them as one body, their aromas fused: Sickert's own that of phosphorus, from matches, and Scottish heather; Kelly's patchouli as ever; Stride's some kind of spiced seafish long harbored in a rolled-up pinafore. They were walking off the human map, he thought, three of the most endangered people in London, putting a brave front on things. It was a lovely night for fisticuffs, he thought; a few quick slashes with his knife and they would be free. Could they run? He thought so, asking the women to try it, so they now advanced in a badly managed sprint, broke ranks briefly and ran their separate ways, Sickert easily going ahead. After this, gasping and perspiring, they settled back into a sedate step, and he at once thought of Dieppe, how he had strolled there with Marie Kelly and Alice Margaret and Annie Crook, cock of the walk, the Impressionist *en famille.* Still, London would have to do. Embraced, as now, by two of those beyond the pale, he felt at home, restored gently to earth, his spry intellectuality leavened and curbed; if only what cheered them cheered him: Gull's inactivity for two and a half weeks. Sickert knew what was to come, in all likelihood, and it was going to come for them, not for close neighbors or intimate friends, but for them, and he was almost certainly going to have to be one of the ghoulish trio. Go to Dieppe, he said to them, until at least Christmas. "We'll get the money somehow. We'll borrow it." They laughed, appalled by his ignorance of whoring, thinking he meant them to go out and earn their fares. "Lord," Stride gasped, "even with the whole of London tupping us, me boy, we'd never get enough." But it was more than that: something he had never quite understood in spite of his long sojourns with prostitutes, some irony that made them sitting ducks. He called it inertia, but they had no word for it, instead thinking of it as, while shifting from bed to bed, doss house to doss house, man to man, staying put in the vocation and the neighborhood, as if expecting a sudden call from God, or rescue, or reprieve. They wanted to be near their friends too, even where those of them now dead had plied *their* trade. "If I were rich," he said.

"But you're not," Kelly snapped, breathing hard. "Be said."

"I will."

"You won't," Kelly told him.

"Don't you know," Stride asked. "Can't you tell?"

"Tell what?"

"Painters never have it," Kelly said. "Money."

"Well, Whistler does, then."

"Who's Whistler," Stride said, "when he's at home?"

"Daft name," Kelly sighed, at the end of her tether, "let's rest." They did, holding each other up in Islington, faced inward as if not to be recognized, heaving into one another's faces while the evening and the crowd flowed round them, unaware of the fear, pride and recklessness that made them compatible and made them warm their hands with death.

In his head they would always be running now, either from something or someone, or for the sake of exercise, just in case. How many assassins would there be in the crowd they were passing through? Five hundred perhaps, each of whom in the course of a year would put paid to one woman as if he were eating a lump of exotic fruit. How many potential murderers had they brushed past this very night? Not doctors skulking in hansom cabs, but nature's gentlemen unredeemed, born to the knife, the club, the broken bottle? How many of those they three had brushed against had had the faintest idea that he was one of the evil three who had already done in the Nichols woman and Dark Annie Chapman? No, he smiled, I had a woman on either arm, so I brushed against nobody at all, my vicarious lethal nature touched no one, and how lucky for them. I am not a bad man, only a man wandered too far away from the discipline he understands and needs. I should have abstained from altruism, which got me into this pickle in the first place, converting me into the reluctant inviter, the dapper enticer, an effete role to be sure. I need to break out of this before it's too late, but all I can hope for is that Gull has done, is going to let them off, these very two, with not even a chin-wagging.

He knew now that he was not the sort from which heroes and saviors were made; he could see himself taking them both off to Bath, on the theory that no woman was ever likely to be disemboweled while taking the waters or playing slap and tickle in a vat of healthful mud, or indeed taking tea with a cucumber sandwich in the enormous atrium while cripples flowed past in wheel chairs like multiple siblings. He would never do it, though, perhaps because he still did not believe that Gull would slouch back into action, having made his point, and slaked his thirst. Sickert trusted to an incalculable providence in which he did not quite believe, much as, when drawing before painting, he drew a grid of squares on his canvas so as to get the perspectives right. It would come out congruous if he only did that instead of leaping to paint at once in the hope of capturing some fugitive impression of irresistible allure. When he was workmanlike, providence came out on his side, but he knew himself only too well, much more interested in the uncoordinated buttocks of a nude woman walking away from him, with that faint fume of hair showing in the join, than in making proper allowances for depth and scale. He well knew he was an opportunist of a painter, which rather suggested he was a man of action, a virtuoso of the spontaneous; but his imagination was not his body—it could go into all kinds of perilous places and come home unscathed, indeed manured and enriched beyond his calculation, whereas his body hung back, not from fear or diffidence even, but simply to be the thing, the entity, that did not go forward. For sheer contrast, while the mind advanced, some other part of him had to hold back. In a sense, it was his mind that entered *The Crusader* and drank in the ghoulish deeds therein, enticing the Polly Nicholses and the Dark Annie Chapmans, whereas his body, seeming present, held itself in abeyance, out of almost theological austerity, declining to touch, trying not to smell, willing itself never to flinch: to be present at its own absence while the transcriptional whirligig of the mind went on noting and tabulating, taking down the evidence, but no more fleshly, no more substantial, than a spider's web arranged across the right angle of a trapeze flying over the floor of a circus.

It had indeed been said of Sickert that his most forward quality was his aloofness, that at his most dangerous he was a man turned abacus, capable, as he himself knew, of observing frightful things without taking up a stance toward them, refusing to give to baleful phenomena the reputation, the epithets, they merited. This meant that, for much of the time in which he watched Gull, or thought about him, Gull was not sadistic, ghoulish, brutal, but merely the man who shoved in this needle, went for the throat with that knife, rummaged deep in a dead woman's belly for some visceral prize not long dreamed of but taken almost as a matter of course. That Sickert could be so appalled him, but he had always assumed that his nominal callousness was part and parcel of an artist's makeup, a sine qua non of the kit. Cold and scrupulous watcher that he was, he nonetheless could go off at the wrong angle, finding sudden grief in the smiling faces of Cockney urchins or almost intolerable joy in certain funerals. His responses were mixed up, and this had bothered Ellen whereas it struck Marie Kelly and even Long Liz, who still did not know him very well, as the funniness of an arty gentleman, akin to the oddity of those who purchased smeared underwear for much more than it was worth or paid to be whipped, scalded, touched with hot lead. The prostitute's approximately tolerant response to the world about her was exactly the kind of appraisal he needed: seen by Kelly or Stride in her rough and ready, undidactic way, he was normal; appraised by the decent folk of the world, he was an inherent monster of passive appetite, as likely to go berserk as to bend his face to any ferocious smell; in short, a man on the skids, not doomed to go down to perdition, but likely to give up on fondled shibboleths merely because he itched, or he was fed up. Sickert was always a man in transit, committed to views not yet even thought of, but committed in principle because they were new, and that included, whenever he thought about it, unfamiliar twists of emotion, of depiction; he thought of the human as the open-ended animal who cultivated certain feelings for the sake of having them, not for their usefulness, their decorum, their nobility. More hospitable than most men and even most artists to what came next, he might wake up one morning with his mouth full of ordure and, before having the obligatory retch, calm his mind and nerves so as to savor in full the incongruity, the fatuity, the wild-card aspect of it. Extremes he associated with excellence and moderation with mediocrity. Gull could not have had a more attuned observer or one more qualified to watch the transit that had led the eccentric doctor from the punitive crudity of The Pudding Club to the insensate barbarism of *The Crusader*, onward to whatever Gull was to do next, having like a toy been overwound.

"Glum chops does move no mops," said Stride. "Not here, love, don't you see? This here is Flower and Dean Street, where truth told I have lived off and on, but cause of my Mike, Mister Kidney, I've been elsewhere, Flower Street sometimes, darlin', but most often at 35 Dorset Street, where I can't bear to go again. Who would? It's where poor old Dark Annie Chapman, used to live. Dossing there would be like going into a grave, wouldn't it now?" Heavens, Sickert thought, they're all on top of one another. They're incestuous neighbors.

"You come with me, Flower, to Miller's Court. First, though, let's have a drink at the Ringer's." Sickert fished out enough coins to pay for their rum and their doss, wondering why painters had to be altruists to the world at large, and then took his leave. "You walk straight, now, luv," Marie Kelly called after him after smooching him hard. "I'm walking on air, girls," he shouted back. "I'll save one for you, duckie," Stride shouted. "It was grand." He strolled away, wondering if anyone in London loved walking as much as he did, noting how the jingle in his pocket had lost its bright and varied tune. It would be easy, he thought, to restart his ailing marriage for financial reasons; after all, it was for those reasons he had entered into it. Should he send a telegram to Ellen, down in Midhurst? No, he would wait until the coast was clear, and all Gulls gone. What would happen if he asked Gull himself for money, playing the starving artist? The man would no doubt offer grapes of one kind or another. How could he sell half a dozen canvases, all at once, so as to have a nest egg? Aiming for Cleveland Street, he yearned for a chop and potato, but fought the urge down, bought an apple instead and so arrived at his studio in a somewhat appeased state only to find a note from Gull under the door, smeared from Netley's hand, telling him when to be ready: midnight, three days hence. He felt his heart stop as if smacked and then resume untidily.

4

Having spilled rum on gin, both Stride and Kelly had become roaring affable, but not to Michael Kidney who, after a long day laboring at the docks in a pall of smoke, had stopped by the Ringer's for a pint, but also in hope of seeing Long Liz, who only the day before had left him, as she often did. "My mind's all Dark Annie," she had told him. "I'm off." "Go and live in a bucket if you want," he said. "You'll be back sure as houses is houses."

"Look who it is, Flower," Marie Kelly said.

"I'm not going," Long Liz shouted. "No fear. That house has a curse on it."

"Then don't," Marie said. "There's always me. Half the time I never know who else's been in the bloody room most of the night. Come in, I tell them, it's a shop. You're welcome to my shop any time."

"Well," said Michael Kidney, "look who's here."

"You snap your braces, Mister Kidney, and bugger off." Kelly defended with zeal. "*We*'ve just had some drinks with a proper gentlemen, see. A real champion. French-like."

"Ten a penny, proper gennerman," Kidney said. "Please yourselves. Home, horse."

"Now," said Kelly, "wasn't Mister Sickert a bobby-dazzler? You should have seen him lording it about in France with me."

"I no doubt should," Stride said wanly. "But I didn't."

Life, she was thinking, isn't a bad old bugger so long as you are willing to do your bit. Having to turn out into the streets at midnight and after isn't so rotten if you only remember what it is like to do it in winter. This was warm for September. Long Liz was alone, willing to remain so, although she knew she had to earn something this night or she would have to go back to Michael Kidney, something she was not yet ready to do. That little jaunt over to Hampstead with Marie, to meet Sickly, had been a peck of fun; if only life was more like that every day instead of one in fifty. She was quite willing to walk all night, but only for her own exercise, hoisting her tall back high and stepping out in almost military fashion: out for a walk, as the saying went, she felt inexplicably pleased with herself, what with the streets having quieted down again and streetwalking gone back to almost normal. In her pocket, making a faint rattle in a small tin that once held cigars, some pawn tickets kept her company, a link to things she did not have to carry around with her, neither the biscuit barrel nor the shoe-repair last, a weird cast-iron thing like a letter L but with a half L sticking out on one side so that the whole thing would sit on the floor without wobbling when the Michaels hammered the nail in; if not the Michaels, then the drowned husband of the moment. She felt lighter for having pawned such things. Perhaps that was why she had bought a little twist of cachous to sweeten her breath while walking. Some clients liked to kiss and some complained when she stank of fish or just ordinary bad breath, and she often told them: "A girl can't go gargling her life away unless she has something to gargle with, my man. You supply the necessary and the worst I'll stink you up with is rum or gin. You can't blame a woman for breathing, can you now, or for being a bit snotty at the best of times." Few clients argued with Long Liz, who had a knack of drawing herself up to her full height and butting the client with her bosom in the region of the heartspoon, unless the man was truly tall. She was beefy too, one of her favorite tricks being to lean forward during the act, shoving the client off balance, so much so that some of them had fallen backwards cursing and fumbling at their loins. "A bad case of uptipped cock," she would sometimes say, or "John Thomas taking a little nap again." They found her a pushy, demanding, almost haughty tart, a woman of too much energy and spirit for the role she pursued, and her face had that settled, experienced look as if she had seen everything several times over; her standard expression was one of sedate worldliness tinctured with smile. She suited herself and, being Scandinavian, thought herself tough enough to go without two meals in a row, knowing she could live off her body fat, even her muscle, if she had to.

Tonight, perhaps in happy memory of the night out with Sickly in Hampstead, she was sporting flowers, red and white carnations, one of each, against the moldy fur collar of her black coat. Even in summer she always went out in her overcoat; it was the best way of carrying it and she sometimes thought how women of the night dressed as if there were no seasons but only one. Kelly had given her the flowers, telling her to watch out for the late-summer wind, but Long Liz knew that it was the permanent wind of London neither warm nor cold, neither dusty nor wet, the exclusive property of street-walkers, those clothes-horse nomads of the ghetto bounded by Hanbury Street to the north, Commercial Road to the south, hemmed in by Commercial Street to the west and the London Hospital to the east. To them a wind was always blustery just as Brussels sprouts were always rather searching (a good laxative, that is) and a spoonful of arrowroot was good for the trots or runs. In some ways she, who had often turned her hand to something better than whoring, enjoyed the reduced quality of her life, of a life on the game, not being responsible for too much, knowing only one kind of human being (the woman of loose morals, so called), and therefore responding like a saint in an ecstasy to such transient delights as carnations, cachous, her own bottle of gin, a chunk of hotel soap, a secondhand bonnet pushed up to look like new. Somehow, she suspected, being on the game made her more appreciative, but she wanted her flesh to be as young and ripe as Marie Kelly's, and she took to blaming the London breeze for drying her out before her time: "Always a wind, a *blustery* wind, in my attic," she said in summary, "and here I am going about with all my windows closed." The time of swooning adorations was over, fifteen years over, but she kept intact some piece of her heart for what, in her cups, she stylishly called "hand-me-down pleasances," never quite sure what she meant, but indicating a modicum of joy in coal-black circumstances. Perhaps because she was tall and could see over the heads of others to a greener prospect up the road, she remained buoyant and boisterous, not yet humbled by her calling to the point of the mouth's being in-sucked, the mind shut off, the eyes tightened to a querulous squint. Her big, abrupt gaze made men quail, but they got used to it and came for more, and, when she took the time to talk with them, she regaled them with her vision of herself as a wasted woman who could have been a nurse, run a café, or a doss house even. They agreed and tipped her almost as much as they tipped Marie Kelly for her roaming forefinger.

5

Going up Commercial Road with a swing in her gait (it was still early), Long Liz became aware of a cab right behind her, keeping pace with her until she halted, looked to her right and saw, of all faces, Sickert's, looming at her from the window, half-smiling to indicate hello, then coughing hard, the nasal voice of one with a full-blown cold saying to her something conventional, by no means a request or an invitation; indeed he seemed to be saying, deep in his clogged throat, "Sorry we can't give you a lift this rainy night we're full up, Flower. It's an invention of the devil, to be sure. You freeze in winter, you smother in summer. It loosens your teeth and ruins your hats. Give my love to Miss Kelly." Netley heard none of this and paid no attention until Sickert settled back into the cab and gestured exasperation at Gull. Netley had spotted Stride and warned Sickert they were overtaking her; but now she resumed her drunken waltz up Commercial Road, swiveling her hips from the pride of having been greeted by Sickly of the other night from his coach. Things were looking up in spite of the wet.

"Tell Netley," Gull said, unrolling something he had been warming in his lap. "He knows what to do." He did, parking the cab in a back street and motioning Sickert to come and help him, but Sickert hung back while Netley forged on ahead, eager to reach Long Liz Stride before the night swallowed her up again. It was hard to miss her, though, her shambling lollop like no one else's, her head held high as if ready for the knife he held. Then she saw him, saying to herself Here he comes, not Sickly, the other one, he must have been taken short, he wanted it something fierce, they sometimes do, they would put it into their mothers sometimes, it must be like when you have to go and piddle something cruel and nothing else will do, you have to go. He saw me and I took his fancy even if I am not on the first flush, nice breath and all mingled with the scent of carnations, I'm a walking nosegay, I am a street-walking nosegay. Here he comes, with his horn at the ready, I'll be bound, the money in his hand. Well, he will not be putting it up a duck tonight. Yes, dear, can I do something for you? Say it, Liz. My, what a noise.

At this point Israel Schwartz was turning into Berner Street from Commercial Road. As he was passing the enormous wooden gates at the entrance to Berner Street he paused, catching sight of a man and a woman by the little wicket gate cut into one of the main gates, their voices drowned by singing. The man was tugging at the woman to get her into the street, but she was putting up a considerable fight and seemed to have physical bulk; she was not playing hard to get, it was more than a token fight, he said, the woman was getting angry. At this point the man managed to spin the woman around and threw her down in one simple, contemptuous movement, at which she screamed three times. Now Israel Schwartz became aware of another man standing lighting his pipe on the other side of the street, apparently unconcerned by the scene enacted in front of him. Now the man who had felled the woman looked up, saw Schwartz and shouted "Lipski," the usual term of opprobrium for an unknown Jew ever since a Jew of that name had been hanged the year before. The screams had not been as loud as the shout, Schwartz decided as he moved away, anxious not to be involved; but the second man began to follow him, so he ran all the way to the arches of the London, Tilbury and Southend Railway, and at some point the pursuer gave up. He kept wondering if the shortness of the attacker had made the other man appear so tall, or vice versa. Two young men, he thought, the shorter one dark, the other fair, both with mustaches. It was about a quarter of one in the morning and within moments Netley and Sickert were back in the cab on their way to an appointment with the person Gull called "the Kelly woman," due to be released, Netley said, from the Bishopsgate Police Station soon after midnight, drunk or not. They raced away from the loud International Workers' Education Club at 40 Berner Street, into whose yard Netley had shoved Stride's body after cutting her throat in full view of Walter Sickert, who now kept waiting for pain to strike home to him as if he were human and had really been on the rug in Hampstead with this same woman only two days ago. Death, he thought, could not be inflicted so trivially, like the clincher to an argument; it just could not be so impromptu, so casual, something you could watch while enjoying a good pipe. He was smoking because someone had told him that the warm air from a pipe's stem soothed the sore throat that went with a cold. "Or makes it worse," had been Sickert's response. He tried it nonetheless, destined to become a cough on legs even on this night of nights. He had expected Long Liz to get up and go waltzing away in her high-handed fashion, but she did not move and he did not cross the road to look at her. Now he knew what Netley was made of, though about Walter Sickert less and less. How could he have stood and watched, half knowing what was to come? How could he have followed Netley as he accosted Stride? Why had he not intervened, doing the obstructive equivalent of the deceit he had practiced while talking to her from the cab? If he found murder so repugnant, why had he on one occasion done his best to forestall any such thing and then, on another, gone along meekly to the slaughter to smoke his pipe? Had Stride, Marie's good friend, counted for nothing? Was he under such a potent threat that he had not dared to lift a finger? Back in the cab with Gull, he thought he had mounted the wrong conveyance because, by the gaslight as they passed successive lamps, he saw Gull now attired in a bright yellow or even white set of fisherman's oilskins, from rubber boots to a sou'-wester with its brim folded back. Gull was dressed for work.

"Finally," Gull was saying to himself, but Sickert was too busy wondering if Netley had been obliged to throw Long Liz Stride to the ground because she was too tall for him to cut her throat standing. Why had he, Sickert, gone after the Jew whom Netley had reviled as Lipsky? What had been that splash of red and white in the decrescendo of Stride's falling down? Had Netley mutilated her? No, he had hardly had time, he had rushed away. Sickert's fingers found in his jacket pocket a piece of chalk he had been experimenting with, to lighten certain shades, to draw on rough dark paper with. Was it billiards chalk? No, he knew it wasn't, it was white, round, short, snapped in two: a stick of chalk snapped in two. If he had a brain, it was not functioning. Something appalling had happened, and the wind still blew, the East End still smelled bad, the noise of the slaughterers' drays had gone on, his own blood had continued to flow, contained, conserved, whereas Long Liz Stride's had flowed out on to the flagstones, he had seen the beginning of that. Now here was Gull dressed for mayhem to be committed upon the body of Marie Kelly, with whom he had also disported himself in the Hampstead house, on the rug, and walked home across London with. He should never have let them out of his sight. This very second, they should all three have been in Dieppe; indeed, two days ago, prolonging their cockahoop walk to the coast, the Channel, and somewhere safe. Gull's task was almost done.

He knew now that a man might engage in unspeakable things and still survive, retain his grasp of the cursive line or colloquial French. It was not the same, though, as if he had been hunting for deer or boar; after even that, something in him would be broken, would it not, irreparably spoiled at the same time as he recognized the need for such violence. Hunting in the mean streets of London was something quite different: it had to come to an end. Even Gull wanted it to come to an end, he wanted to round things off this very night, which was why *The Crusader* was going at speed to the right police station, the right street, in which Marie Kelly would appear after being discharged. It was as if she had commanded a cab to meet her after some weighty appointment to take her to a fashionable hotel, *The Metropole* or *The Fleece.* He could see it now, why men joined the masons, wanted to join them, for if you went beyond the law you needed to belong to some cadre that made a fetish of going beyond it, of being always above it, of being the law above the law. It was savagely lonely otherwise, he could see that. Already he was in a trance, being carried along by the superior will of others, as unable to refuse as to think. It could never be happening: the object of this harum-scraum chase through London was to get to the music hall on time; that was how civilized people lived, people who did not go disemboweling in stark holy righteousness. Then he thought again as some dreadful black seepage from the river got into his veins and cells, converting him to the theatrics of horror. As well to develop a passion for toasted snow as to try and hold on to his old, decent self, certainly in the company of Gull and Netley, Gull the mad healer in oilskins, Netley the cutter of throats. Why am I here, Sickert wondered. I am here simply because of Alice Margaret and the threat to me. It is a choice between death and complicity. Why, they may even kill me off later on, once their loathsome foray is over; after all, I might blab, I might tell it all in my old age and become a nine-day wonder. If I were they, I would remove Sickert along with the rest, I surely would, and they have the stomach to do it. He It had been an uproarious night at the International Working Men's Educational Club; semi-disciplined debate about the issues of the time (poverty and republicanism) had given way to shouting and that to dancing and singing, all of it some nuisance to the cigarette makers and sweatshop tailors who lived in the terraced cottages opposite. Into their windows poured a big avalanche of light from the Club, and it was toward this that the Club's steward, Louis Diemschutz (a name that made folk suspicious, he said: a communist Jew agitator, perhaps?) drove his pony and barrow, shaking his head at the things his wife allowed. She ran the club both night and day while Louis worked as a costermonger, infiltrating his cheap costume jewelry into the better-off suburbs of London. She burned in gas, he grumbled, what he made with his barrow, but how could he be in both places at once? His pony balked at something and pulled left, causing him to tug hard on the reins, and then it shied again, so Louis poked at the obstruction with his whip, knowing he would have to get down and shift it, but reluctant to do everything in one motion. He struck a match, but it was still windy and the match blew out. He had seen enough, though, to recognize a female body drunk or dead, right in his path, so he halted, rushed into the club, came out with a lighted candle from his stock and several club members whose levity struck him as possibly inappropriate, depending on what they found. Of course they found Long Liz Stride, dead and wet in a pool of blood, and still warm. It was only 1 a.m. The next few hours saw the thorough search of all houses and rooms in the vicinity and the inspection of hands for blood, including even the indignant merrymakers from the Club. No one knew who she was, but they knew what she had been, and their hysterical cries were mainly for themselves, not for those it had already happened to. How many more like himself, Louis Diemschutz wondered, would be finding murdered women in the small hours of the morning, and wondering why they came from Europe to London, supposedly a haven of safety. Sooner or later, he mused, everything gets found, although not solved. You could so easily have your throat cut in the back alleys, for reasons the police would never discover, and you would not be long remembered, not even by the Working Men's Educational Clubs of the World, but if you were a member of *nothing* you were even less than one, weren't you? Safety in numbers had something to commend it, he decided, and the bigger the number the better. Would his pony have walked over the woman? He doubted it, but it might have walked right past without shying, in which case he might have gone to bed in the usual way with the dead woman lying there all night. He did not like the element of chance in all this, haunted as he was by the thought that the world of the future, in which working men read books for a purpose and not just to better their minds, would have to be based on corpses, the yield of all revolution. Surely this woman's murder had not been political, just an act of revenge and unbridled sexuality, yet she did not look interfered with, poor big slop of a baggage in her musty black, one of the thousands who haunted him, who could and should have been doing useful work instead of trading their vulvas for pennies.

At this time, the fourth victim of Gull and Netley (and even of Sickert too since he was with them if not of them) was telling the jailer, George Hutt, at Bishopsgate Police Station that she would go straight home to Spitalfields and sleep off the remainder of her hangover. "I'll get a damned fine hiding when I land there too," she told him. It was too late to go and sleep it off at her sister's place in Thrawl Street, and she was still feeling a bit wobbly.

"Or with your brother," George Hutt said in his friendly yet austere fashion. "At least you has folks arsking arfter you. That's more than many do, mark my words."

"Brother?" she said. "I haven't got a brother, "so who?"

"Wanting to know when you was due out, arsking right as rain for Mrs. Mary Ann Kelly. Sounded right to me."

"Well, then," she said, "I have a friend. It wasn't my gentleman friend, I'm sure, Mr. Kelly. My husband, I mean. He never does things like that."

"Thousands wouldn't, dear," he said. "You can go whenever you want." He signed her out and expressed the hopeless wish not to see her again in the state she arrived in. She was a perky, garrulous little bird of a woman. Yes, he thought, Chirpy is the name for her. Ever a little quip like a touch of birdseed. She proved it by twitting him as she went out, still reeling slightly. "I've the Queen's garden party later on today," she chortled, "rain or no rain, wind or no wind. I'd better be off."

"You had," he rumbled, "Her Majesty likes her tarts on time, she does that. Good morning, M'am." Out she went and was seen at once by Netley the lookout, her false brother from his high perch. One tap of his whip on the superstructure of *The Crusader* and they were off, snailpace, to pick her up out of the windblown rain. When Sickert, his face trembling in every part, peeked out, he could not have been happier even if he had been praying for such an outcome. In fact the woman in the street was Catherine Eddowes, who, as she had intimated to her jailer, lived with a man named John Kelly and therefore passed herself off as Mary Ann Kelly, less often as Mary Jane. She lived only fifty yards from Marie Kelly, but did not know her and had certainly not signed the letters. Now she saw Sickert leaning out, his face quite composed, inviting her to step in out of the rain. Well, she thought, I am not much of a sight tonight, this morning, but I don't get many takers, I'm more than a bit past it, if they have the spirit to want me then they can. Even if it was only a ride, it would be better than walking home in the rain at the mercy of cutthroats, whoever they were. These were toffs, doing what toffs ought to do a damn sight more often. Of course she would. She mounted, sat, smiled, and took the grapes, only slightly put out by the sight of a toff opposite her in a yellow oilskin for the rain of course, who handed her the grapes, patting her on the knee, while the other man kept saying *Oh it is, it is, take my word for it.* Then Gull was upon her with pent-up savagery, less a mason, Sickert thought, than a barbarian, making the blood fly far from the muslin, as if he hated this total stranger, this frail body, with all his heart. She was the last one, the cause of all the trouble, and he fell upon her like a yellow thunderbolt, cutting away her nose as if it had antagonized him for years, even as her linnetlike mind saw some resemblance between being invited into their carriage by toffs and, long ago, in some twisted parody of a high-class evening out, going all dolled-up with her parents to the home of Uncle Reginald for high tea, but not really for that: the deep purpose of their visit had been to hear Uncle Reg belch after eating, in the course of which he made those near him flinch right out of their chairs. An evening out, but of an unusual kind: that had been virtually her last thought as she took the grapes and bit home, nodding indulgently at the flavor, the kindness of the fisherman fellow, the good manners of the tall young one. She felt stunted and bedraggled, this Eddowes-Kelly otherwise known as Conway, a Welsh name she had always thought, aged fifty looking sixty, therefore astounded to be accosted when she had virtually given up on the game, not from desire but because she was no longer physically appropriate, not even within the generous limits tolerated by the East End. She gave a chuckle, a gurgle, a long serrated sigh and she was gone from life, much too easily, as if all she needed was a slight tap and she was over the edge, Gull and his knife whittling her down as she fell, killing her three times over for being Kelly.

I am watching, Sickert told himself, I cannot be watching this.

I have a knife in my stocking, I can kill him for doing it; but he did not, not even as the lobe of Eddowes's right ear fell and dangled, the knife hit the face and the lower eyelids, then the throat. He closed his eyes against what happened to the pathetic, shrunken body, instructing himself that this would have been Marie Kelly but for luck and Sickert. When Gull found out he had butchered the wrong woman, he would be furious, and the hunt for Kelly would begin all over again. The dreadful thing was that Sickert now had developed a sense of series; a vile tradition had begun to form; experience had ordered itself into a pattern such as he would never have dreamed of, and it might extend itself, with ease, to little Alice Margaret or himself. When he opened his eyes again he could see that Eddowes, whose name he did not even know, was open from the breasts to the groin, and Gull was tussling with something inside, yet without moving his shoulders or back. The hands and wrists were doing it all and his crouch was almost that of someone hunched in prayerful reverence. He wanted to leap from the cab and cry out to all of London that murder was going on, right among them, sealed away in a little moving abattoir, but he could not move. His vocal cords had gone dead, his eyes were aswill with some caustic untearlike fluid, and his body was frozen into an intimidated cramp. All he could think of were some pages from a pamphlet Gull had given him to acquaint him with the ways of masons, but he remembered the details incoherently, such as the word *Juwe*, which had nothing to do with Jews but recalled a salient killing by three famous apprentice masons. Arches and lodges and squares and miters and lambskin aprons moved about in his mind, yet to no point; he wanted to remember nothing, especially the rank stench of decomposition that filled *The Crusader*'s interior as Gull began to finish up, slashing quick triangular flaps of flesh from the face of the once perky little woman stranded beneath him. All this time, Netley had kept the horse trotting about Aldgate and Whitechapel Road. Anyone peering in would have seen only the bunched-up form of Gull in yellow and the anguished, blanched face of Walter Sickert, new convert to mayhem although, as he had begun to suspect, not utterly against it. In their travels, they actually passed the real Marie Kelly several times as, finally certain that the streets had become safe again, she plied her trade, standing still, then moving ten yards along, cursing the rainshowers, wondering how Long Liz was faring tonight, happily recalling their night out and in together up in Hampstead with

Sickly, as Stride called him, and resolving never to write letters to people above her station. She had to earn her doss, but with all her heart she wished she were Marie Jeanette, earning it in France, with Camembert and that lovely French bread to go home to, and some wine, the real stuff, to wash it down, and almost any toff to see her through the night: Sickert, Eddy or even Bertie the Prince of Wales, a man with an unfailing eyes for a pretty woman. Saint mercy, she thought, you're not thinking like a woman who's knocked up, Marie girl: you have the divil of a time keeping anything down, don't you now? Is there going to be solid months of *that*, then, or does it leave you be after a while, once you're punished enough for what you did? In God's mouth, it's a penance, what you pay for in the wind-up. She changed from one pitch to another, but business was slow, although, without in the least dreaming, she did think she saw the same carriage go past her and come back, then go past her again as if touting but not quite able to decide on her or somebody else: one of those Mary-Ann John Thomases, she thought, who want the thrill without any of the infection, without the bad breath and the need to speak or pay. That was it. Next time it came past her, if it did, she would bang on the cab with a bottle plucked from the dozens in the gutter, against one of which the cab's wheels had jingled merrily when going by. And she would shout in at the window, "Get it out and polish it, old cock. Make your bloody mind up, there's hundreds waiting as can't hold it any longer. Do you have a taste to thrump or don't you?" She had been outdoors for hours, within the space of only one of which Long Liz and Catherine Eddowes-Kelly-Conway had gone to their Maker undone, trapped forever with an unambitious thought in mind, gone for ever from their beloved sisters, only one of whom, Stride's, had had a vision of Long Liz at the moment of the murder, leaning over her bed in walking-out clothes, telling her not to worry, but she had to leave her now. What odds would anyone have given that the homeless carriage patrolling the filthy streets had within it a furnace of sorts, a mad doctor and a dithering painter. If there was hope for London, it was not at the hands of such men as these: Netley asking where to drop the packet, as he said; Gull, being devoutly masonic tonight as this final one was Kelly, the brains behind it all, and telling Netley beforehand "Mitre Square, of course, where else?" Then he could rest, go back to his Pudding Club, release young Stephen into the world again (or had he done that already?). The fatigue of doing two in less than an hour had blunted and sapped him, but he was glad about the oilskins, initially his wife's idea against the rain, especially as he pressed the heaps of muslin on the seat, marveling at his luck that Stride had been dealt with outside; otherwise the cab would have been aswill with blood when Kelly entered, and she would have balked, oh she would have yelped a mouthful at the sight of that. These sluts had no composure, not even at the sight of the operating table; the only way was to accept things in the same way as the doctor did, putting all outside. Now Netley could take the oilskins and clean them for himself or burn them, it made no difference to Gull, who would never need them again, not once they had disposed of the packet in Mitre Square, a place drenched in masonic references, not least since it was the site of another murder, that of the woman praying in the Priory in the sixteenth century, slaughtered by a mad monk who then killed himself. She had been killed in a holy place, just like Hiram in Solomon's Temple. He wanted the violent connection as well as the masonic one: Hiram's Lodge had met there, and at the Mitre Tavern the Union Lodge and the Lodge of Joppa met, and the Lodge of Judah in Mitre Square only a *stride* away. He liked that, grateful for the adventitious labors of the sweated brain. His very own lodge, The Royal Alpha, when it did not meet in the West End, met either in Leadenhall Street or at the Mitre Tavern. It was hint enough: there was not a mason who would not know that he had paid his debts, had been obediently grateful in the twilight of his august career. Read it, Salisbury, he thought, as a parvenu's payment, or his praise. Netley had stopped the coach and even now, as Gull had instructed him to do, was scanning the neighborhood for policemen. Fortunately for Gull, the rain had begun again, and the wind was gusting, so the usually busy square was more or less empty. It was one-thirty. Out Sickert clambered, still retching, holding on to the piece of chalk in his pocket as if it linked him to a better world. Netley got down, went inside *The Crusader* and hoisted the remains toward the door where Sickert, in a costive frenzy, took hold of Eddowes's legs. Out she came, broken at two places, and down she went, left there with her insides slapped against her right shoulder. A small square of her bloodstained apron fluttered down beside her while Sickert, out of his mind and frantic to do almost anything, went to the bottom of a nearby stairway and wrote on the wall there the first thing that came into his mind: anything to disrupt the symmetry of the ritual, the preconceived arrangement of it all. "The Juwes are," he scrawled, "The men That," and then he paused even as Netley exhorted him to get a move on, "Will not"—one last flurry of the chalk—"be Blamed for nothing." There, he had done it, set it out as a poem: a sign that he had been there, disagreeing even while grateful that this other woman, not Kelly, had come along at the right time. Gull was bound to hear about his mistake, by which time Sickert wanted to be gone at least as far as France. The wind blew the bloodstained bit of cloth away from the body toward the wall he had written on in the passage of Wentworth Dwellings, Goulston Street. Eddowes, who had dreaded arriving home to the mercies of John Kelly, had received a hiding she did not deserve.

NOTES ON CONTRIBUTORS

Forthcoming from Sun and Moon is BRUCE ANDREWS' *I Don't Have Any Paper So Shut Up (or, Social Realism)*. Potes and Poets will be bringing out *Executive Summary* this Winter.

RAE ARMANTROUT's latest book is *Necromance* (Sun & Moon). She lives and teaches in San Diego.

JOHN ASH's *The Burnt Pages*, will be published in England by Carcanet in Spring and by Random House in Fall 1990. British-born, Ash now makes his home in New York City.

JOHN ASHBERY's *Flow Chart* is coming out this Spring with Knopf.

JOHN BARTH is the author of *The Last Voyage of Somebody the Sailor*, which is due out with Little, Brown this February.

MARTINE BELLEN's first book, *Salt in a Saltless Land* was published by Lines. She has just finished *Lunar Tire*, her second collection.

CHARLES BERNSTEIN's collaborative adaption of Olivier Cadiot's *Red, Green & Black* is just out from Potes & Poets.

MEI-MEI BERSSENBRUGGE's *Empathy* (Station Hill Press) won the 1990 PEN Western Writer's Prize.

CATHERINE BUSH is completing work on her first novel, *Up There*.

JAY CANTOR's first collection of essays, *On Giving Birth to One's Own Mother*, is coming out in February with Knopf. He is author of two previous novels, *The Death of Che Guevara* and *Krazy Kat* (also Knopf).

NORMA COLE is the author of *Mace Hill Remap* and *Metamorphopsia*. Her new collection, *My Bird Book*, will be published by Littoral Press.

PETER COLE's first book, *Rift*, came out earlier this year with Station Hill Press.

LYDIA DAVIS's collection of stories, *Break It Down*, was published by Farrar, Straus, Giroux in 1986. She is presently at work on another collection and a novel.

BARBARA EINZIG is working at the Centro de Romulo Gallegos in Caracas, Venezuela, completing *One and All*, a novel about the time of Christopher Columbus.

Love and Science, THEODORE ENSLIN's new title, is just out with Membrane Press.

GEORGE EVAN's selected poems, *Sudden Dreams*, is forthcoming with Coffee House Press.

PHILLIP FOSS edits *Tyuonyi*.

FORREST GANDER's recent publications include *Rush to the Lake* (Alice James) and *Eggplant and Lotus Root* (Burning Deck).

PETER GIZZI is co-editor of *O.blek.*

BARBARA GUEST's most recent book is *Fair Realism* (Sun & Moon).

JOHN HAWKES's *Whistlejacket* is available from Collier Books. "The Horse Killers" is from a novel-in-progress told in the first person by a twenty-two-year-old former racehorse. Hawkes is a recent recipient of a Lannan Foundation Literary Award.

SUSAN HOWE's most recent books of poems are *Singularities* (Wesleyan University Press), *The Europe of Trusts* (Sun & Moon), and *A Bibliography of the King's Book; or Eikon Basilike* (Paradigm).

RONALD JOHNSON has been work on *ARK* for the past twenty years. *ARK* consists of: Book I, *The Foundations*; Book II, *The Spires*; Book III, *The Ramparts*, whose first eighteen sections appear here for the first time. He is author of several cook books, including *The American Table* and *Simple Fare* (Simon & Schuster).

ROBERT KELLY's *Cat Scratch Fever* (McPherson) was published in October. Forthcoming is a collection of his poems 1985–1988, *A Strange Market* (Black Sparrow).

ANN LAUTERBACH's latest collection, *Forgetting the Lake*, will be published in 1991 by Viking.

SARAH MENEFEE is the author of *I'm Not Thousandfurs*; her forthcoming collection of poetry is *The Blood About the Heart* (both from Curbstone Press).

LAURA MORIARTY's *like roads* is available from Kelsey Street Press. Her *Rondeaux* will soon be out with Roof Books.

YANNICK MURPHY's first book, *Stories in Another Language*, was published by Knopf in 1987. She has recently completed her new collection, *The Beauty in Bulls.*

MICHAEL ONDAATJE's books include *The Collected Works of Billy the Kid* (Penguin), *Coming Through Slaughter* (Penguin), *Running in the Family* (Penguin) and *In the Skin of the Lion* (Knopf). He co-edits the literary magazine, *Brick*, and has recently edited a collection of Canadian stories, *From Ink Lake*, which is just out with Viking.

MICHAEL PALMER's most recent collection is *Sun*, from North Point. His translation, with Norma Cole, of *French Surrealist Poets on Painting* has just been published by Lapis Press. He is currently translating the poetry of Aleksei Parshchikov and working on a book of prose fragments, *Deck*.

In 1990, RACHEL BLAU DuPLESSIS published *The Selected Letters of George Oppen* (Duke), *The Pink Guitar: Writing as Feminist Practice* (Routledge), the co-edited *Signets: Reading H.D.* (Wisconsin), and *Draft X: Letters* (Singing Horse Press).

DAVID RATTRAY's *Opening the Eyelid* (Diwami) has just been issued. A book of translations, *Black Mirror: Selected Poems of Roger Gilbert-Lecomte* will be published in January 1991. He is currently engaged in a collaboration with the painter James Nares, entitled *R/G*.

JANET RODNEY runs the Weaselsleeves Press in Santa Fe. Her *Orpthydice* came out with Salt Works Press in 1986.

LESLIE SCALAPINO's book *The Return of Painting /A Trilogy: The Return of Painting, The Pearl, & Orion* will be published by North Point next Spring.

CHARLES STEIN's most recent book, *The Secret of the Black Chrysanthemum*, was published by Station Hill Press in 1987. He is currently at work on his long-term poetic project, *theforestforthetrees*.

JOHN TAGGART's *Loop* is forthcoming from Sun & Moon.

Seeing America First, NATHANIEL TARN's new book of poems, came out this year with Coffee House Press.

WILLIAM T. VOLLMANN's *The Ice Shirt* is just out with Viking. It is the first book of his seven-volume saga, *Seven Dreams*.

KEITH WALDROP's *The Opposite of Letting the Mind Wander: Selected Poems*, was just published by Lost Roads. His book of fictions, *Hegel's Family*, was published by Station Hill last year.

Station Hill published ROSMARIE WALDROP's novel *A Form—of Taking—It All* earlier this year. *The Reproduction of Profiles* was published in 1987 by New Directions.

DIANE WARD's *Relation* was issued last year by Roof Books.

MARJORIE WELISH's *The Windows Flew Open* will be published in Spring 1991 by Burning Deck Press.

PAUL WEST has two forthcoming books: *Portable People* (Paris Review Editions) and *The Women of Whitechapel and Jack the Ripper* (Random House).

DIANE WILLIAMS's first book, *This is About the Body, the Mind, the Soul, the World, Time and Fate*, was just published in paperback by Grove Weidenfeld.

Back issues of CONJUNCTIONS

"A must read" —*The Village Voice*

A limited number of back issues are available to those who would like to discover for themselves the range of innovative writing published in CONJUNCTIONS over the course of the last decade.

CONJUNCTIONS:1. *James Laughlin Festschrift.* Paul Bowles, Gary Snyder, John Hawkes, Robert Creeley, Thom Gunn, Denise Levertov, Tennessee Williams, James Purdy, William Everson, Michael McClure, Octavio Paz, Hayden Carruth, over 60 others. Kenneth Rexroth interview.

CONJUNCTIONS:2. Nathaniel Tarn, William H. Gass, Mei-mei Berssenbrugge, Walter Abish, Edward Dorn, Paul West, Kay Boyle, Kenneth Irby, Thomas Meyer, Gilbert Sorrentino, Carl Rakosi, and others. H.D.'s letters to Sylvia Dobson. Czeslaw Milosz interview.

CONJUNCTIONS:3. Guy Davenport, Michael Palmer, Don Van Vliet, Michel Deguy, Toby Olson, Coleman Dowell, Cid Corman, Ann Lauterbach, Robert Fitzgerald, Jackson Mac Low, Cecile Abish, and others. James Purdy interview.

CONJUNCTIONS:4. John Ashbery, Luis Buñuel, Aimé Césaire, Armand Schwerner, Rae Armantrout, Harold Schimmel, Gerrit Lansing, Jonathan Williams, Ron Silliman, Theodore Enslin, and others. Excerpts from Kenneth Rexroth's unpublished autobiography. Robert Duncan and William Gass interviews.

CONJUNCTIONS:5. Coleman Dowell, Kenneth Gangemi, Paul Bowles, Hayden Carruth, John Taggart, Guy Mendes, John Ashbery, Francesco Clemente, and others. Lorine Niedecker's letters to Cid Corman. Barry Hannah and Basil Bunting interviews.

CONJUNCTIONS:6. Joseph McElroy, Ron Loewinsohn, Susan Howe, William Wegman, Barbara Tedlock, Edmond Jabés, Jerome Rothenberg, Keith Waldrop, James Clifford, Nathaniel Tarn, and others. The *Symposium of the Whole* papers. Irving Layton interview.

CONJUNCTIONS:7. John Hawkes, Mary Caponegro, Leslie Scalapino, Marjorie Welish, Gerrit Lansing, Douglas Messerli, Gilbert Sorrentino, and others. *Writers Interview Writers*: Robert Duncan/Michael McClure, Jonathan Williams/Ronald Johnson, Edmund White/Edouard Roditi.

CONJUNCTIONS:8. Robert Duncan, R.B. Kitaj, Paul Metcalf, Barbara Guest, Robert Kelly, Claude Royet-Journoud, Guy Davenport, Kenneth Rexroth, and others. *Basil Bunting Tribute*, guest-edited by Jonathan Williams, nearly 50 contributors.

CONJUNCTIONS:9. William S. Burroughs, Dennis Silk, Peter Cole, Paul West, Laura Moriarty, Michael Palmer, Hayden Carruth, Mei-mei Berssenbrugge, Thomas Meyer, Aaron Shurin, and others. Edmond Jabés interview.

CONJUNCTIONS:10. *Fifth Anniversary Issue*. Walter Abish, Bruce Duffy, Keith Waldrop, Harry Mathews, Kenward Elmslie, Beverley Dahlen, Jan Groover, Ronald Johnson, David Rattray, Leslie Scalapino, George Oppen, Elizabeth Murray, and others. Joseph McElroy interview.

CONJUNCTIONS:11. Lydia Davis, William T. Vollmann, Susan Howe, Robert Creeley, Charles Stein, John Hawkes, Charles Bernstein, Kenneth Irby, Nathaniel Tarn, Robert Kelly, Ann Lauterbach, Joel Shapiro, and others. Carl Rakosi interview.

CONJUNCTIONS:12. David Foster Wallace, Robert Coover, Georges Perec, Norma Cole, Jonathan Williams, Joseph McElroy, Yannick Murphy, Diane Williams, Harry Mathews, Trevor Winkfield, Gilbert Sorrentino, Armand Schwerner, and others. John Hawkes and Paul West interviews.

CONJUNCTIONS:13. Maxine Hong Kingston, Ben Okri, Jim Crace, William S. Burroughs, Guy Davenport, Rachel Blau DuPlessis, Walter Abish, Jackson Mac Low, Lydia Davis, John Ashbery, Fielding Dawson, Eric Fischl, and others. Robert Kelly interview.

CONJUNCTIONS:14. *The New Gothic*, guest-edited by Patrick McGrath. Kathy Acker, John Edgar Wideman, Jamaica Kincaid, Peter Straub, Clegg & Guttmann, Robert Coover, Lynne Tillman, Bradford Morrow, William T. Vollmann, Gary Indiana, Mary Caponegro, Brice Marden, and others. Salman Rushdie interview.

Send your order to: CONJUNCTIONS, Bard College, Annandale-on-Hudson NY 12504. All issues $10.00 each, plus $1.00 per issue for postage. For a complete set: $125.00 postpaid.

ALGONQUIN BOOKS OF CHAPEL HILL

Volume I, Number I
Fall, 1989

THE VIEW FROM ALGONQUIN

Short musings on books, authors, and publishing, prepared from time to time by Algonquin Books of Chapel Hill

On "regional publishing," local talent... and literature that transcends geography

We were pleased to accept, some time back, a citation from the Ernest Hemingway Foundation for Kaye Gibbons' first novel, *Ellen Foster*—but were slightly bemused by the language:

> "In honoring *Ellen Foster*, we also pay tribute to the small regional presses now flourishing throughout this country..."

Not to seem ungrateful, and we do appreciate the kind words, but—Algonquin may be small, but we are not a regional press any more than Random House or Doubleday are regional presses because they are located in New York City.

The idea that our books are written for people in a specific area is absurd. Take Mississippian Larry Brown's new novel, *Dirty Work*, for example. Written fifty years after Dalton Trumbo's famous antiwar novel *Johnny Got His Gun*, *Dirty Work* bears comparison on many levels, for the same issues are at stake: war and peace, life and death, love. And while Brown's approach is as different from Trumbo's as the eighties are from the thirties, his novel achieves the same kind of universal power, delivers the same shocking recognition of human loss. What, then, is so all-fired "regional" about that?

Having said all that, it occurs to us that we *do* publish more than our share of outstanding Southern writers, especially in *New Stories from the South.*

The Algonquin Literary Quiz

Identify the sport played by the following fictional characters, and the book in which each appears: (a) Rabbit Angstrom; (b) The Citizen; (c) Labove; (d) Jordan Baker. *Answers, inverted, at bottom of page.*

Uncle Maxwell's Publishing Clinic

Uncle Maxwell will endeavor to answer your questions about publishing and related subjects.

Q. *Why do books cost so much these days? Several decades ago, books cost $3, $4, and $5. You'd think that with computerized typesetting and photoprinting, books could be printed more economically. It is getting so that I cannot afford to buy anything but paperback books.*

—*N.L., New York, NY*

A. The envelope in which you enclosed your letter has a 25¢ postage stamp on it. Back in the Good Old Days, the same letter would have taken a 3¢ stamp. Does that answer your question?

TO BE CONTINUED...

Address correspondence, if any, to Algonquin Books of Chapel Hill, Post Office Box 2225, Chapel Hill, N.C. 27515-2225

(a) Basketball, Updike, *Rabbit, Run*; (b) Shotput, Joyce, *Ulysses*; (c) Football, Faulkner, *The Hamlet*; (d) Golf, Fitzgerald, *The Great Gatsby*.

ALGONQUIN BOOKS OF CHAPEL HILL

THE PUSHCART PRIZE

1989
1990

BEST OF THE SMALL PRESSES

Edited by Bill Henderson with the Pushcart Prize editors. Introduction by Tess Gallagher Poetry editors: Sandra McPherson and Laura Jensen

XIV

A DISTINGUISHED ANNUAL LITERARY EVENT.

— *THE NEW YORK TIMES BOOK REVIEW*

"...There may be no better combination of overview, entertainment, invention, and play between hardcovers each year than the Pushcart collections."

World Literature Today

JUST PUBLISHED
540 PAGES
CLOTHBOUND
$28

PUSHCART PRESS
P.O. BOX 380
WAINSCOTT, NEW YORK 11975

George Robert Minkoff, Inc.

RARE BOOKS

20th Century First Editions, Fine Press Books,
Letters, Manuscripts & Important Archival
Material Bought & Sold
Catalogues issued

Rowe Road, RFD, Box 147
Great Barrington, MA 02130
[413] 528 - 4575

Milton Avery Graduate School of the Arts

BARD COLLEGE

ANNANDALE-ON-HUDSON, NEW YORK, 12504 TEL. (914) 758-7481

MASTER OF FINE ARTS

MUSIC • FILM/VIDEO • WRITING • PHOTOGRAPHY • SCULPTURE • PAINTING

Our unusual interdisciplinary approach to work in the arts has changed the nature of graduate education:

Four radical differences:

• Direct personal one-to-one conferences with artists in your field are the basic means of instruction—no impersonal classes.

• Response and interaction of students and faculty in all the arts.

• Residence requirements can be fulfilled during the summer.

• Our intensive sessions lead in three summers to the degree of Master of Fine Arts.

SUMMER 1991 JUNE 24–AUGUST 16

Resident faculty: Perry Bard, Alan Cote, Lydia Davis, Jean Feinberg, Arthur Gibbons, Regina Granne, Peter Hutton, Kenneth Irby, Robert Kelly, Nicholas Maw, Tom McDonough, Adolfas Mekas, Archie Rand, Anne Turyn, Stephen Westfall, The Meridian String Quartet burning deck books

WALTER ABISH
99: The New Meaning
with photographs by Cecile Abish
Five collage "entertainments" by the author of *How German Is It* and *Alphabetical Africa.* Playful probes into the nature of fiction, narrative, even the concept of authorship, they do not give us a make-belief "world," but invite the reader to come onto the scaffolding and participate in the process of construction.
112 pages, offset, cloth $20, signed $30, smyth-sewn paper $8

TINA DARRAGH
Striking Resemblance
4 texts that are experimental in the scientific sense of testing premises and questioning procedures. "What is most distinct is the degree of disclosure, including explanation of procedure... There is the warmth of the personal, but the privileged placement of the ego-centric voice is entirely absent." –Joan Retallack, *Parnassus*
64 pages, LP, sewn, paper $7; signed paper $15

MEI-MEI BERSSENBRUGGE
The Heat Bird
1984 American Book Award (Before Columbus Foundation). Four long poems accumulate into an intricate narrative. "In the brilliant light of her poems, things never lose their pungence." Marjorie Welish, *Poetry Project Newsletter.*
64 pages, 2nd ed., offset, paper, sewn, $6

LISSA MCLAUGHLIN
Troubled by His Complexion
Stories "almost just forming as the reader enters them. A quality that makes writing enchanted."—Russell Edson.
128 pages, LP, sewn, paper $8; signed paperback $15
Seeing the Multitudes Delayed. 76 pages, offset, signed cloth $15, paper $4.

DALLAS WIEBE
Going to the Mountain
"In these stories Wiebe strengthens his position as one of our best writers of innovative fictions."— *American Book Review.*
192 pages, LP, sewn paperback $10

HARRY MATHEWS
Out of Bounds
A poem cycle by the author of *Cigarettes.* *"An important poet" —Booklist.* 28 pages, LP, 2 colors, $5

Burning Deck has received grants from the National Endowment for the Arts, the Rhode Island State Council on the Arts, the Fund for Poetry and the Taft Subvention Committee.

71 Elmgrove Ave. #1C
Providence, RI 02906

Post Hoc

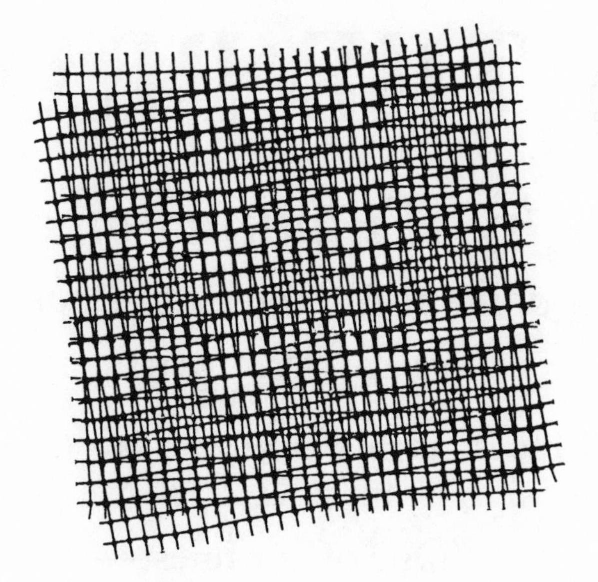

new poems by
Michael Davidson

Avenue B

P.O. Box 542, Bolinas, CA 94924

// DEATH IS THE PLACE

by William Bronk

winner of the 1982 American Book Award
for Life Supports

"He is, at this moment, our most significant poet." *The Nation*

"One of our finest—though largely uncelebrated—poets."
New York Times Book Review

Cloth, $13.95

Other recent volumes of poetry from North Point Press: *What Light There Is and Other Poems* by Eamon Grennan, Cloth, $21.95, Paper, $10.95; *Bitter Angel* by Amy Gerstler, Paper, $12.95; *Variable Directions* by Dan Pagis, Cloth, $21.95, Paper, $9.95; *Riprap and Cold Mountain Poems* by Gary Snyder, Cloth, $19.95, Paper, $9.95

NORTH POINT PRESS

850 TALBOT AVENUE, BERKELEY, CALIFORNIA 94706